Emotionally Attached
Wooing and Taking Vows with Customers

Edited By

Professor Mohamed Zairi

European Centre for
Best Practice Management

PUBLISHING HOUSE

Emotionally Attached
Wooing and Taking Vows with Customers

1st Edition 2009
ISBN 978-1-906993-07-8

Published by:
European Centre for Best Practice Management
1, Carriage Fold
Cullingworth
Keighley. West Yorkshire
BD13 5DW
UK
Tel: +44-1535-275030
www.ECBPM.com

Cover Design
UpStart Design & Media
25 Aireville Crescent
Bradford
BD9 4EU
UK

Contents

List of figures

List of tables

List of co-contributors

Dr Mohammed Al Ajlan (Chapters 1, 2 and 4)

Mr Ali Bilal Mohammed (Chapter 3)

Mr Osman Khan (Chapters 5, 6 and 8)

Miss Wafa' Abu Snieneh (Chapters 7 and 9)

Acknowledgements

No book is ever written alone and no research endeavour is ever carried out in solitude.

First and foremost, my greatest appreciation has to go to my research teams past and present, and in particular, the individuals involved in these compilations and whose research projects I have enjoyed leading and closely supervising. In particular, my sincere thanks and deep appreciation go to my co-contributors: **Dr Mohammed Al Ajlan, Mr Ali Bilal Mohammed, Mr Osman Khan and Miss Wafa' Abu Snieneh** for making the book on *Emotionally Attached – Wooing and Taking Vows with Customers* possible.

My sincere thanks also go to my support teams, past and present, who make our work possible every day of the week, all months of the year and who have helped sustain our focus and our determination to continue pioneering.

Lastly, my thanks and appreciation go to my wife Alweena and my children Adel, Bilal and Nadir for their unconditional love and unwavering support.

Dedication

But when I searched, I found no work so meritorious as the discovery and development of the arts and inventions that tend to civilise the life of man. (Francis Bacon)

This book is dedicated to all the men and women whose mission in life is to pioneer, validate and enlighten others with knowledge and the discovery of facts and the truth. It is also dedicated to all those who can help by developing solutions to problems and finding answers to enquiries. Dr Joseph Juran once said: 'My job of contributing to the welfare of my fellow man is the great unfinished business.'

It is therefore hoped that the content of this book will help move forward the human thinking capacity, will assist in the development of the enquiry mind and will support future quests for knowledge and advancement of theory and practice in the field of Total Quality Management and related topics.

Our biggest thrill would be to see that the content of this book is used, the knowledge presented consumed and the various ideas applied. It may of course be wishful thinking but we remain hopeful that the efforts made in putting this text together are not futile and that there will be some positive use of the various concepts presented.

As Rita C. Richey (October, 1999) wrote:

Ideas often take a substantial amount of time to be appreciated, and even for those few that attract attention quickly, there is an assumption that one needs the perspective of hindsight to determine their lasting value. Consequently, an intellectual inheritance is usually determined by the survivors rather than by the donor, and the labels that describe the merit of one's ideas are affixed by subsequent generations.

Introduction

Experience and the tribal customer

The meaning of customer experience in the 21st century is equated with the new quality. Indeed the customer experience is one that is defined by the customer, in many cases designed by the customer, the delivery aspects are dictated by the customer, and the fulfilment is judged by the customer. In a sense this new dimension of quality is owned by the customer in its entirety. For organisations wanting to provide excellence in customer service, they will therefore have to face the following challenges:

- Significantly changing the culture of the organisation so that it is truly customer centric, and addressing the voice of the customer, both in upstream activities and downstream activities.

- Ensuring that the customer experience resonates throughout the organisation. In a sense to make it the corollary that everyone owns.

- Ensuring that the process change is to create a seamless progression of value creation for the end benefit of the customer.

- Ensuring that there is discipline in ensuring smoothness, reliability, consistency, quality and dependability. These features used to be competitive parameters that all organisations used to use to impress their customers and compete with. However, in the 21st century these parameters are nothing but a baseline dimension, which the customer expects to receive and expects the providers of services to have integrated internally.

- Ensuring integration between upstream activities, which are mainly creative in nature and downstream activities, which are mainly operational.

- Involving employees at all levels as the providers of services and as the creators of the unique, individual experiences that customers are going to enjoy.

- Ensuring executive involvement at all levels and determining criteria for ensuring that their involvement transcends throughout the organisation.

Without active involvement of senior executives in driving customer centric cultures, the approach adopted for providing unique customer experiences will undoubtedly fail. How do we therefore ensure that executives at all levels have a key role to play in amplifying the message for customer centricity and in ensuring that unique experiences happen every day, at all levels within the organisation.

The following challenges need to be addressed:

Challenge number 1

Senior executives have to design a strategic agenda to have customer experience at its core. This therefore means that all aspects associated with the creation, delivery and the evaluation of customer experience are discussed and decisions are made upon the discussions for ensuring that optimal approaches are deployed.

Challenge number 2

Ensuring that internal communications between the CEO and the rest of the leadership team include all aspects of the customer experience, and not just discussion of internal business matters.

Challenge number 3

To ensure that customer experience is explicitly discussed in the strategic plans of the organisation and to have specific reports being submitted on a regular basis on the level of maturity, the degree of impact generated, and the loyalty aspects of customer experience provision.

Challenge number 4

Perhaps creating the senior position in the form of the Chief Customer Officer, or The Chief Customer Experience Officer: This means that there is total commitment to ensuring that the voice of the customer is relayed back right to the very top of the organisation and that the customer is not going to be ignored or neglected in the bowels of the organisation.

Challenge number 5

To link the performance of executives directly with the degree of customer satisfaction and the level of loyalty and retention achieved, and the growth of the business in relation to experiences provided.

Impediments to great customer experiences

Having argued in the previous section the importance of senior executives in driving and leading the customer centric philosophy and building a momentum for delivering great customer experiences, there is however, a lot of evidence to suggest that in reality most organisations fail to drive the voice of the customer in a consistent, disciplined and meaningful manner. Research conducted by Forrester in 2006 (Temkin, 2007) determined that 85% of customer experience is considered to play a very important and critical role in organisations' competitiveness. However, given the importance of customer experience, participants did not rank this item (i.e. customer experience) as the number one agenda.

Figure 0.1 Customer experience plays an important role for most firms

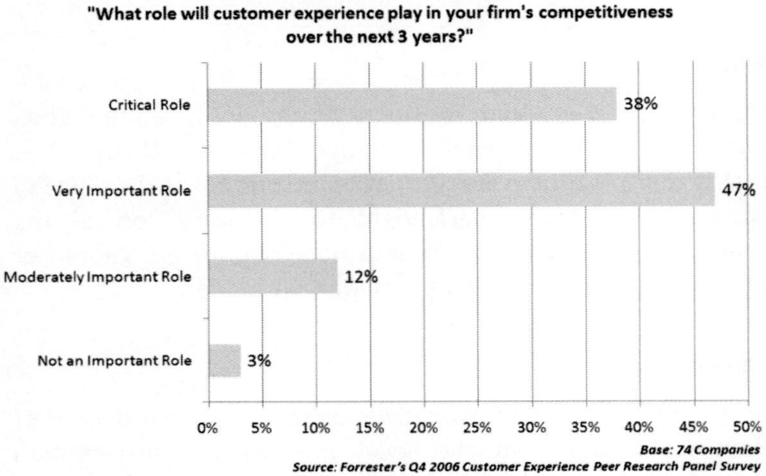

"What role will customer experience play in your firm's competitiveness over the next 3 years?"

Base: 74 Companies
Source: Forrester's Q4 2006 Customer Experience Peer Research Panel Survey

Source: Temkin (2007)

As Figure 0.1 indicates, 47% of respondents agreed that this was a very important aspect in their organisations, while only 38% mentioned it as a critical one. This survey also revealed that most organisations still adopt an ad hoc, undisciplined approach to customer experience management (Figure 0.2). The lack of discipline demonstrates that the systematic implementation of customer experiences is low in terms of implementation and many key activities tend to be ignored or neglected (Figure 0.3).

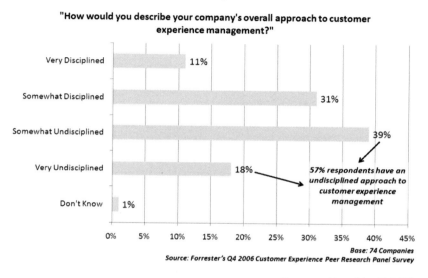

Figure 0.2 Most companies do not have a disciplined approach to managing customer experience

"How would you describe your company's overall approach to customer experience management?"

Source: Temkin (2007)

It is very clear that most organisations are still very poorly equipped for driving great customer experiences. As Figure 0.4 indicates, 73% of the respondents to the Forrester survey 2006 acknowledged that a lack of clear customer experience strategy is a major impediment to them achieving their desired goals and objectives. In terms of designing robustness and internal capabilities for driving customer experiences, 59% of respondents acknowledged that they still have not managed to prepare management processes that can ensure smoothness and seamlessness for delivery of great customer experiences. Amongst the other factors acknowledged to be a major impediment, were the silo mentalities that impede the translation of the voice of the customer and the conversion of needs into great customer experiences. 53% of respondents reported the lack of cooperation across the organisation as one of the key factors.

5

Figure 0.3 Few firms have customer experience initiatives

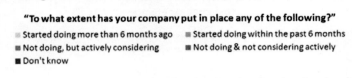

"To what extent has your company put in place any of the following?"

- Started doing more than 6 months ago
- Started doing within the past 6 months
- Not doing, but actively considering
- Not doing & not considering actively
- Don't know

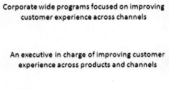
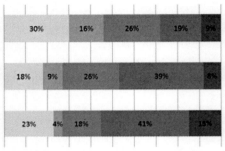

	Started doing more than 6 months ago	Started doing within the past 6 months	Not doing, but actively considering	Not doing & not considering actively	Don't know
Corporate wide programs focused on improving customer experience across channels	30%	16%	26%	19%	9%
An executive in charge of improving customer experience across products and channels	18%	9%	26%	39%	8%
A single set of customer feedback score (E.g., NetPromoter) that are used across the company	23%	4%	18%	41%	15%

0%   10%   20%   30%   40%   50%   60%   70%   80%   90%   100%

Base: 74 Companies (Percentages may not add up to 100% due to rounding)
Source: Forrester's Q4 2006 Customer Experience Peer Research Panel Survey

Source: Temkin (2007)

With this in mind, it is clear that technology is evolving much faster than the capability of organisations and the rate of change and preparedness for absorbing technology and in particular the internet, is much slower than the expectations from customers and the outside world. As we continue to progress in the 21st century with DIY practices, the customer in the driving seat mentality and the 'pull' approach provided by opportunities through technology, organisations will continue to wrestle in dealing with internal issues of change, re-engineering, adaptation, capability building, and discipline.

Figure 0.4 Firms lack a customer experience strategy

"Which of the following are significant obstacles to dramatically improving the customer experience your firm delivers across all channels?"

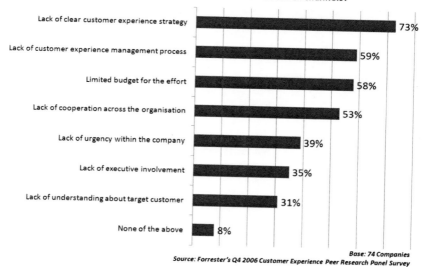

Base: 74 Companies
Source: Forrester's Q4 2006 Customer Experience Peer Research Panel Survey

Source: Temkin (2007)

The magic wand phenomena: How to progress to creating unique customer experiences

Faced with the reality of slow change momentum and having to radically change the ethos of business in order to create better absorption of technological innovation, and to prepare business organisations that are adaptable to the rapid change that is taking place outside, and to prepare them for the regular and extremely demanding customer, and also for having to deal with severe competition caused by globalisation and open markets, it is clear that the best way forward is to create a gradual but safe and positive approach, rather than to deal with a 'blitz' mentality.

Figure 0.5 suggests a strategy which will enable organisations to create the required transformational thinking for delivering great customer experiences, but also which can be used as a roadmap for doing the re-engineering and the radical changes necessary to be close to the tribal customer.

Figure 0.5 Strategy for creating great customer experience

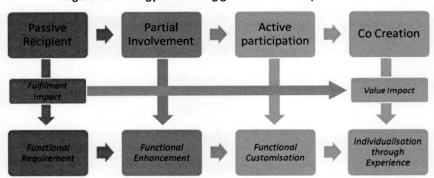

Principle 1

As a new mindset for providing value based experiences it is important for organisations to redefine the nature of value that they provide their customers with. Traditionally, they tended to use the transactional based approach, which measures value on the basis of physical fulfilment by providing products and services which meet specific needs and which are defined through technical parameters; this is a very narrow basis upon which to measure value.

Principle 2

To acknowledge, in the 21st century, with e-commerce being a growing phenomenon, that the notion of having the customer as a passive recipient of functional requirement, will no longer be valid as a business concept.

Principle 3

Organisations must start to operate as an open system and gradually transfer power to the customer through partial involvement in order that they have the ability to customise needs and gradually move into an active participation where customers can receive specific services and value tailored for their individual needs.

Principle 4

To create a new business ethos where the customer is put in the driving seat, which will enable the customer to design, deter, determine, decide, and influence the delivery aspects of the total experience. This, therefore, means a radical shift from a 'push' mentality to a 'pull' mentality, where customers' experiences are truly individualised, and where the concept of value is also to be changed radically.

Principle 5

In terms of value, to move away from economic value to individually designed value. This means that the customer could be more interested in the social aspects of the experience, rather than the economic benefits of what they receive from the provider or organisation.

The transformation discussed in Figure 0.5 means that the focus from here on is going to be on experiences rather than on products and services. It is important for organisations and senior management to start to believe a true differentiation is going to come from a focus on experiences rather than on the traditional capabilities they used to deploy for providing quality products and services. This also means that the approach to innovation is going to change radically, and in the 21st century organisations will have to create what is referred to as an 'open' source innovation, or a 'pull' innovation model, as opposed to the traditional 'push' model of innovation. The life cycle of a 'pull' innovation model means that there is a true spirit of co-involvement, co-development for the production of a new generation of innovations, and the customer has a direct, clearly acknowledged and defined role in this (Figure 0.6).

Figure 0.6 Transforming to open source innovation

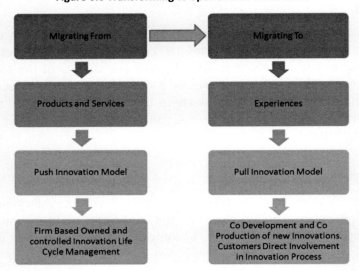

The concept of co-creation explained

It is desirable, of course, to have customer input in the design and development of new products and services that can be fit for purpose, but more importantly it is significantly important to have the customer in the driving seat, managing the whole life cycle of their individual experiences. Organisations will have to be more daring if they strongly believe that the reigns should be handed over to the customer and that in the future the customer is going to remain king, and remain in the driving seat. Figure 0.7 suggests a series of factors which are proposed to be critically important for ensuring that aspects associated with co-creation and direct involvement can lead to truly unique, great and very fulfilling experiences.

- Ensuring that the customer is well heard, the voice of the customer is listened to, and exploring all kinds of possibilities through dialogue and dual communication flow, as to what is really needed, what is a dream for the customer, where to focus innovativeness, and how to help the customer experience pleasurable and impactful experiences.

- *Customer engagement:* this means that the mentality of organisations will have to move from control to collaboration, and it means that collaboration is a truly riveting cycle, where the knowledge exchange is enhanced and where the customer input facilitates the enrichment process. This can only happen, of course, if the customer is encouraged and empowered to have direct input, to suggest changes and to propose new ideas.

- *Create customer centric experiences (CCE):* this means that an internal pool of talent for delivering great customer experiences needs to be available. Furthermore, it means that all organisations wishing to provide great customer experiences must have customer centric capabilities that will enable them to provide, in an able manner, and in a consistent, reliable and dependable way, great customer experiences. Furthermore, it also means that they have to develop the right work environment, propelled on by the application of customer centric practices.

- *Customer orientation:* means that the collaborative knowledge exchanged between customers' need to be stimulated, so as to enrich the process of receiving feedback, capturing ideas and

11

suggestions that can be used for future strategies and plans that will enable organisations to remain capable of delivering great customer experiences. This needs to be supported by world class IT infrastructure that will enable connectivity on a one to one basis and across the network of customers.

- **Appointing a Chief Customer Officer (CCO):** This means having an executive position that will represent the voice of the customers, but more importantly this position would ensure that there are customer driven strategies, with customer based performance measures and KPIs that have owners across the organisation.

- **Customer vertical integration:** it means that that the customer role and responsibility is clearly defined, mapped and documented, and it also means that the value chain is to be extended and re-defined so that the seamless approach transcends the voice of the customer upstream and downstream, and it also means that the customer touch points occur during all aspects of value adding.

Creating the right infrastructure and focus on the factors discussed in Figure 0.7, may not be sufficient for involving the customers and empowering them to make decisions on their individual experiences. The challenge for organisations wanting to delight their customers and involve them at all stages of value creation activities, is to ensure that the customer will have capabilities in terms of knowledge and competencies as they are more and more encouraged to be involved in designing their own experiences, and empowered to decide for themselves.

Figure 0.7 Factors in the co-creation process

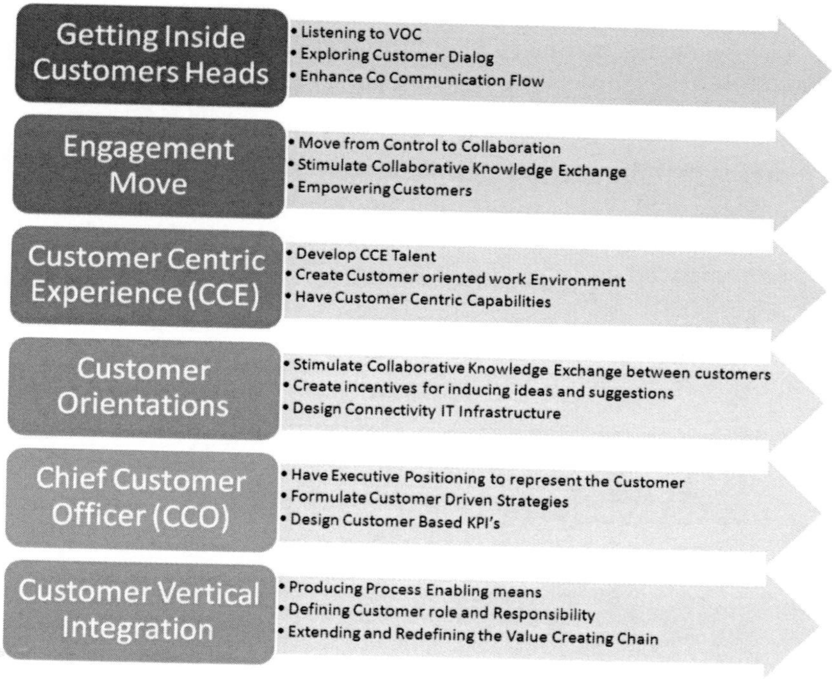

Getting Inside Customers Heads	• Listening to VOC • Exploring Customer Dialog • Enhance Co Communication Flow
Engagement Move	• Move from Control to Collaboration • Stimulate Collaborative Knowledge Exchange • Empowering Customers
Customer Centric Experience (CCE)	• Develop CCE Talent • Create Customer oriented work Environment • Have Customer Centric Capabilities
Customer Orientations	• Stimulate Collaborative Knowledge Exchange between customers • Create incentives for inducing ideas and suggestions • Design Connectivity IT Infrastructure
Chief Customer Officer (CCO)	• Have Executive Positioning to represent the Customer • Formulate Customer Driven Strategies • Design Customer Based KPI's
Customer Vertical Integration	• Producing Process Enabling means • Defining Customer role and Responsibility • Extending and Redefining the Value Creating Chain

These are the following transformations in the approaches adopted by providers and also the competencies that customers must have.

- Customers need to have the ability to speak the same language as their providers. Organisations wanting the customer to be involved must develop absorptive capabilities for having meaningful dialogues with their customers, and must provide an education process that will enhance the knowledge of customers in relation to methods, technologies, management approaches, involved in providing them with their unique experiences.

- Creating deep trust with customers: this means that the customer should not feel inhibited in terms of proposing changes or suggesting ideas, or feeling empowered in terms of decision making. Provider organisations need to have a comfortable dialogue with customers where there is an open sharing capacity with the customer being part and parcel of that process.

• Motivating customers in the knowledge creation process: this means that the provider organisation has a defined, documented process that will capture the knowledge received from the customer and have the deployment capacity for those ideas to be translated and carried out at various stages of value creation (Figure 0.8).

Figure 0.8 Capabilities for customer knowledge co creation (between firms and customers)

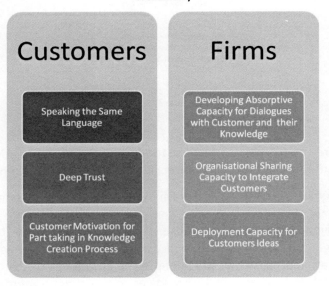

Customer advocacy and intimacy

The desire of most organisations is not to have just customers who are satisfied, but to ensure that long term survivability and competitiveness is heavily reliant on their loyal customers. This means that the first challenge that organisations have is to ensure that loyalty exists within their customer base. In particular they will wish to have the most valuable customers being retained and being depended upon for the future. There are several challenges associated with moving the boundaries of customer loyalty so that future success can be guaranteed. The open system perspective suggested earlier is the only means by which organisations can start to appreciate the positive impact that they can receive from the power of being close to their customers, and the impact that the latter can create for the future of the provider businesses concerned. At the onset, and as discussed previously, organisations must create an open dialogue with their customers and must radically move the momentum from a transactionally based relationship, driven by products and services, to experience based relationships which are driven by the customers themselves. Furthermore, having the organisation as an open system means that the mentality of 'push' will gradually give way to a new paradigm of a 'pull' mechanism triggered by customer needs, and customers wanting to cater for their own individual requirements. The theme of customer advocacy, therefore, is a direct consequence of having created the necessary changes and the radical transformations of operating a business with the following characteristics in mind:

- An open system where innovation is based on co-creation and is not under the control of the provider organisation.

- The value chain is redefined so that it reflects the voice of the customer at all stages of the value creation and translation aspects.

- The key catalyst for ensuring that great, individualised experience is customer engagement and empowerment at all stages.

- The communication is defined as a dual dialogue of open sharing, knowledge transfer, education and pro-active efforts, to capture ideas and propose schemes for the future.

- The measurability of values to be radically shifted from the transactionally based approach which tends to measure value through economic means into a new mindset where value is measured by fulfilment according to individual customer needs (i.e. beauty is in the eyes of the beholder).

- Trustworthy relationships: this means that trust is a mutual currency that both parties concerned value immensely. From the point of view of the customer, they trust the brand and they trust the provider organisation in catering for their needs for the present and for the future. From the point of view of the provider organisation, this is to trust that the customer will be advocates for the brand and they will promote the interests of their preferred brand, or preferred provider in the best way possible.

Figure 0.9 From passive recipient to brand advocate: the role of the tribal customer

Trust that is mutually appreciated and preserved by both parties concerned, will mean that there is an intimate relationship at all levels within the exchanges, whereby the interests of the other party are protected and where the growth of outcomes is to satisfy all necessary needs of each party concerned. This will represent the start of customer advocacy as a practice and as a concept. Customer advocacy will not ensue if there is suspicion, if there is dissatisfaction, if there are blockages which prevent customers from being engaged and involved, and if the communication is not open and the knowledge transfer is not appreciated and captured in a systematic and proper way. There are six principles proposed in Figure 0.9, which would enable organisations and customers alike to indulge in a fulfilling relationship triggered by the concept of advocacy and intimacy.

- Empowering customers: this is an essential requirement for any organisation wanting to build long term relationships with its customers. It means that the customers have to feel that they are in the driving seat and it also means that fulfilment moves away from the utilitarian, hedonic to emotional aspects.

- Putting customers in the driving seat and engaging them at all levels of value translation so that they can achieve their own optimal experiences.

- Creating an advanced form of customer orientation, not just by creating social networks enabled by IT solutions, but more importantly facilitating the requirements of customers to act as brand advocates and to use the brand for their own needs, for the customer network needs and also for the provider organisation's requirements as well.

- Creating authentic customer relationships: this means that authenticity is a concept that needs to be appreciated by the provider organisations as a necessary means for indulging in one to one long term relationships, where the customer is king but also where the experience provided to the customer is real, unique, individualised, and more importantly is fulfilling emotionally as well as fulfilling in other dimensions.

- Learning to use the role of customer mentorship and consultancy roles: this means as the 'pull' mentality starts to grow, provider organisations will need to assist the customers with information, ensure that the knowledge that the customer has is adequate for them making the right decisions and as they are involved more and more in the processes of innovation and co-creation, the role of consultancy and advisory capacity is considered to be valuable and extremely critical.

- Fostering knowledge creating partnerships: this means that the cumulative experiences, innovativeness and ability to exchange ideas and to enrich the process is to be considered to be an asset that needs to be safeguarded and also for the knowledge received to be mapped, to be documented, to be deposited and transferred across the organisation so that the future is a joint future and so that the relationship between provider organisations and customers is a long term positive one.

Professor Mohamed Zairi

Editor

Reference

Temkin, B.D. (2007) *Obstacles to Customer Experience Success*, Forrester Research, Inc., Cambridge, USA.

Chapter 1

CRM: The 'left brain' of customer focus

Introduction

In the future, success in business will continue to depend on how effectively organisations meet their customers' needs. If the company can listen to those needs carefully, and respond to them with creativity and flair, then it will certainly be able to win the competitive race and make an acceptable profit from what it does. In the future, even more than in the past, the customer must be king (Quinn, 1996).

No business can any longer succeed in distinguishing itself through operational excellence, customer intimacy, or product innovation without understanding the needs and desires of its customers. Successful enterprises will offer products and services defined by individual customers and achieving excellence in the vital customer touch points of marketing, sales and service, through mass customisation (Galbreath and Rogers, 1999).

CRM definitions

Customer relationship management (CRM) is a highly fragmented environment, and has come to mean different things to different people; it is rare to see a unified perspective for CRM. Bull (2003) reveals that CRM systems can be viewed as information systems aimed at enabling organisations to realise a customer focus.

On the other hand, Bradshaw and Brash (2001) defined CRM as a management approach that enables organisations to identify, attract and increase retention of profitable customers by managing relationships with them.

Ang and Buttle (2002) defined CRM from different levels. At a strategic level, CRM is seen as a core business strategy. They argue that CRM is a business strategy combined with technology to manage effectively the complete customer life cycle. At an operational level, CRM is concerned with automating chunks of the enterprise, they add that a good CRM programme enables customers to access the information they need easily at any time. At an analytical level, CRM is focused upon exploitation of customer data to drive more highly focused sales and marketing campaigns. Therefore, CRM is the core business strategy that integrates internal processes and functions and external business networks to create and deliver value to targeted customers at a profit.

In general, from the previous definitions and from other literature sources, e.g. Galbreath and Rogers (1999), Hamilton (2001), Swift (2001), Law et al. (2003), Al-Ajlan and Zairi (2005), Javalgi et al. (2006), Payne (2006), CRM can be defined as an approach that combines people, process and technology, which allows organisations to understand their customers and retain the most profitable (see Figure 1.1).

Figure 1.1 What is CRM?

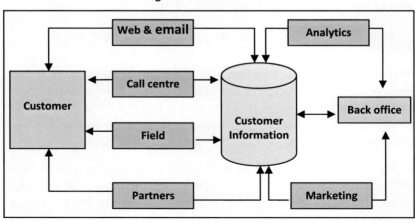

Source: Adopted from Siebel (2006)

Therefore, CRM is more than the automation of traditional sales, marketing, supply-chain, back-office or service functions using technology and process reengineering; CRM is also more than customer service or service quality issues. CRM is about the transformation of the entire enterprise and how it views and conducts business with its customers. Therefore, CRM is a strategy for competitive advantage (Galbreath and Rogers, 1999).

As has been mentioned before, everyone who profits from CRM has his/her own definition. The first step to recognising the meaning of any concept is to scrutinise its different perspectives. Here, three definitions show the paradoxes among them. Galbreath and Rogers (1999) define CRM as what a business performs to identify, qualify, acquire, develop and retain increasingly loyal and profitable customers by delivering the right product or service, to the right customer, through the right channel, at the right time, and at the right cost. CRM also integrates sales, marketing, service, enterprise resource planning (ERP) and supply chain management (SCM) functions through business process automation, technology solutions, and information resources to maximise each customer contact. Therefore, CRM facilitates relationships among enterprises, their customers, business partners, suppliers and employees.

Swift (2001) defines CRM as an enterprise approach to understanding and influencing customer behaviour through meaningful communications, in order to improve customer acquisition, customer retention, customer loyalty, and customer profitability. In contrast, Hamilton (2001) interprets CRM as the process of storing and analysing the vast amounts of data produced by sales calls, customer-service centres and actual purchases, supposedly yielding greater insight into customer behaviour. CRM also allows businesses to treat different types of customers differently; in some cases for instance, by responding more slowly to those who spend less or charging more to those who require more expensive hand-holding.

Each of these three perspectives offers its own definition. The first is a kind of holistic definition as it includes many ideal actions. The second can be viewed as the simplified version of the first, but with the emphasis of customer behavioural modification through meaningful communications. The last is focused on the use of data processing for customer differential treatment.

CRM evolution

Bose (2002) argues that during the 1850s, businesses could sell almost anything they made. Consequently, it was a seller's market and businesses focused on production. Early in the 1900s, competition began to creep up and businesses realised customers manipulated more power and firms had to find reasons for people to buy their products. This brought about a sales orientation. By the 1950s, businesses began to realise that they had to make what people wanted instead of trying to persuade them to buy whatever they had to sell, which led to the marketing orientation. This orientation focused on addressing the needs of market segments (see Figure 1.2).

Figure 1.2 Business orientations of the last 150 years

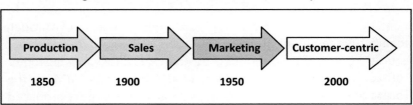

Source: Adopted from Bose (2002)

During the same era, Drucker (1954) asserted that creating a satisfied customer is the only justifiable definition of business purpose. While the marketing discipline was attracting increasing attention among scholars, a realisation of the significance of the customer was also emerging within the marketplace. Moreover,

McKitterick (1957) augmented the development of the marketing concept by advocating that the purpose of a business is to respond to the customer rather than to attempt to change the customer to suit the firm's purposes.

In the 1960s and 1970s, large corporations began to look at accounting and finance and realised there were tremendous opportunities for productivity gains using computers. They would observe their accounting department and see hundreds of clerks with adding machines doing manual calculations to maintain customer accounts, ledgers, etc. So they decided to automate.

Camdell (2002) argues that, at that time, the only option was to call in a large vendor like IBM, and have an entire system customised for the way they did business. Mainframes, terminals, operating systems, onsite computer experts, and software were all part of the equation. These implementations were hugely expensive, and only made sense for the largest companies and organisations.

In the following sections, CRM evolution will be discussed starting from relationship marketing, the emergence of CRM as a concept, e-CRM as a new phenomenon, and it will conclude by discussing the future of CRM.

Relationship marketing (RM)

The precise meaning of relationship marketing is not always clear in the literature, and the attempts to define it have been many and varied. Persson (2004) defines relationship marketing as being 'to establish, maintain and enhance relationships with customers and other partners, at a profit, so that the objectives of the parties involved are met. This is done by a mutual exchange and fulfilment of promises'. Thus, the essence of relationship marketing is to put the customer at the heart of the organisation.

Relationship marketing emphasises that customer retention affects company profitability, therefore it is more efficient to maintain an existing relationship with a customer than create a new one (Reichheld and Teal, 2001). The idea of relationship marketing within CRM is fairly strong, and has led others such as Newell (2000) to explore strategic methods for maintaining or improving customer retention (Bull, 2003).

It is impossible to ignore the striking similarities between CRM and relationship marketing. Relationship marketing is based on the idea that the happier customers are with a relationship, then the greater the likelihood they will stay with an organisation. There is also strong evidence that customer retention and profitability are correlated (Light, 2003). As a result, CRM evolved from business processes such as relationship marketing, and the increased emphasis on improved customer retention through the effective management of customer relationships.

Emergence of CRM

As discussed, CRM as a concept existed for a long time, but the term CRM gained more consideration when technology emerged. Therefore, CRM is a consequence of business that demanded more automation in order to facilitate business processes and get closer to the customer. Chase (2001) mentions that CRM evolved from the sales force automation (SFA) market, which was in turn born of contact management. Contact management gave salespeople a place to keep information about their prospects; things like addresses and phone numbers.

However, the first wave of CRM, which came to prominence in early 1990, centred on traditional channels supporting front-office personnel communicating mainly by telephone, but also by fax and mail, as well as field personnel (Bradshaw and Brash, 2001). Then in the mid-1990s, the web emerged. It changed both the CRM market and customer-related business requirements of all sizes of companies. New CRM systems mean that existing and potential customers are now able to interact and communicate with corporations.

More importantly, Xu *et al.* (2002) indicate that the client/server architecture behind existing CRM applications will disappear. The big vendors such as Siebel and SAP were slow to respond to the internet. This left more opportunities for start-ups. A new market segment of e-CRM emerged, which will be discussed in more detail in the next section.

Over recent years, the amount invested in CRM technology has exploded worldwide. It was estimated that worldwide investment in CRM would to grow to $148 billion by 2005 according to the International Data Corporation. In the United States, the near-term annual growth rate in CRM investments is expected to be around 9%, and in Europe, 25% (Ang and Buttle, 2002).

E-CRM

The internet has changed the ways of many businesses. Organisations have to recognise the internet revolution in order to survive in this fierce competitive environment. It was estimated that 59% of UK households would have internet access by 2006 compared with 21% at the beginning of 2000, and that the value of consumer transactions over the internet – fixed and mobile – would top $21 billion by 2005 compared with under $750 million in 2000 (Bradshaw and Brash, 2001).

This in turn emphasises the importance of recognising e-business. To provide a good customer experience in e-business, the company has to integrate the internet with its front office (sales, marketing and service). Therefore, e-CRM is designed to help the organisation to get in touch with its customer (Gurau, 2003).

In reality, e-CRM is just part of a comprehensive CRM strategy and implementation. According to Sterne (1996), internet-based CRM has three general areas: presales information, e-commerce services, and post-sales support. An unpublished study at the Center for Customer Driven Quality highlights the potential savings: for one particular retailer, the cost of an in-store customer contact was estimated to be $10, the cost of a phone contact $5, and the cost of a web contact $0.01 (Feinberg *et al.* 2002). Therefore, it appears that most companies will rely on e-CRM to lower their costs and to serve their customers more effectively and efficiently.

The internet has allowed companies to reach their customers in an easy way that previously was impossible. Consumers who do not have web access today will have access tomorrow. Those who have web access but have never purchased today will try tomorrow. Those who have tried yesterday will do more on the web tomorrow. It is logical to state that the growth and importance of e-CRM are guaranteed (Reda, 2000).

Future of CRM

According to Bose (2002), there seems to be three trends that will affect CRM in the near future. However, Bose (2002) highlights that 'no one can predict the future with certainty'. These trends are explained below.

- Extend CRM to channel partners: Companies are increasingly collaborating with other parties along the value-chain, as a result, there is a need for channel relationships. So, the next step is to extend CRM to business partners within the product value-chain, this is called partner relationship management. Partner relationship management (PRM) can be defined as: 'a business strategy to select and manage partners to optimize their long-term value to an enterprise. In effect, it means picking the right partners, working with them to help them become successful in dealing with your mutual customers, and ensuring that partners and the ultimate end customers are satisfied and successful'.

- Visual tools: More visual tools for analysing customer data are available. These tools are better than traditional online analytical processing (OLAP) technologies.

- Consolidation of CRM vendors: There is common vendor consolidation within the CRM industry. To ensure a smooth integration of hardware and software, companies offering core technologies are acquiring or partnering with CRM specific vendors.

On the other hand, Greenberg (2004) mentions verticalisation as a trend that will affect the evolvement of CRM. There is no ideal way of designing a CRM system, since each company has its unique needs depending on what customers they are aiming at and in what market they compete. As a result, the functionality of a CRM system differs significantly from industry to industry, even if they may follow the same basic principles when reviewed briefly.

However, today, most CRM vendors do not aim at any particular vertical industry niches, instead the adaptations are made during the implementation phase. Consequently, there is an increasing need of specialised solutions, since it implies less tailoring of the system to fit to your business. In addition, it is valuable to engage a CRM vendor who really knows and understands your specific business. As would be expected, some analysts speculate that the underlying software of e-CRM will soon become a less important factor than the industry expertise of the vendor (Greenberg, 2004)

Fundamental characteristics of CRM

There are four fundamental characteristics of CRM that the company may choose. Selection from those characteristics depends on the organisations' needs and requirements. These characteristics can be executed as a separate solution, or they can be integrated together (Gupta and Shukla, 2001). The major characteristics of the

CRM are sales force automation (SFA), customer service (CS), marketing automation (MA) and field service (FS) (see Table 1.1).

Sales force automation (SFA)

Sales force automation (SFA) is an electronic tracking and management of account activities by individual salespeople, which integrates the data at the corporate level to provide the company with a rich view of its customers and prospects (Dyché, 2002). SFA increases productivity and provides consistent information, which in turn helps organisations to sustain a competitive weapon.

Table 1.1 Characteristics of CRM

Characteristics	Impact
Sales force automation (SFA)	Greatly empowered sales professionals.
Customer service (CS)	Customer problems can be solved efficiently through proactive support.
Marketing automation (MA)	Remote staff can efficiently get help from customer service personnel to meet customer expectations.
Field service (FA)	Companies can learn clients' likes and dislikes to better understand customers' needs. Consequently, these companies can capture a market before their competitors.

Source: Adopted from Xu *et al.* (2002)

Gray and Byun (2001) argue that SFA is initially designed to support salespersons in managing their touch points, and to provide them with event calendars about their customers. SFA's meaning expanded to include opportunity management that supports sales methodologies and interconnection with other functions of the company such as production.

In CRM systems, current customer, deal, product and competitor information are all stored in the CRM central database for sales force retrieval. The customers' sales process is configured into the application. Order placement and tracking are integrated, so that each customer's sales cycle can be monitored and tracked. This provides a singular view of each customer, which contains all contact information and sales history, available to everyone who has access to the system. This also allows data to be summarised by views such as region, territory, customer and product for target marketing campaigns (Xu et al., 2002).

Zeng et al. (2003) add that the functions include automation of sales promotion analysis, automatically tracking a client's account history for repeated sales or future sales, and coordinating sales, marketing, call centres, and retail outlets to realise the sales force automation

Customer service (CS)

The second characteristic of CRM is customer service and support (CS). Customer service is an activity that deals with the customer after sales and satisfies customers' needs. This service varies from a web-enabled service via a website or self-service, it supports the customer with solving problems and handling guarantees (Dubrovski, 2001).

The goal of CS is to resolve internal and external customer problems quickly and effectively. By providing fast and accurate answers to customers, a company can save cost and increase customer loyalty and revenue. Customer services include call centre management, field service management, and help desk management (Gray and Byun, 2001)

CRM helps companies to incorporate an exemplary customer service into its core. It improves the organisation's abandonment rate by configuring the functions of tracking, monitoring and measuring customer service responses. It also makes it possible for the company to assign each query to the appropriate expert, who can resolve the customer call once the query from the customer comes up. Customer problems can be solved efficiently through proactive customer support (Xu *et al.,* 2002).

Marketing automation (MA)

The third characteristic of CRM is marketing automation. It targets the whole market, involves collecting information from various types of data warehouses, and exploiting the data into a marketing plan. It supports customers and organisations with information on products, campaigns, customer profiles, etc. (Cho *et al.,* 2002). MA should allow the user to establish, monitor and modify marketing campaigns across multiple channels. The user should be able to distinguish among the different marketing channels, helping it to establish the most effective way to approach customers with new products and services (Rodgers and Howlett, 2000).

CRM provides the most up-to-date information on customers' buying habits so that the most effective marketing campaigns to cross-sell to current customers and attract new customers can be achieved. By using CRM, marketing intelligence, customer database and interactive communication technologies are combined to enable companies to better address customers' individual needs (Xu *et al.*, 2002).

Field service (FS)

The fourth characteristic is field service. Here, Dyché (2002) emphasises that the customer touch points occurring while performing field service should be recorded as part of the customer portfolio in the CRM system. Therefore, the need for field service automation functionality is growing fastest within the area of CRM. By using the CRM system, remote staff can quickly and effectively communicate with customer service personnel to meet customers' individual expectations.

Why companies are adopting CRM

The foremost goal of CRM is to build a long-term relationship with customers to enhance value shares for both partiers (Krueger, 2000). Organisations that adopt CRM may do so for a variety of reasons, mostly improving customer retention and customer satisfaction. A published research found that lifting customer retention rates by 5% of customers could increase company profit by 25% to 95%. This is due to the high cost of acquisition, plus the fact that in the early years, customers are often unprofitable (Reichheld and Teal, 2001).

It is only in the latter years, when the volumes purchased increase, that customers become profitable. This leads to the idea that a customer should not be viewed from a single transaction, but as a lifetime income stream (Ang and Buttle, 2002).

Figure 1.3 Customer profit contribution over time

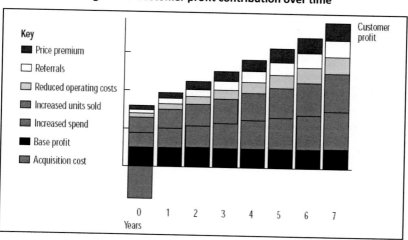

Source: Adopted from Duffin (1997)

Duffin (1997) indicated an important customer retention model. By using this model, you will see how keeping a customer for a number of years really does increase their value as spend grows. They purchase more products, they refer the product to others, they tend to become less price sensitive, and servicing costs become reduced (Figure 1.3).

From a purely economic point of view, firms learn that it is less costly to retain a customer than to find a new one. In industrial sales, it takes an average of 8 to 10 physical calls in person to sell to a new customer, but 2 to 3 calls to sell to an existing customer (Gray and Byun, 2001). Hildebrand (1999) argues it is 5 to 10 times more expensive to acquire a new customer than obtain repeat business from an existing customer.

However, the key driver is to find out more about customers and the way they interact with the organisation. This relationship can then be exploited by cross-selling (of products or services that the customer has not yet bought from the organisation), by extension selling (of products or services that relate to those already bought), or by some other transaction offering additional revenue to the organisation (Bolton, 2004).

Gray and Byun (2001) mentioned that another driver for having CRM in the organisation is the change introduced by e-commerce. Rather than the customer dealing with a salesperson in a physical location or on the phone, in e-commerce the customer remains in front of his/her computer at home or in the office. Thus, firms do not have the luxury of someone with sales skills to convince the customer. Whereas normally it takes effort for the customer to move to a competitor's physical location or dial a free number, in e-commerce, firms face an environment in which competitors are only a few clicks away.

So, managers using CRM software to support their sales, marketing and service activities report several benefits, for example higher levels of customer satisfaction, enhanced customer retention, reduced customer acquisition costs, and higher share of customer spend (Ang and Buttle, 2002).

Furthermore, Mohammad (2001) argues that CRM allows companies to gather and access information about customers' buying histories, preferences, complaints, and other data, so they can better anticipate what customers will want. The goal is to instil greater customer loyalty. Other benefits include:

- Faster response to customer inquiries.

- Increased efficiency through automation.

- Deeper understanding of customers.

- Increased marketing and selling opportunities.

- Identifying different customers.

- Identifying the most profitable customers.

- Receiving customer feedback that leads to new and improved products or services.

- Obtaining information that can be shared with business partners.

Besides, CRM not only helps to reduce overall business costs, but it helps companies provide better customer service and earn long-term customer loyalty. It allows companies to gain a better understanding of customer needs and build individual customer solutions, and link departments and give them access to the same information (Mukund, 2003).

Thus, CRM is a business philosophy that lets the organisation understands its customers' needs and requirements based on their histories and preferences, which in turn helps the organisation to predict and anticipate their future actions. Today more than before, success in this digital era will rely on those organisations that adopt the CRM strategy efficiently and effectively.

CRM is creating a customer-centric culture

There is no doubt that the customer has to be the king of any business; the customer is the only source for ensuring the success of an organisation. The organisation's revenues, profits, market share, and staff salaries also come from only one source, the 'customer' (Curry and Curry, 2000). Therefore, CRM adds value to the company by enhancing the customer experience of the service and product offering, by improving profit, by managing relationships across all channels, and by getting to one-to-one marketing.

Ang and Buttle (2002) presented one prominent case of Royal Bank of Canada (RBC), which won the first international award for CRM excellence in large corporations. RBC started its CRM initiative in 1995. To date it has invested over $100 million. Today, the Vice-President for CRM claims 'We no longer view CRM as a program. It is our core strategy'. Revenue growth is running at 10-15% p.a., and profit growth at 25%. He went on to say: 'We absolutely conclude the CRM is paying us back in spades. It enabled us to grow both top of the house revenue line and at the same time achieve huge cost savings'. RBC's retention of customers is exceptionally high in an industry where some 22% of commercial customers change banks every five years.

The following sections will show how CRM can create a customer-centric culture, and has a superior role in customer acquisition and satisfaction, which in turn leads to customer loyalty and retention.

Understanding the customer

Recently, many companies have become adept at the art of customer relationship management. They have collected and sifted mountains of data on preferences and behaviours, divided buyers into different segments, and honed their products, services and marketing pitches. Harvard Business School (2002) emphasises that it is vital not only to concentrate on the point where the customer is exposed to the company but also to get inside the customer's life. In the other words, understand customer scenarios. For example, one customer may buy a product for personal use, but another may buy it as a gift. Each of those customers appears to be same for the salesperson, but in reality, each has a different motivation for buying the product.

CRM helps a business to understand which customers are valuable to acquire, which customers to keep, which have untapped potential, which are strategic, which are important, which are profitable, and which should be neglected. To achieve the goal of focusing a business on the right customers, a creative mix of strategies, processes, technologies, information resources and people are essential (Galbreath and Rogers, 1999; Lee and Sohn, 2006).

Therefore, if we understand who our customers are, or who we would like to be our customer, identify the segments within our customer base, and understand the needs of these groups, we will be in a position to create products and services that can satisfy the customers (Institute of Directors and Oracle Corporation, 1999). Consequently, CRM is a great concept that allows the organisation to understand their customers' needs and requirements based on their histories and behaviours.

Acquiring and targeting the customer

Not every customer is needed; only the profitable customer has to be at the heart of the organisation. CRM is a strategy that identifies and attracts profitable customers, tying them to the company or product by efficient relationship marketing to guarantee profitable growth (Kracklauer *et al.*, 2001).

According to Newell (2000), CRM is a useful tool in terms of identifying the right customer groups, and for helping to decide which customers to serve. The idea that you cannot have a profitable relationship with all customers, and the practice of targeting customers with a differentiated product or service, is already widespread in many financial services. One method for identifying customer groups is the notion of distinguishing between transaction and relationship customers (Bull, 2003). Peck *et al.* (1999) argue that for many organisations it would be beneficial to distinguish between the two types of customer and focus on relationship customers.

Figure 1.4 Customer pyramid

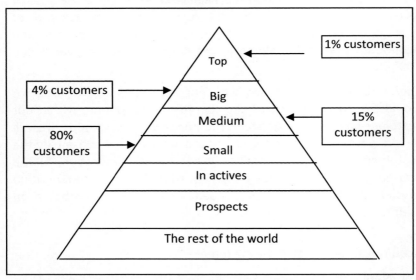

Source: Adopted from Curry and Curry (2000)

Curry and Curry (2000) used the customer pyramid to help the organisation visualise, analyse, and improve profitability of customers. The customer pyramid indicates that there is a differentiation in importance of customers in terms of revenue generation (Figure 1.4). Based on the Pareto principle, the customer pyramid indicates that 20% of the customers represent 80% of the revenue and incur only 20% of the selling cost. Therefore these customers are profitable.

In contrast, small customers (80% of the customer base) are attached to a large portion of the costs, and therefore might not be valuable at all. Improvement schemes have the objective to move customers up the pyramid. If small customers have no growth potential, they should not be served any more. Efforts to try to change their purchasing pattern and have them buy somewhere else could be attempted.

Newell (2000) identified three distinct types of relationship customers: the top, middle and lower groups. The top group (top 10 %) consists of customers with excellent loyalty and of high profitability for the organisation. CRM is needed to retain and offer them the best possible services in order to avoid their defecting to other competitors. Middle group customers (next 40-50 %) are ones delivering good profits and who show good potential for future growth and loyalty. These customers are probably giving some of their business to competitors.

The idea is to use CRM to target middle group customers effectively as they are the greatest source of potential growth. Lower group relational (bottom 40-50 %) customers are those who are only marginally profitable. Some may have potential for growth, but the expense and effort involved in targeting such numbers hinders the effectiveness of servicing existing relational customers in the top and middle groups.

CRM should be used to identify this group and seriously consider the response required. Transactional customers contribute either nothing or have an adverse effect on profitability. The consensus therefore is that CRM needs to identify transactional customers to help organisations respond appropriately

Satisfying the customer

In an increasingly competitive environment, companies must be customer-oriented (Kotler, 1997). After all, the underpinning of the marketing concept is that identification and satisfaction of customer needs leads to improved customer retention. It is thus not surprising that companies spend substantial resources to measure and manage customer satisfaction (Day, 1994).

Customer satisfaction has been related to perceived performance and expectations. If performance matches expectations or exceeds them, the customer is satisfied or highly satisfied, respectively. If performance falls short of expectations, the customer is dissatisfied (Stefanou *et al.*, 2003).

However, satisfaction is not enough to ensure the future success of a company. For example, many companies (e.g. Whirlpool) that score well on customer satisfaction have done poorly financially (Grant, 1998). Recently, Coles and Gokey (2002) have argued that it is not enough to manage customer defection alone. They suggest that it makes better sense to monitor customer buying behaviour, and to identify customers who have reduced their spending. This is often a signal that defection may be about to happen.

In applying a CRM system within the firm, the customer data profile needs to be expanded in order to include non-transactional data, such as general enquiries, suggestions and complaints (Bose, 2002). These data help the company to tailor its products and services to fit the customer's needs and requirements, which in turn enhance the relationship and build the satisfaction.

Galbreath and Rogers (1999) believe that, in moving to the twenty-first century, there will be three distinct areas that businesses should focus on to satisfy customer needs and wants: customisation, personal relationships, and after-sales service/ support (Figure 1.5).

High satisfaction does not necessarily predict retention. The reason is that satisfaction has mainly to do with meeting customers' minimum requirements and, in many industries, that is simply not enough (Crosby, 2002). Thus, satisfaction is not enough; you have to make your customer a loyal one to ensure future success. This supports the Storbacka *et al.* (1994) research which found that between 65% and 85% of customers who defect say they were satisfied or very satisfied with their former supplier.

Figure 1.5 Three distinct areas of focus for customer satisfaction

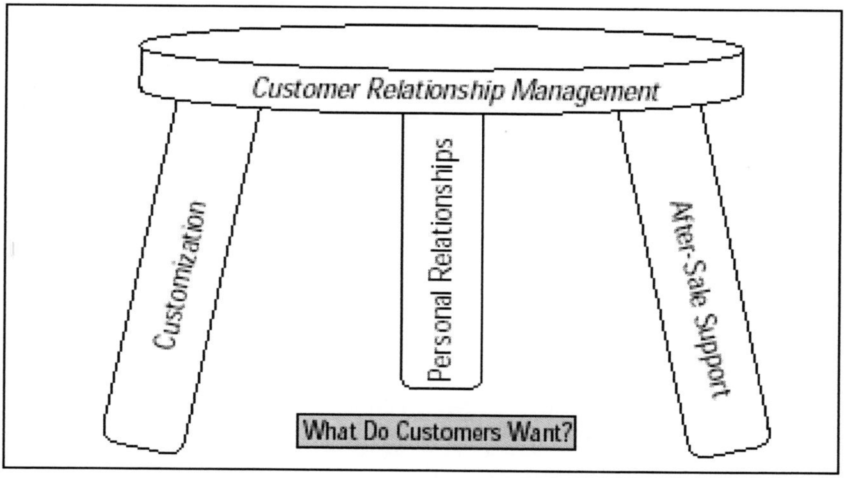

Source: Adopted from Galbreath and Rogers (1999)

Achieving customer loyalty

It is impossible to have loyal customers without satisfying them; customer satisfaction is the main driver to achieving customer loyalty. A loyal customer is more profitable than the non-loyal customer. The loyal customers cost less to serve, in part because they know the product and require less information; Raman (1999) states that they even serve as part-time employees.

The increased profit from loyalty comes from reduced marketing costs, increased sales, and reduced operational costs (Gurau, 2003). Loyal customers are less likely to switch, and they make more purchases than similar non-loyal customers do; loyal customers will also help promote your products. They will provide strong word-of-mouth, create business referrals, provide references, and serve on advisory boards (Bowen and Chen, 2001).

Quinn (1996) states that:

> CRM helps to build customer loyalty by serving the customer's needs properly, at a price that offers value. If we do that successfully, we can create not only loyal customers but also customers who will become enthusiastic missionaries for the business and indeed, become more effective salespersons for the organization more than their employees do.

The profits usually rise as a customer's relationship with a company lengthens. Customer defections have a surprisingly powerful impact on the bottom lines. When defections are cut in half, the average growth rate becomes more than doubled (Young and Stepankek, 2003).

In conclusion, CRM plays a main role in keeping and retaining customers. Griffin (1995) found that 68% of customers left for no special reason, which means that many customers, in fact a majority, leave because of benign neglect. This is supported by Jobber (2001), who points out that research on customer loyalty in the service industry showed that only 14% of customers who stopped patronising service businesses did so because they were dissatisfied with the quality of what they had bought. More than two-thirds stopped buying because they found service staff indifferent or unhelpful.

Major CRM vendors

A few years ago, technology vendors had their own specialties. For example, Siebel was in sales force automation, Remedy focused on helpdesk systems, Davox specialised in call centre systems. Today, however, there is no specific boundary of vendors. All vendors are trying to expand their products over the entire CRM area. For example, Siebel says it can do everything, Davox moved into customer contact management, and Broad Vision is trying to integrate backwards with ERP.

Today, CRM has grown and matured to become one of the most significant and fastest growing software segments of the past five years. It was predicted that the total aggregate revenue of the CRM market was anticipated to grow from $1.2 billion in 1997 to $76.5 billion in 2005, with an annual growth of more than 50%. CRM licence revenue reached $7.5 billion by 2002 against $762 million in 1997. CRM applications and market penetration are expected to significantly grow to new levels as the market is continuing to strive to leverage strategic advantages. Now CRM is becoming one of the hottest areas in enterprise applications (Xu *et al.*, 2002).

Gray and Byun (2001) show that CRM vendors come from different origins, back-end applications like traditional ERP vendors (SAP, Oracle Corporation, Baan and PeopleSoft) acquire, build, and partner their CRM application for ERP functionality, this is in contrast with front-end applications; some companies started with front-end solutions such as personal information management system (PIMS). Siebel, BroadVision, and Remedy are in this category. In the following section, the major CRM vendors will be presented.

Siebel

Arguably, the best-known CRM vendor in the marketplace, it holds a commanding share (approximately 36%) of the market, both in terms of software and mind share. Siebel products originate in customer service. Its product line is called Siebel e-Business 2000. Siebel targets the following broad areas of CRM: call centres, field sales and service, marketing, channel management, dot-coms, and niche verticals such as finance, energy and telecommunications. Their solutions are horizontal, vertical, wired, wireless, big, handheld, expensive to implement, and flexible to customise. Additionally, in mid-2000, Siebel released Siebel e-Business 2000 Midmarket Edition, a product aimed at the smaller part of the enterprise market.

Oracle

Oracle is the second largest software company in the world, and the leading provider of specialised database products. Oracle delivered the first version of its CRM application in 1999. Due to Oracle's dominant market position in the database sector, the first release of its CRM product suite captured 2.2% of the total CRM market within approximately 18 months. The most recent product, Oracle CRM 11i, has evolved to be an e-CRM solution comprising modules like Oracle Sales, Oracle Marketing, etc. The product features consist of sales online, telesales, incentive compensation, marketing online, and marketing intelligence. Additionally, another CRM solution, Oraclesalesonline.com, has been primarily targeted to medium-sized companies in the worldwide.

SAP

Founded in 1972, SAP is the world's largest inter-enterprise software company, and the world third-largest independent software supplier overall. Its renowned product SAP R3 has taken a leading position in the ERP market. It is also the recognised leader in providing collaborative e-business solutions for all types of industries and for every major market. MySAP branded suite of applications features a CRM component that includes marketing, sales, configuration/commerce, order management, interaction management, and customer/field service functions. Although SAP entered the CRM market later than other leading vendors like Siebel, Clarify, and PeopleSoft, SAP has released a fully functional suite of products that has brought it back into the mainstream within the course of two years or so.

Conclusion

CRM is a vital weapon to gain and sustain competitive advantage and companies can reap great benefits from adopting such a concept. It can be concluded that CRM is necessary for most organisations especially in this digital era where competition is increased.

References

Al-Ajlan, M. (2003) *Building and sustaining a competitive advantage through effective brand management and customer loyalty a case study of the Saudi garments industry*, Ph.D. Thesis, University of Bradford.

Ang, L. and F. A. Buttle (2002) ROI on CRM: a customer-journey approach, *IMP-conference*, Industrial Marketing & Purchasing, Perth, Australia.

Bolton, M. (2004) Customer centric business processing, *International Journal of Productivity and Performance Management*, 53, 1.

Bose, R. (2002) Customer relationship management: key components for IT success, *Industrial Management & Amp*, 102, 2.

Bowen, J. T. and Chen, S. L. (2001) The relationship between customer loyalty and customer satisfaction, *International Journal of Contemporary Hospitality Management*, 13, 5.

Bradshaw, D. and Brash, C. (2001) Managing customer relationships in the e-business world: how to personalise computer relationships for increased profitability, *International Journal of Retail & Amp*, 29, 12.

Bull, C. (2003) Strategic issues in customer relationship management (CRM) implementation, *Business Process Management Journal*, 9, 5.

Camdell, S. (2002) *The History of CRM*, Camdel Software.

Chase, P. (2001) Why CRM implementations fail and what to do about it, *CRM Knowledge Base*.

Cho, Y., Im, I., Hiltz, S. and Fjermestad, J. (2002) An Analysis of Online Customer Complaint: Implication for Web Complaint Management, *The 35th International Conference on System Sciences, Hawaii*.

Coles, S. and Gokey, T. (2002) Customer Retention is Not Enough, *The McKinsey Quarterly*, 2, 1-7.

Crosby, L. A. (2002) Exploding some myths about customer relationship management, *Managing Service Quality*, 12, 5.

Curry, J. and Curry, A. (2000) *The customer marketing method: how to implement and profit from customer relationship management*, Free Press, New York; London.

Day, G. (1994) The capabilities of market-driven organizations, *Journal of Marketing*, 58, 4, 37-52.

Drucker, P. (1954) *The Practice of Management*, Harper & Row, New York, NY.

Dubrovski, D. (2001) The Role of Customer Satisfaction In Achieving Business Excellence, *TQM World Congress*, 6, 325-331.

Dyché, J. (2002) *The CRM handbook a business guide to customer relationship management,* Addison Wesley, Boston.

Feinberg, R. A. and Kadam, R. (2002) The state of electronic customer relationship management in retailing, *International Journal of Retail & Amp*, 30, 10, 470-481.

Galbreath, J. and Rogers, T. (1999) Customer relationship leadership: a leadership and motivation model for the twenty-first century business, *The TQM Magazine*, 11, 3.

Grant, L. (1998) Your customers are telling the truth, *Fortune*, 164-166.

Gray, P. and Byun, J. (2001) *Customer Relationship Management*, Irvine, CA, Centre for Research on Information Technology and Organisation, University of California.

Greenberg, P. (2004) *CRM at the speed of light essential customer strategies for the 21st century,* McGraw-Hill/Osborne, Berkeley, Calif.

Griffin, J. (1995) *Customer Loyalty*, Jossey-Bass, San Francisco, CA.

Gupta, M. and Shukla, S. (2001) Implementation Issues in CRM: A Study in the Indian Banking Sector, *Productivity*, 42, 1, 26-38.

Gurau, C. (2003) Tailoring e-service quality through CRM, *Managing Service Quality*, 13, 6.

Hamilton, D. P. (2001) Making sense of it all, *The Asia Wall Street Journal*, T4.

Harvard Business School (2002) *Harvard business review on customer relationship management*, Harvard Business School Press, Boston.

Hildebrand, C. (1999) One to a Customer; Customer Relationship Management, *CIO Enterprise Magazine*.

Institute of Directors and Oracle Corporation (1999) *Customer relationship management how directors can build business through improved customer* relations, published for the Institute of Directors and Oracle Corporation UK Ltd by Director Publications, London.

Javalgi, R. R. G., Martin, C. L. and Young, R. B. (2006) Marketing research, market orientation and customer relationship management: a framework and implications for service providers, *Journal of Services Marketing*, 20, 1, 12-23.

Jobber, D. (2001) *Principles and practice of marketing*, McGraw-Hill, London.

Kotler, P. (1997) *Marketing management analysis, planning, implementation and control,* Prentice-Hall, Englewood Cliffs, NJ.

Kracklauer, A., Passenheim, O. and Seifert, D. (2001) Mutual customer approach: how industry and trade are executing collaborative customer relationship management, *International Journal of Retail & Amp*, 29, 12.

Krueger, M. (2000) Fulfilment: The gateway to customer loyalty, *Manufacturing Systems; Wheaton*, 18, 9, 32.

Law, M., Lau, T. and Wong, Y. H. (2003) From customer relationship management to customer-managed relationship: unraveling the paradox with a co-creative perspective, *Marketing Intelligence & Amp*, 21, 1, 51-60.

Lee, J. S. and Sohn, S. Y. (2006) Cost of ownership model for a CRM system, *Science of Computer Programming*, 60, 1, 68.

Light, B. (2003) CRM packaged software: a study of organisational experiences, *Business Process Management Journal*, 9, 5, 603-616.

McKitterick, J. (1957) What is the Marketing Management Concept? *Proceedings of the American Marketing Association Conference*, Chicago, IL.

Mohammad, A. B. (2001) CRM implementation an empirical study of best practice and a proposed model of implementation, *TQM*, Bradford.

Mukund, A. (2003) *The Customer Relationship Management Champion*, ICFAI Centre For Management Research, Hyderabad.

Newell, F. (2000) *Loyalty.com: Customer Relationship Management in the New Era of Internet Marketing*, McGraw-Hill, New York, NY.

Payne, A. (2006) *Handbook of CRM achieving excellence in customer management*, Elsevier Butterworth-Heinemann, Oxford.

Peck, H., Payne, A., Christopher, M. and Clark, M. (1999) *Relationship Marketing Strategy and Implementation,* Butterworth-Heinemann, Oxford.

Persson, P. (2004) Customer Relationship Management: How a CRM system can be used in the sales process. *Department of Business Administration and Social Science,* Lulea University of Technology, Stockholm.

Quinn, F. (1996) Becoming a customer-driven organisation: three key questions, *Managing Service Quality*, 6, 6.

Raman, P. (1999) Way to create loyalty, *New Straits Times,* Kuala Lumpur.

Reda, S. (2000) Customer relationship management, *Stores Magazine*, 6-33.

Reichheld, F. F. and Teal, T. (2001) *The loyalty effect the hidden force behind growth, profits, and lasting value,* Harvard Business School, Boston, Mass.

Rodgers, K. and Howlett, D. (2000) *What is CRM?* GoldMine Software (Europe) Limited, Berkshire.

Stefanou, C. J., Sarmaniotis, C. and Stafyla, A. (2003) CRM and customer-centric knowledge management: an empirical research, *Business Process Management Journal,* 9, 5, 617-634.

Sterne, J. (1996*) Customer Service on the Internet: Building Relationships, Increasing Loyalty, and Staying Competitive,* John Wiley and Sons, New York, NY.

Storbacka, K., Strandvik, T. and Gronross, C. (1994) Managing Customer Relationships for Profit: The Dynamics of Relationship Quality, *International Journal of Service Industry Management,* 5, 5, 21-38.

Swift, R. S. (2001) *Accelerating Customer Relationships: Using CRM and Relationship Technologies,* Prentice-Hall, Englewood Cliffs, NJ.

Xu, Y., Yen, D. C., Lin, B. and Chou, D. C. (2002) Adopting customer relationship management technology, *Industrial Management & Data Systems Management,* 102, 8, 442-452.

Young, M. and Stepankek, M. (2003) CRM Strategies: Loyalty Programs That Are Working, *Enterprise News & Review.*

Zeng, Y. E., Wen, H. J. and Yen, D. C. (2003) Customer relationship management (CRM) in business-to-business (B2B) e-commerce, *Information Management & Computer Security,* 11, 1, 39-44.

Chapter 2

CRM implementation: The key factors

Introduction

As competition increases, an organisation needs to be customer-focused to survive in any market, since the customers make or break the organisation's success. Gartner group predicted that worldwide spending on CRM would reach $76.5 billion in 2005, up from $23.26 billion achieved in 2000 (Starkey and Woodcock, 2002).

Even though CRM systems are proving an incredibly popular choice for implementation, success is proving illusive. However, effectively implementing such an approach requires radical changes in processes, technologies and employees if a business is not already somewhat customer-focused.

Bull (2003) reports that one study of 202 CRM projects found that only 30.7% of organisations said that they had achieved improvements in the way they sell to and service customers. Furthermore, Tanoury (2002) indicates that in sophisticated consulting organisations and in Fortune 500 companies, projects continue to fail, with some industry experts claiming a project failure rate of 60% to 70%. He further adds that failure is defined as a project that does not meet its business objectives.

Most CRM projects in larger companies take between 3 and 5 years to implement. Ang and Buttle (2002) argue that the technology component typically is a large investment at the outset. However, over the full term of the CRM project, technology costs account for between one-third and one-fifth of overall costs. Other costs are incurred in changing two other core elements of CRM strategies: people and process. People may need to be re-skilled or retrenched; talent may need to be recruited. Consultants may need to be brought in to conduct some of the project, such as systems integration and data warehousing. Front and back-office processes may need to be re-engineered.

The organisation may need redesigning around customers or segments. Thus, applying CRM is a complicated task that needs to have a big consideration from the top-level management in the organisation.

CRM development life cycle

Many authors and practitioners have introduced a CRM life cycle from various perspectives. Some of them, for example, have outlined CRM development from the viewpoint of practical use of the data source (Ahn *et al.*, 2003). In contrast, Tie (2003) has indicated that the CRM life cycle comprises three phases: acquiring, enhancing and retaining the customer. Each phase supports increased intimacy and understanding between a company and its customers. On the other hand, Bose (2002) outlined the CRM development life cycle from a holistic view that includes eight phases, each one is described in turn.

Planning phase

CRM has to receive commitment from the top management. In this phase, it would be wise for management to consider the uniformity of their product offering and the value that customers will put on a customised interaction with the firm. Additionally, identifying how managers at various levels of the organisation will use the information is critical. Wells *et al.* (1999) suggest several components for such interaction. First, the firm must identify how, when and where it will be interacting with customers. The key is to initially identify all of these interaction points and, then, determine whether to retain, modify or remove the points. The IT manager should focus on how these interactions can be recorded into an information system.

Moreover, Pavlin (2004) argues that during the planning stage, the scope of the project is reviewed in detail, and an analysis of the business processes is initiated for all customers facing departments that will use the CRM solution. Business requirements and processes are approved and mapped to CRM. The planning phase takes into account how training, testing and support for the deployment will be done.

Research phase

In this phase, Bose (2002) argues that methods for addressing the CRM needs of the organisation must be recognised. For example, addressing important questions such as why they need CRM would be vital. Lipscomb (2004) agrees and stresses that the CRM objectives have to be determined before the implementation. It would be important to recognise the current organisational structure, culture, hardware, software, vendors, etc. A careful assessment of resources and market conditions is critical in this phase. Therefore, the company has to define the benefits for deploying the project and whether the project goes hand in hand with the business objectives and goals or not.

System analysis phase

In this phase, careful and thoughtful planning is the most critical element. The system analysis phase combined with the previous planning phase are arguably the most important steps (Bose, 2002). During it, several critical factors need to be considered.

CRM is customer interaction

It is important to provide all necessary information to users in order to have a good interaction with the customers. Bose (2002) has outlined two ways in which a CRM system may interact with the customer: IT-assisted or automated interaction. In IT-assisted (manual), an employee becomes the intermediary between the CRM and the customer (see Figure 2.1). Usually, in this case, the interaction between employee and customer is the key, and CRM is a tool used to assist the employee. An example of such interaction is a telephone support centre.

In automated interaction, the customer is placed in complete control of the interaction (see Figure 2.1). This would mean empowering the customer through technologies such as the World Wide Web, kiosks, or automated phone systems. In this case, the customer would interact directly with the CRM system.

Figure 2.1 Assisted vs. automated interaction

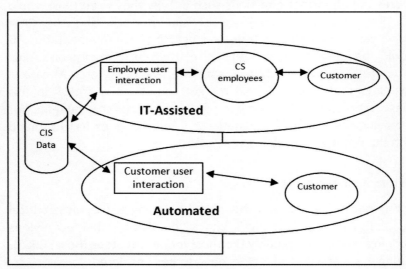

Source: Adopted from Bose (2002)

Obtain outside expertise

When developing a CRM system, the company has to engage an expert to support the CRM project. The reason for this is because CRM implementation requires additional technical staff and experienced consultants who can ensure the successful implementation (Bose, 2002).

Furthermore, Market Force (2000) reports that selecting a CRM vendor is as critical as selecting the CRM software. When choosing a vendor, CRM experience is a crucial element. Choosing an experienced vendor that you have strong confidence in, can communicate easily with, and is responsive to your needs and requests is essential as he/she will be with you for the life of your CRM system. An experienced vendor will:

- Identify specific business automation requirements.

- Train project teams.

- Design, document and configure the system.

- Provide implementation and technical support.

- Train users, managers and support staff.

- Roll-out the CRM system to user workgroups.

- Provide ongoing support services.

Consider implementation in stages

Bose (2002) says that the CRM implementation can be of more benefit if it can be implemented in stages, even if the company has the available resources to implement it in a short period. Prior requirements need to be recognised before the CRM implementation takes place (e.g. data warehouse, data mining, integrated phone systems, etc.). The implementation of CRM can be obtained gradually, and with increasing functionality comes increasing value (Dyché, 2002). Thus, to avoid risk and complexity in the project managers need to consider the implementation in divided stages. This is supported by Tanoury (2002), who argues that expecting a project to deliver all required functionality in one-phase increases complexity and risk.

Re-design of customer data

It is important to reconsider how data are stored in the company. Three major aspects of CRM data have to be considered: integrating customer data across the entire firm, expanding the customer data profile, and integration with legacy systems (see Figure 2.2).

Figure 2.2 Fragmented vs. integrated view of customer data

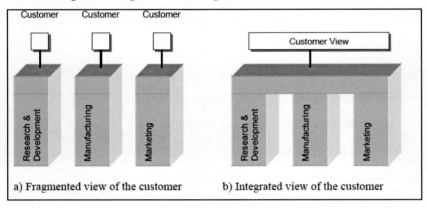

Source: Adopted from Bose (2002)

Scalability

Because CRM is such a new technology, it is nearly certain that firms will be working overtime to keep up with changes. Given the enterprise scope and the evolving nature of CRM, it will be important to create a system that can be scaled to meet the changing needs of the future. Selection of hardware or software that has limited connectivity or scalability should be avoided. Buttle (2004) agrees and indicates that as a CRM system grows, and is used by more internal and external people, the scalability of the system becomes vital. Therefore, the system has to be customised to suit customers' needs and requirements.

Feasibility study

Before starting to develop a CRM system, it is vital to decide whether the CRM implementation is feasible or not. CRM requires a lot of support and resources from all levels in the organisation, and needs fundamental changes in the company. A CRM project can be quite expensive. Bose (2002) indicates that 38% of current CRM users plan to spend more than $1 million on systems, and final approval usually comes from the most senior management, while 42% indicated the CEOs would have the final decision. As CRM implementation always involves enormous amounts of money, people and resources, it is crucial to the company to execute cost-benefit analysis of the CRM project in terms of business value (Knox 2003; Tie, 2003).

Design phase

In this stage, CRM involves detailed specifications on the design. Consideration of what software package has to be involved alongside the core technologies, such as data warehouse, decision support system (DSS), etc. A common complaint seems to be the lack of easy integration between CRM and ERP packages.

Construction phase

This stage entails the execution of the design plan. It is a difficult and large task unless the company has divided the implementation into different stages; the company has to rely on vendors and consultants to ensure smoothness. Brandon (2005) states that firms should closely review the depth and breadth of consulting services provided by CRM vendors under consideration. A company thus has to make sure that the vendor that it selects can provide experienced and dedicated consulting staff members who will work with its team to ensure success.

Implementation phase

It is essential that the workers realise what CRM entails, and the goals with it. A critical component in the implementation phase is training. CRM implementation may involve major IT and business process changes that all users must fully understand. A solid training programme will therefore go a long way in helping employees to understand not only the goal of CRM, but also to understand how the system will help to better serve the customer.

Maintenance and documentation phase

Maintenance is an imperative phase, since a company must always be seeking to learn more about its customers. Because the marketplace is dynamic, CRM requires continual evaluation of the system performance, and data quantity and quality. IT should work continuously with other functional areas such as marketing, management and production to ensure that the system meets the needs of the decision makers in the firm.

Adaptation phase

This is a critical component, as CRM is still in its infancy: as a company learns more about its customers (through use of the CRM system), it will change. In the past, adding a new product or sales channel may have meant only minor changes for an IT department. However, a new sales channel or product may alter the customer interaction points or the types of data that need to be collected. If

IT fails to make changes, the company will quickly lose the competitive edge of the customer-centric orientation.

Critical success factors in CRM implementation

In this era, the CRM concept has emerged as a new phenomenon to many organisations around the world. CRM implementation is not off-risk and needs a customer focused organisation; it may also need re-engineering of the current business processes to support the implementation (Xu *et al.*, 2002; Bull 2003; Kotorov 2003; Bolton, 2004). It has also become, for many companies, an IT project rather than driven by the marketing department; the real problem with CRM is that it is not a marketing-driven concept (Cuthbertson and Laine, 2004).

Furthermore, having CRM software installed, by itself does not ensure a successful customer relationship. For this to happen, business processes and company culture have to be redesigned to focus on the customer needs and requirements. Baumeister (2002) points out that CRM software can be only an enabler to implement a customer strategy.

The reason a CRM project fails lies in the way companies regard CRM systems. Light (2001) argues that if companies view CRM as a technological project that is bounded by time and budget, instead of regarding CRM as a long-term commitment to efficiency and improvement, the project will definitely fail. Ryals and Knox (2001) have the same opinion, and contend that the CRM project has to be seen as a holistic approach, including strategy and organisational process.

A number of authors and practitioners have established many studies regarding CRM implementation (Galbreath and Rogers, 1999; Mohammad, 2001; Radcliffe, 2001; Ang and Buttle, 2002; Dyché, 2002; Bull, 2003; Gurau, 2003; Knox, 2003; Kotorov, 2003; Newell, 2003; Greenberg, 2004; Lawler, 2006). Nevertheless, most of these studies have not covered a holistic approach for the implementation of CRM.

For instance, some studies have focused generally on the operational side of the implementation, while others have concentrated on the strategic level only (see Figures 2.3 and 2.4). These studies however ignore the overall CRM project implementation (e.g. communication or integration between departments inside the organisation) (Mohammad, 2001; Trestini, 2001; Bull, 2003; Newell, 2003; Pavlin, 2004).

Figure 2.3 CRM implementation phases

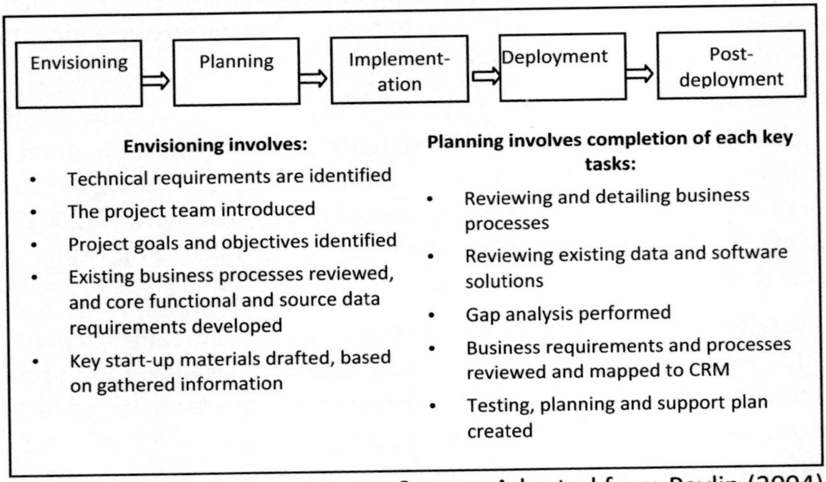

Envisioning	Planning	Implement-ation	Deployment	Post-deployment

Envisioning involves:	**Planning involves completion of each key tasks:**
• Technical requirements are identified	• Reviewing and detailing business processes
• The project team introduced	• Reviewing existing data and software solutions
• Project goals and objectives identified	• Gap analysis performed
• Existing business processes reviewed, and core functional and source data requirements developed	• Business requirements and processes reviewed and mapped to CRM
• Key start-up materials drafted, based on gathered information	• Testing, planning and support plan created

Source: Adopted from Pavlin (2004)

The investigation of factors potentially affecting the success of CRM implementation is of great importance, because the CRM software market worldwide according to a Gartner group prediction would reach $76.5 billion in 2005, up from $23.26 billion achieved in 2000 (Starkey and Woodcock, 2002).

Figure 2.4 Roadmap for implementing CRM

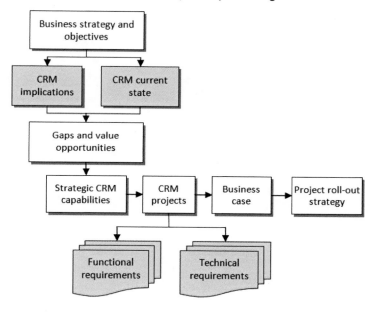

Source: Adopted from Mohammad *et al.* (2002)

Furthermore, Radcliffe (2001) and Kotorov (2003), for example, mention the critical success factors (CSFs) of CRM implementation from strategic and tactical perspectives, but did not cite the level of project implementation (see Figure 2.5).

Figure 2.5 Eight building blocks of CRM

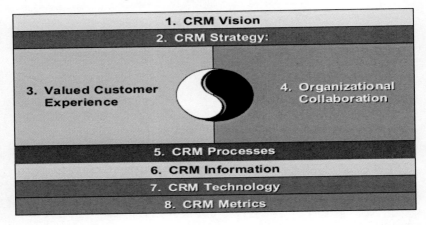

Source: Adopted from Radcliffe (2001)

Figure 2.6 CRM implementation model

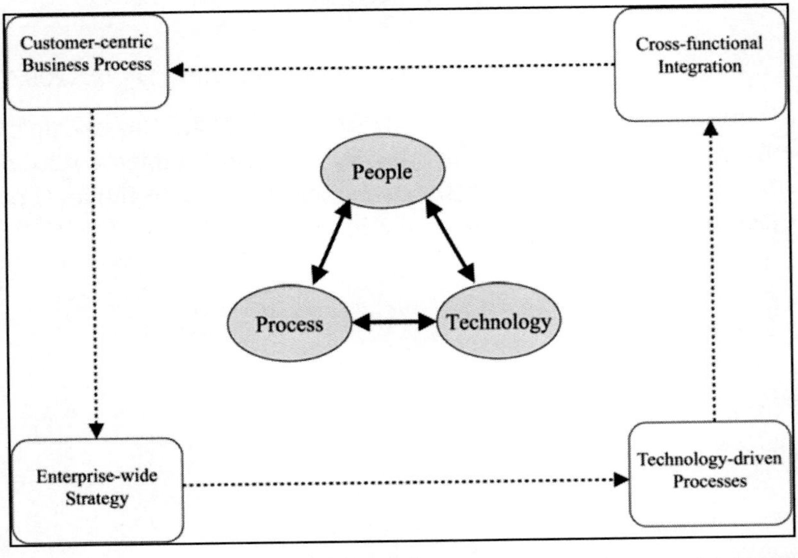

Source: Adopted from Chen and Popovich (2003)

Chen and Popovich (2003) depicted a CRM implementation model that aligns the people, process and technology together, but without considering the importance of project plan or benchmarking in the implementation (see Figure 2.6). On the other hand, Newell (2003) designed eight steps to CRM success: design CRM to meet the customer's needs, establish a benchmark, define measurable goals, create strategy, re-engineer the processes, be able to change technology, and finally select the right tools. However, Newell did not identify project plan or top management involvement.

Some authors discussed the strategic and tactical levels together as critical factors for the CRM implementation (see Table 2.1). Silva and Rahimi (2003) presented the CSFs of CRM implementation based on the Holland and Light (1999) model of ERP implementation, and they think that ERP and CRM implementation processes are similar. They believe that the implementation of both systems is executed from a strategic perspective, and is not a software implementation. They think also that the major difference lies in the fact that each system focuses on a different element. ERP focuses on internal processes and resource management (e.g. employees and finance, manufacturing certain products, etc.), while the CRM approach focuses on the customer, and to that end consists of marketing, selling, customer service, and call centre models.

Keen (2000) suggests that in order to have a successful CRM implementation, we should go over the ERP implementations and evaluate them. He mentioned that what makes the ERP implementation successful would be the same in the CRM implementation, and what had been expected or underestimated has to be considered in the CRM project.

Table 2.1 Revised essential strategic and tactical CSFs for CRM implementation

Strategic CSFs	Tactical CSFs
• CRM philosophy • Project mission • Top management commitment • Project schedule and plans	• Client consultation • Connectivity • Skilful personnel • Technical tasks • Client acceptance • Monitoring and feedback • Communication • Troubleshooting • BPS and software configuration

Source: Adopted from Silva and Rahimi (2003)

Furthermore, Trestini (2001) depicts the CRM implementation life cycle from the operational side. It however neglects the overall project issues such as integration and data or information.

There are many practitioners and authors (Radcliffe, 2001; Bose, 2002; Rigby *et al.,* 2002; Tanoury, 2002; Myron, 2003; Newell, 2003; Lindgreen *et al.* 2006) who have investigated why CRM projects failed. Others (Corner and Hinton, 2002; Greenberg, 2004) have identified sets of risks associated with CRM implementation. However, there is little or no scientifically solid research published on factors affecting the success of CRM. This study will focus on the CSFs that help the organisation to implement CRM project successfully.

Figure 2.7 CRM implementation lifecycle

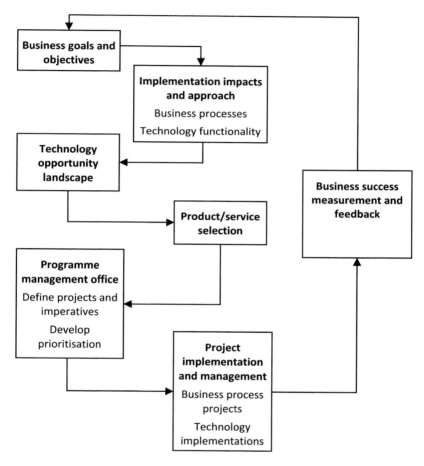

Source: Adopted from Trestini (2001)

In essence, there are critical issues that must be carefully considered to ensure successful implementation of CRM project. Based on a vast literature review conducted on CRM implementation, this study has derived a framework of CRM system project implementation, depicted in Figure 2.8. This conceptual framework will be tested through a complementary empirical investigation using a combination of qualitative and quantitative methods to ensure whether these factors have an impact on CRM implementation or not.

Figure 2.8 CRM conceptual framework

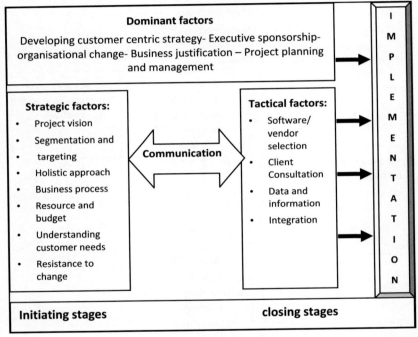

Source: Al-Ajlan and Zairi (2005)

In general, a CRM project is complex and not easy to adopt if the organisation does not consider several factors that contribute directly or indirectly to the success of its implementation. The following sections will discuss the dominant factors, the strategic factors, and the tactical factors of CRM implementation.

Dominant factors

The dominant factors have to be recognised throughout the implementation phases, as they have a considerable impact on the process of implementation.

Developing customer centric strategy

CRM is both a business and technology strategy; most of those companies which have failed to implement CRM, think that the software would be the only solution to their problems. Most implementations fail because the organisation fails to adopt a clear strategy and fails to make appropriate changes to its business processes (Crosby, 2002; Xu et al., 2002; Bolton, 2004; Teo and Pan, 2006).

One key point that managers should understand is that although CRM depends on, and is driven by cutting edge technology, it works only when supported by the corporate culture that embraces customer-focused aims (Xu et al., 2002). Thus, without the comprehensive understanding of customer-focused objectives, the company will find it very difficult to really leverage this cutting-edge technology (Baumeister, 2002; Xu et al., 2002; Cuthbertson and Laine, 2004). Ang and Buttle (2002) and Harvard Business School (2002) agree with this opinion, and point out that CRM does better in organisations that are already customer-centric, therefore this factor is the cornerstone for adopting such a concept.

Lee (2002) mentioned that developing customer-centric business strategies is also known as the step most want to avoid, because it is all about planning. Who has the time and patience for planning will have a successful CRM implementation. However, this is not enough; a CRM strategy is not an implementation plan or road map. A real CRM strategy takes the direction and financial goals of the business strategy, and sets out how the enterprise is going to build customer loyalty. The objectives of a CRM strategy are to target, acquire, develop and retain valuable customers to achieve corporate goals (Radcliffe, 2001).

Cho *et al.* (2002) have the same opinion; they have indicated that successful CRM requires a clear strategy that concentrates on customer loyalty and uses complaint-handling data to solve customers' problems. If a CRM strategy can be shown to improve profitability, then the organisation is obviously on the right path and succeeding (Bull, 2003).

On the other hand, Newell (2000), Rigby *et al.* (2002), and Gurau (2003) all concur that the company has to create a customer strategy before starting to deploy the CRM programme; it has to identify the customers with which it wants to build a relationship and those customers it does not want to have. Not every customer is profitable; the company has to define its customers based on their profitability. Before spending the smallest amount on CRM, executives therefore need to make sure they have the right targets in their sights (Harvard Business School, 2002)

Finally, the CRM concept is frequently misunderstood. Many organisations struggle with attempting to define who their customers are, and fail to address their customer relationship model. While a CRM tool can be designed to accommodate most business processes, doing so will many times circumvent CRM best practices (Tanoury, 2002).

Executive sponsorship

CRM implementation is a hard task; it involves business process change and the introduction of new information technology. Consequently, effective leadership is important. The top management has an influence to make or break the project (Galbreath and Rogers, 1999; Silva and Rahimi, 2003; Kristoffersen and Singh, 2004; Brandon, 2005; Lee, 2006). Successful CRM must start from the top down; getting involvement from upper management as well as all key areas of the business will reduce risk and ensure the success (Buggy, 2001; Chen and Popovich, 2003).

Bull (2003) has emphasised that the role of the leaders is of importance, and because leaders monitor the external environments of an organisation they are often the best placed to set the vision or strategic direction for CRM projects. Pinto and Slevin (1987) add that they are also influential in terms of controlling the expenses, monitoring performance and motivating the personnel. Ang and Buttle (2002) and Tanoury (2002) go along with this opinion; and stress the responsibility of executive level sponsorship. Without the active sponsorship of top management, it is difficult, if not impossible, to obtain the level of commitment and participation necessary from the staff that has the required expertise at a functional level to support the needs of a CRM project.

The difference between informal support and active leadership can be the difference between success and failure. Executives have to be prepared to engage personally in the implementation process. They also need to communicate to their employees and ask them how this project would improve customer satisfaction, reduce work frustrations and make employees jobs easier (Brendler and Loyle, 2001). Unless the management team is fully committed, it is not worth starting the CRM initiative. Commitment usually begins with the redesigning of sales and marketing processes, and is a key strategic challenge (Saviano, 2004).

Sanchez (2003) points out that many think that the need of leadership for CRM projects is a figurehead role; they think their involvement ends with the signing of the cheque to purchase the software. But in fact, CRM requires an executive sponsor who is informed about customer strategy and involved in the project.

Chen and Popovich (2003) agree with this, and point out that top management commitment is an essential element; this commitment, however, is much more than a CEO giving his or her blessing to the CRM project. They also believe that a customer-centric management requires top management support and commitment to CRM throughout the entire CRM implementation. Executive involvement is also critical to steer the project, so that it is continually in alignment with the company's strategic objectives. As a result, everyone knows and understands his/her role in the success of the initiative and its overall importance to the firm.

A query survey of more than a dozen project managers found that lack of executive sponsorship is the biggest risk factor in any project. For a CRM project to be successful, it must have the support and commitment of key executives within the organisation. Executive sponsorship ensures that the project has high visibility and buy-in across all ranks of users (Bordoloi, 2000). Therefore, it is very important that the organisation ensures the sponsorship of the key executives whose areas are going to be affected by the CRM implementation.

Communication

Lack of communication can be categorised as one of the leading strategic mistakes in a CRM project (Tanoury, 2002). Therefore, communication between departments is vital to ensure the success of the implementation. CRM involves improved and increased communication between a company and its customers, as well as within the company itself (Xu *et al.*, 2002).

Tanoury (2002) argues that communication is vital to the success of a project. At the onset of a project, the vision and goals need to be communicated to all employees who will be impacted by it. It is not enough for departments to communicate between each other (e.g. sales, marketing, customer service, etc), but every point of contact with the customer must be enhanced. He also adds that regular communication throughout the project will ensure that a project stays on track and does not take any unnecessary deviation. Lack of project status updates can create major problems for a project.

When there is no communication regarding the status of a project, everyone assumes there are no outstanding issues and everything is on schedule.

Chase (2001), Ang and Buttle (2002), Kotorov (2003), Meltzer (2004), and Teo and Pan (2006) all point out that, to ensure the success of any CRM system implementation, especially those that involve human interaction, the organisation must design a robust communications strategy that permeates the whole programme. Communications are not merely tacked on but are the core of any CRM implementation.

Regular communication should be delivered throughout the company highlighting 'where we are' in the project, sharing milestones, and informing staff what happens next. The reasons for process change, where the company wants to be and why, should be communicated to all employees. Organisations that fail to communicate this may experience limited success when the CRM solution is initially deployed (Tanoury, 2002)

Organisational change

Implementing CRM is likely to cause some organisational change in terms of reforming business units, acquiring new staff, and changing existing business activities (Radcliffe, 2001). Many organisations believe that the current business process is the only way the business can run, and as a result do not feel the need for change. Tanoury (2002) opposes this perspective; he points out that unwillingness of an organisation to change can destroy a CRM project. Failure to re-engineer the current business process is a classic mistake that organisations make. Newell (2003) claims that the change has to take place in re-engineering the process to move from the goal of improving efficiencies and reducing costs to the goal of transferring power to the customer.

On the other hand, Rigby *et al.* (2002) believe that having a customer strategy is not enough; a CRM rollout will succeed only after the organisation changes its processes (job description, performance measures, compensation systems, training programmes, etc.) in order to meet customers' needs.

Furthermore, Dyché (2002) points out that CRM creates business change; a successful CRM programme not only changes the way a company deals with its customers, but also changes the way customers deal with the company. Gillies *et al.* (2002) state that to make a success of a CRM programme the company has to ensure it is aligned with its customer strategy. One of the reasons more than half of all CRM programmes fail is because a CRM software solution is parachuted into a company in the vain hope that it will resolve on its own a business's customer relationship problems.

Tie (2003) indicates that some CRM studies have shown that most small companies will choose fast and simple implementation of a CRM system, that needs as little customisation as possible because of limited financial and IT resources. Small companies should be aware of what kinds of organisational change might occur when adopting CRM strategy and technologies, identifying possible cost drivers from those changes, and developing proactive business models to deal with changes as well as contingencies.

According to a survey conducted by the online resource centre, CRM Forum, when asked what went wrong with their CRM projects, 4% of managers cited software problems, 1% said they received bad advice, but 87% pinned the failure of their CRM programmes on the lack of adequate organisational change (Rigby *et al.*, 2002).

Simpson (2002) points out that 75% of the investment in a CRM project is related to organisational change, and only 25% is the software implementation and consulting. He also adds that organisational change is a painful process requiring new perspectives, responsibilities, team set-ups, and behaviours, and it is essential that HR and training are highly involved in synchronising and supporting these activities.

Business justification

The CRM implementation always involves an enormous amount of money, people and resources. Therefore, it is imperative to the company to perform cost-benefit analysis of a CRM project in terms of business value (Knox, 2003; Tie, 2003). In this booming CRM market, some companies rush to get CRM products before they really understand how these products can make any difference for their companies. When the leaders in some companies were asked why they decided to install CRM products, they responded that it was because this is the most advanced technology (Xu *et al.*, 2002). Consequently, the company has to identify the needs of the CRM before starting the project.

Lipscomb (2004) thinks that the company should answer this important question: what are my customer relationship management objectives? From there, it should be able to formulate its policy and extract the high-level requirements necessary for selection of a CRM system that best fits its needs. It is also extremely important that customers understand the importance of the underlying technology platform in their selection.

On the other hand, Mohammad (2001) states that CRM is not suitable for every company. The company should begin by clearly defining its business issues and needs, and then determine whether CRM can and should be a part of the solution. CRM strategies that are clearly linked to business objectives have a much greater likelihood of success.

Myron (2003) argues that the project leader must start by crafting a valid business case for CRM before selecting a vendor, upgrading software, or launching a new project. The primary elements of a CRM business case are: how does it benefit us, tangibly and intangibly, and what will it cost us? That cost can be financial or the cost of risk (Greenberg, 2004).

According to the Gartner Group, however, more than 60% of companies that have implemented CRM did not have mutually agreed upon goals for their projects prior to the installation. This in turn will lead to destroying the project at the beginning, and create a disaster for the company.

Project planning and management

As described earlier, CRM implementation is complex, costly, and needs time. As a result, it has to be managed and monitored carefully. Thus, project planning and management is deemed a vital factor in implementing a CRM project. According to Mohammad (2001), good CRM implementation begins with up-front planning. He argues that developing parameters for the project is important in maintaining schedules, managing scope and utilising resources.

The company has to create its project in stages, and an organisation's desire to implement everything at once should be discouraged and prohibited (Tanoury, 2002). To reduce costs and the risk of introducing CRM at a company, a CRM solution should be established not in one big step, but in several small steps in a company. This, of course, requires software that has to integrate into the current IT infrastructure, and that can be extended in a modular fashion (Baumeister, 2002).

According to Pavlin (2004), planning is the most important phase for successful CRM implementation. During this phase, the key tasks that will dictate the implementation process are researched and discussed. And, in order for the implementation to be successful, each of these key tasks needs to be completed:

- Reviewing and detailing the business processes.
- Reviewing existing data and software solutions.

- Performing a gap analysis.

- Reviewing and mapping business requirements and processes to CRM.

- Creating a testing, planning and support plan.

Furthermore, Mohammad (2001) introduced four steps for successful project planning and management:

- Define project.

- Review current systems environment.

- Formulate grounds for evaluation.

- Develop recommended systems architecture.

The lack of an effective project plan is crippling to a project. It creates an environment without a common frame of reference for the project team, and clients as well (Tanoury, 2002).

Strategic factors

As discussed before, the CRM project is affected at the strategic level, which is considered to be the foundation of the whole implementation processes. According to Ang and Buttle (2002), at a strategic level, CRM is seen as a core business strategy, which is combined with technology to effectively manage the complete customer life cycle. Consequently, the decisions regarding CRM implementation have to be considered at this level.

Silva and Rahimi (2003) state that the CRM philosophy, top management commitment, project mission, and project schedule and plan are CSFs at the strategic level. On the other hand, Brendler and Loyle (2001) include communication, training and understanding the culture as critical at this level. Communication, executive sponsorship, project schedule and planning have been introduced as dominant factors that have to be monitored during the implementation processes. The following section covers other factors that affect CRM implementation at the strategic level.

Clear project vision and scope

Pinto and Slevin (1987) defined the project vision as the initial clarity of goals and general direction. To have a successful CRM implementation, the CRM has to go hand in hand with business vision. A CRM project should coincide with the corporate mission and vision, and the CRM solution should be viewed as a major catalyst in achieving the corporate vision. The vision and how the CRM solution supports it must be clearly communicated to all areas of the company. If this is not done prior to the launch of the CRM project, confusion can arise, and the cooperation required from the staff who will be directly affected by the CRM project can be elusive (Tanoury, 2002).

Brendler and Loyle (2001) and Xu *et al.* (2002) all agree with this opinion, and point out that a CRM system that does not meet the organisation's goals is a disaster to a company. Furthermore, Tanoury (2002) emphasised that not only has the overall project to take into consideration the business vision to ensure success, but every single phase in the project should contribute to the company's vision. Lester (2003) also states that a successful CRM initiative starts with the end goal in mind to understand clients and prospects from all perspectives.

On the other hand, Stewart (2004) warns that the result of having a multi-faceted organisational vision of what CRM is and how it affects the business will lead to confusion and chaos, as what is required to make CRM a success, and why, is collectively misunderstood. Therefore, the company should attempt to unify the shared vision with its employees. This supports the Galbreath and Rogers (1999) perspective, who state that the first step a leader must accomplish is to facilitate a shared vision. He or she cannot impose a vision, because it will likely be dismissed by front-line employees as another heavy-handed management tactic. The vision must come from within (e.g. employee task forces and focus groups), and spread throughout the firm to create a sense of grassroots' ownership.

Alternatively, Radcliffe (2001) argues that successful CRM requires a clear vision, so that a strategy and implementation can be developed to achieve it. The CRM vision is how the customer-centric company wants to look and feel to its customers. He also states that without a CRM vision, the company will not stand out from the competition, target customers will not know what to expect from it, and employees will not know what to deliver. A successful CRM vision is the basis to motivating staff, generating customer loyalty, and gaining a greater market share.

Segmentation and targeting

As described earlier, CRM is a strategy that identifies and attracts profitable customers, tying them to the company or product by efficient relationship marketing to guarantee profitable growth (Kracklauer *et al.*, 2001). The core of any customer relationship strategy is customer segmentation, which is why some of the world's pickiest companies have the most successful CRM programmes (Gillies *et al.*, 2002)

According to Newell (2000), CRM is a valuable tool in terms of identifying the right customer groups and for helping to decide which customers to neglect. The idea behind that is to have a relationship only with the profitable customer.

Mohammad *et al.* (2002) agree with Newell's perspective, and they state that CRM initiatives are designed to drive better relationships with customers. In addition, the relationships that are most important to a company are those that provide the greatest profit potential. To make smart decisions about CRM strategy, it is critical that a company understands its customers' values, needs, requirements and behaviours. This understanding allows the company to build systems and processes based on customer requirements, and to allocate their CRM expenditures towards customer segments that are likely to yield the greatest returns.

In an age of one-to-one marketing, many people neglect the market segmentation, but in fact, CRM strategy depends and begins with segmentation and ends with the individual customer (Crosby, 2002). Furthermore, Bull (2003) points out that one of the most popular aspects of CRM is the issue of targeting profitable customers. Ang and Buttle (2002), on the other hand, highlight the importance of CRM as a discipline of customer portfolio analysis in guiding CRM implementations. They argue that the company has to divide its customers into different segments, which in turn will help to identify the most profitable customers.

Before implementing or fixing CRM, focus should be more on the customer relationship, and not on the management. The company should know customer buying behaviours, understand product problems, and interview its customers. This information should then drive the steps that follow. Understanding the company from the customer's point of view is the first step to successful CRM (Chase, 2001).

Therefore, failing to recognise the significance of segmentation and targeting will lead the CRM project to fail. The company has to identify its customers before the selection and implementation of the chosen software (Bull, 2003).

Holistic approach

Because CRM reaches into so many potential parts of the business, Girishankar (2000) suggests that organisations should adopt a holistic approach. The holistic approach is one where CRM involves the entire organisation, and where CRM software tools are integrated with all other corporate information systems. Other authors like Trepper (2000), Dyché (2002) and Tie (2003) claim that CRM includes operational, analytical and collaborative elements. For Mohammad *et al.* (2002), Newell (2003), Greenberg (2004) and Meltzer (2004), CRM goes beyond the front office, it has to be integrated to other systems within the organisation (e.g. back office).

Bull (2003) points out that the holistic approaches to CRM help organisations effectively manage and maintain the growth of disparate customer contact points or channels of communication. He adds two significant issues that highlight the importance of the need to take a holistic approach, and the difficulties associated with doing so. Both issues involve the complexities associated with integration, one with changing operational functions into customer-centric business processes, the other with the problems associated with integrating CRM software into corporate information systems.

Therefore, the company that adopts CRM has to take into consideration the holistic approach, otherwise its absence will lead the CRM initiatives to fail because the CRM is more than technology or just front-office activities.

Business processes

Lack of a well-defined business process is a strategic mistake that will lead to failure of a CRM implementation (Tanoury, 2002; Fjermestad *et al.*, 2003). The current business process must be recognised so that the CRM tool may be utilised to its full potential. Tanoury (2002) points out that once the current business process is documented, all areas of the organisation that are involved in any part of the process need to validate it. Most organisations have departments that follow unique sub-processes that are unidentified to the managers; these processes have to be understood to ensure a smooth deployment of the CRM project.

Chase (2001), Patton (2002) and Tanoury (2002) all agree that a classic mistake that is made when implementing a CRM project is to insist that the current process remains unchanged, and has the CRM solution designed to support the current process. Greenberg (2004) points out that analysing business processes in terms of their benefit to customers will suggest elimination of some, change to others, and additions to fill holes that will become apparent.

Fluss (2005) indicates that new technology is a good thing but does not take the place of effective business process management. He further reveals that the core issue is that the vast majority of CRM systems do not address business process management. CRM is about improving relationships with customers to maximise enterprise profitability, and technology is only a small part of that goal. As automation is not the end-plan but an enabler, enterprises should pay as much, if not more, attention to improving their processes as they do to technology.

Thinking that technology is a solution is a big pitfall, as in most companies there are process gaps. These gaps occur when the customer wants something but the process produces something else. Mohammad *et al.* (2002) argue that managers commonly believe that deploying CRM technology will bridge these gaps. But in reality, the gaps often exist because the processes that affect the customer are poorly designed. They further add that these poorly designed processes cause wait times between the steps a customer has to take to get what he/she wants, for instance:

- Processes that require too many managers' approval.

- Processes that do not add any value to the customer experience.

- Processes that cannot get done properly because of poor organisational culture (i.e. a culture that rewards individuals with information, chilling collaboration).

- Processes that are not done properly because individuals do not understand the goal of the organisation.

Gillies *et al.* (2002) present an example. They state that Tesco (the giant UK grocery retailer) adapted its business processes and then added technology, which in turn leads to thinking through the customer experience every step of the way; that is why Tesco is a distinctive company in delivering the right service to its customers.

The function of process re-engineering in CRM is fairly obvious. In order to put the customer in the centre of the business circle, the departmental roles and responsibilities have to be changed. And when that happens, new work processes have to be adopted. Otherwise, people will do the same work they have always done without new outcomes (Lee, 2002).

Fjermestad *et al.* (2003) suggest that the company has to pay more attention to the end user's involvement; involving the end user at this stage of the project will help to make any process change. Fluss (2005) agrees with this idea, and refers to project failure because the management is focused on their own objectives, and simply neglected to ask the system users, the people who will make or break an implementation, what they need exactly, which is often not a new system but new processes. Therefore, if a company wants to install a new CRM system or is planning to do so, it has to review its business processes to ensure successful implementation.

Resources and budget

When deploying a CRM project, the management has to allocate sufficient resources; this includes monetary, human and technological (Colvin, 2003). He further adds that to fully realise the benefit of the CRM project, sufficient funds must be obtained. Bolts (2002) concurs, and points out that CRM is an expensive project; nothing is more costly in terms of time and money than a failed CRM system. By investing the time and resources required at each stage of the CRM project, the company will soon realise the benefits of CRM success (Market Force, 2000).

Xu *et al.* (2002) argue that cooperating sales, marketing and customer service activities is the first stage in the CRM implementation; these things are of course necessary, but not sufficient. It also requires exploitation of human and organisational resources to support the implementation processes. It is a journey rather than a destination. Kotler (1997), Buggy (2001) and Bull (2003) all agree with this, and emphasise the importance of having sufficient funds to support the implementation process. They also ask to devote not only sufficient resources, but time as well, so that an effective CRM strategy can be deployed.

Trying to implement a CRM programme as cheaply as possible is a big mistake to make. Often, the company ignores including CRM initiatives within its budget, which in turn leads to running a CRM project that does not meet company requirements, and results in a CRM system that will be refused by the users (Chaudhry, 2002).

The company has to include the costs of staffing, process changes, training and communication, as well as installation and deployment. Some of these costs are ongoing throughout the life of the initiative, and must be considered in resource planning. Treating a CRM initiative as solely an IT project, and failing to consider the other organisational costs, can result in under-utilisation of the CRM solution, and depress the ultimate return the firm realises from its investment (Interface Software, 2005).

Understanding customer needs

The main pitfall that most companies face is designing their CRM initiatives according to their business needs, not according to the customers. Gartner Group (2003) points out that the CRM should make things easier for customers, but in fact it does not for many companies. If the CRM programme is only a tool that controls sales process and helps sales management reporting requirements it may not have been designed for the front line people, thus they may not use it. The company has to involve employees as well as customers to ensure that their interests are represented.

Lee (2002), on other hand, argues that the company should plan around the customer's needs, not the company's goals. He also adds that the company has to focus on listening to customers rather than forcing them to listen to you. King (2004) has the same view, and indicates that the company has to talk to its customers, and find out their wants and how the company can meet their needs, which are essential activities, rather than just implement a CRM initiative that abandons people on the outside of the business.

Newell (2003) points out in his book *Why CRM does not work* that most CRM programmes are driven by the desire of the company to improve the efficiency of the business process, and reduce cost while increasing sales. Companies are not asking customers what they need, what they want, or what bothers them. As companies adopt a CRM philosophy, they have to ask customers these questions to find out which processes matter to them, and what the company can change to make their lives easier. Knox (2003) attributes the problem arising with CRM implementation to the fact that the customer relationship is managed by only one partner. He argues that purveyors of new technology encourage managers to think that they can predict and manipulate customer behaviour for their own benefit.

Rigby *et al.* (2002) present one of the main four perils that many companies may face: 'stalking, not wooing, customers'. They argue that many companies invest a vast amount in loyalty programmes in order to increase customers' loyalty. But the question is: 'Does the customer value that?' The answer depends on the kind of relationships that the company wants to have with the customer. When using CRM, companies often end up trying to build relationships with the wrong customers, or trying to build relationships with the right customers the wrong way. They have to build relationships that are valued by the customers, or in other words, ensure that the relationships are two-way.

Thus, failing to design a CRM project that meets customer's needs will lead to destroying the project in its first stages. The company should involve the users as well as the customers once they deploy the project.

Resistance to change

As has been introduced before, CRM implementation requires cultural and people change (Galbreath and Rogers, 1999; Chase, 2001; Ang and Buttle, 2002; Bull, 2003). The people changes may include the need to learn new skills, to work with different functions or even to eliminate positions entirely (King and Tang, 2002). Therefore it is crucial to consider the people factors and, in particular, employees. A critical pitfall to be avoided is focusing too much on process and technology, and not enough on the people who will be using the system. For a CRM system to be successful, everyone must use it (Chaudhry, 2002).

Galbreath and Rogers (1999) argue that introducing such a change into any business can create turmoil among employees if not introduced and implemented carefully. Employees' resistance is one of the major risks associated with CRM implementation. In most companies, CRM efforts often never get off the ground because they encounter such stiff resistance (Xu *et al.*, 2002).

Myron (2003) states that it is natural to resist change. Some employees may ask why they should be forced to change their working habits. Failure to convince employees of the benefits of CRM often results in passive resistance and low employee-adoption rates. Tanoury (2002) argues that usually employees find it very difficult to change a work process they are comfortable with, and resist any change in their daily routine. He further suggests that involving employees in the project can help to break through some of these issues. Crosby (2002) writes of encountering instances of employees avoiding CRM because: they find it too confusing; lack confidence in the direction it provides; or they fail to see its relevance.

Hence, what is the company's role? Dailey and O'Brien (2002) point out that engaging people in the change process speeds up the CRM implementation and circumvents significant resistance from staff. Furthermore, Xu *et al.* (2002) recommend that a well-planned training programme is one of the solutions. Clearly, a system just cannot be put in with the hope that people will figure it out by themselves. In order to eliminate or minimise the resistance to it, companies should also let the end-users become involved early in CRM implementation and spark a grassroots movement.

Moreover, Myron (2003) advises that effectively communicating the benefits of CRM to users should bolster their confidence in and comfort levels with the new system. It is crucial to sell those benefits internally both before and during a CRM initiative. Companies must not only create buy-in, but must also maintain users' enthusiasm. Saviano (2004) points out that historically, companies that involve their personnel in the planning process have a much higher rate of programme success.

In addition, Dailey and O'Brien (2002) believe that embarking on any change initiative, such as CRM implementation requires a parallel strategy of ERM (employee relationship management). They also add that, in helping companies manage change, their experience repeatedly reveals that employees know what the problems in implementation are, usually have strong opinions about them, and honestly want to make their work environment successful.

Tactical factors

Silva and Rahimi (2003) present many tactical factors based on the Holland and Light (1999) model. These include client consultation, skilful personnel, client acceptance, monitoring and feedback, and communication. On the other hand, Kotorov (2003) points out that from a tactical perspective, there are two main challenges that need to be considered: business process integration, and systems/ applications integration.

The following sections focus on the main tactical factors that have an impact on CRM implementation. These include software selection, client consultation, data and information, and integration of the system.

Software/vendor selection

Software selection plays a prominent role at the tactical level. In this step, the company has to look at selecting software that supports (but does not drive) new workflow and work processes (Lee, 2002). Looking at CRM as another software purchase guarantees setting the stage for failure (Alohaly, 2004). Many organisations make the mistake of choosing a CRM package first, and then try to map their business processes to fit it. The search for a software package should come last in a series of sequential steps (Umashankar, 2001).

Before buying the software solution, the firm should assess its goals, and decide which customer information to collect and what to do with it. Umashankar (2001) suggests that CRM software must have certain characteristics:

- Driven by a data warehouse.

- Focused on a multi-channel view of customer behaviour.

- Based on consistent metrics to assess customer actions across channels.

- Built to accommodate the new market dynamics that place the customer in control.

- Structured to identify a customer's profitability or profit potential, and to determine effective investment allocation decisions accordingly.

- Scalable to meet growth and performance needs.

Saviano (2004) recommends that the company has to make the following considerations when choosing a CRM software package:

- Does the software have the features and functionality to implement and drive the processes and overall programme objectives?

- Is the software easy to learn, or will the learning curve be too long and perhaps lead to discouragement with less computer literate personnel?

- Does the software vendor have adequate support after installation and training?

CRM software comes in all shapes, sizes and functions. The decision has to be made according to the company's needs. Gupta and Shukla (2001) strongly recommend having a trial copy to try out before getting the final solution. Lee (2002) points out that once a company has established a list of potential systems that match up with its needs, the best way to get to a selection is to break down its technology needs process step by process step. Then roll up those needs list, and ask software suppliers to show how they will meet the company's needs.

In contrast, Greenberg (2004) argues that the vendor selection is more important than the software selection. He claims that most companies fall into this trap; a CRM application cannot solve its problems and cannot configure its limitations. Also, CRM software cannot take care of a crash of itself, but the company that provides that software can take care of those problems and solve those issues. Therefore, the company has to consider vendor selection prior to choosing an application.

Client consultation

Silva and Rahimi (2003) regard client consultation as a major tactical factor that influences the CRM implementation. Al-Mudimigh (2002) defines client consultation as the communication and consultation with, and active listening to, all affected parties, mainly the client. He further adds that it is essential for an organisation to keep its clients aware of its future project to avoid misconception.

Besides, client opinions are very important for defining the project requirement and designing work flow. It is also critical to involve the enthusiasts in each step of the development and testing, and to ask for their opinion and suggestions. Managing expectations is the key to acceptance (Xu *et al.*, 2002). Tanoury (2002) points out that realistic expectations are critical to project success, and unrealistic expectations are a leading cause of failure.

He also states that consistent and regular end-user participation through all phases of the project is a prerequisite for success. The more user input that is collected and incorporated into developed product functionality, the more likely the end users will regard the project and end product as successful. Projects that do not have a high degree of end user interaction, as well as ongoing involvement in the earliest stages increase the risk of misunderstanding the project requirements, and become highly susceptible to requirements that shift and creep.

Data and information

The CRM system is based on the customer's profile and transaction history, therefore the company needs to collect data about its customers (Kracklauer *et al.*, 2001). The implementation of CRM procedures requires the existence of historical data that are used to identify the main market segments and create an accurate customer profile. Part of the early attraction of CRM systems lay in their ability to deliver real time information to give marketers, salespeople and managers a clear picture of what is happening in the market at any particular moment. Used in the right way, real time information can help companies cope with high levels of complexity in their customer relationship cycle, making priorities clear (Harvard Business School, 2002).

Successful CRM requires a flow of customer information around the organisation and tight integration between operational and analytical systems. Having the right information at the right time is essential to successful CRM strategies, providing customer insight and allowing effective interaction across any channel (Radcliffe, 2001). CRM is all about having the information at your fingertips to understand the client, communicating back to them, and tracking your correspondence (Stimpson, 2003).

Dravis (2003) points out that according to Giga Information Group Research, data quality occasionally has turned out to be the weak underbelly of CRM implementations. Myron (2003) indicates that dirty data or inaccurate and old information can be dangerous to companies. Data are the lifeblood of a CRM system, and incorrect numbers, spelling mistakes, and outdated contact information can infect that system if left unchecked. He also adds that dirty data cannot only cost companies millions in wasted direct marketing dollars, but also it can severely hinder CRM adoption rates.

Kracklauer et al. (2001) argue that data can be obtained either through online-automated systems that register the history of customer interaction (historical data) and/or from buying the necessary data from a third party (usually a specialised market research agency). Furthermore, Galbreath and Rogers (1999) cite that information resources can come from anywhere inside or outside the firm, and this requires successful integration of multiple databases and multiple technologies, such as the internet and the web, call centres, sales force automation, and data warehouses, to name a few, in order to convert information into business intelligence.

A fundamental factor for successful CRM is the efficient linking of customer data to fulfil customer needs better. The proactive use of customer data for improving customer relationships is crucial, as opposed to simply collecting data for future retrieval (Kracklauer *et al.*, 2001). CRM ultimately focuses on effectively turning information, something most businesses are overwhelmed with, into intelligent business knowledge to manage customer relationships more efficiently (Galbreath and Rogers, 1999).

System integration

One of the CSFs of CRM implementation is the integration with the back-office systems. A comprehensive management of marketing, sales and service processes requires the integration of interactive processes in the front-office with the transaction-oriented processes in the back-office (Pushmann and Alt, 2001). This was proved by Umashankar (2001), where 47% of firms said the ability to access all relevant customer information is the biggest challenge in implementing CRM.

The essence of having good communication within an organisation that adopts CRM emerges from the flow of information. A CRM system will change the way information flows within a company (Xu *et al.*, 2002). In the case of CRM, lack of coordination leads directly to failure as it creates an incomplete or distorted customer view. The difficulty arises from the very nature of customer information which can change dynamically in each department or business unit independently of other departments or units (Kotorov, 2003).

Thus, CRM has to be regarded as a project that covers the whole organisation not only a single department. Kotorov (2003) mentioned that CRM projects that start within and as departmental level initiatives run into dead-ends, as the CRM needs to cross the departmental boundaries, and to change processes, functions, and systems in other departments.

One of the basic goals of implementing CRM is that employees can have access to all customer data from within one system. This usually means integrating with all legacy systems the organisation is already using. The biggest challenge is to integrate the CRM system with the website and software that supports other channels of communication (Alohaly, 2004). Customers should be able to use each channel interchangeably and at the same time, without having to explain who they are and what they want each time. Finding a CRM package that can easily export and import data from and to other systems will overcome this problem (Patton, 2002).

From a tactical perspective, Kotorov (2003) states that there are two main challenges: business process integration, and systems/applications integration. Both process and system integration are necessary conditions for achieving better person-to-person service and web-based self-service. Yet, the larger the scope of the project, the more daunting the integration task. Companies that do not adopt the strategic approach often settle for partial integration. Partial integration results not only in an incomplete customer view, but often in a distorted customer view, leading to confusing customer service and poor customer targeting. Successful companies took process and system integration seriously, and did not rush to produce customer level results without having obtained a nearly 360-degree view of the customer first.

Enhancing productivity and efficiency in a company's back-office is the aim of enterprise resource planning (ERP) systems, while CRM systems aim to improve customer relationships in the front-office (Pushmann and Alt, 2001). Therefore, Chase (2001) argues that the CRM has to work in connection with the rest of the enterprise, including ERP systems, the web, and other enterprise applications, to finally unleash its potential.

Chase (2001) state that:

> ... *without integration, placing an order typically involves a series of manual steps across multiple departments, often*

> *resulting in duplicate data entry, wasted effort, and numerous errors. If we cannot give them an accurate price, if we cannot give them a delivery date, if we cannot give them an accurate account status, then we have a dissatisfied customer who can, and will, take their business elsewhere.*

The way to eliminate this problem is to have a complete, unified view of the customer. This means taking all of the information that resides in various systems within the company, and making it available to each person who interacts with the customer. Without this fundamental shift in the approach to CRM, we will continue to see high failure rates.

Additional components for CRM success

As introduced before, a CRM application is complex and not cheap. CRM creates a substantial competitive advantage to most organisations. However, as more firms implement such systems, the advantages will decrease. The company should go a step further to extend the technology (Bose, 2002).

Many authors (e.g. Al-Mudimigh, 2002; Bose, 2002; Corner and Hinton, 2002; Xu *et al.*, 2002; Chen and Popovich, 2003; Stefanou *et al.*, 2003; Hendricks and Stratman 2006) have suggested that CRM needs supportive activities and an infrastructure to ensure its smooth deployment. Among these activities are enterprise resource planning (ERP), supply chain management (SCM) and knowledge management (KM).

Enterprise resource planning (ERP)

Pawlowsiki and Boudreau (1999) define ERP as an umbrella term for integrated sets of business applications that allow companies to control all aspects of operations. Al-Mudimigh (2002) describes ERP as integrated information system software comprised of several applications and modules that share a central database, designed to automate business processes and functions across the enterprise (see Figure 2.9).

It is obvious from the former definitions that the ERP system is concerned with back-office activities (accounting, sales order processing and manufacturing), while CRM is about front-office activities (sales, marketing and customer service) that help to improve the selling and revenue generation processes of organisations (Corner and Hinton, 2002).

Figure 2.9 Overview of ERP system

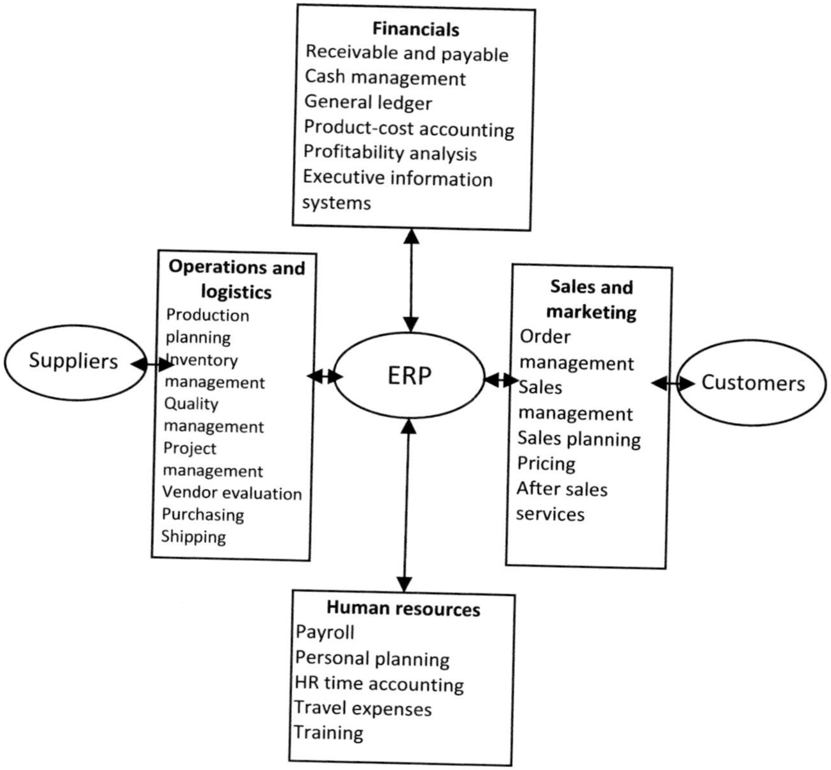

Source: Adopted from Chen and Popovich (2003)

Chen and Popovich (2003) reveal that providing customers, suppliers, and employees with web-based access to systems through CRM will only be beneficial if the underlying infrastructure, such as ERP, exists. On the other hand, Bradshaw and Brash (2001) point out that any company that is doing CRM properly must integrate the front-office, back-office and analytic systems. The back-office executes the customer requirements, and generally the only customer contact functions in the back-office are billing and logistics (for delivery of goods, for example).

Xu *et al.* (2002) provide this scenario:

> *A customer places an order from the Web after being presented with up-to-the-minute pricing and configuration options. That order flows through the manufacturer's inventory and production planning systems, pings a customer database to check credit history, hits a financial system to generate an invoice, and records the details of the transaction, so information can later be leveraged by telesales or support professionals to better service customer requests or cross-sell products.*

This is what is meant by integrating ERP and CRM.

Bose (2002) states that CRM has many similarities with enterprise resource planning (ERP) where ERP can be considered back-office integration and CRM as front-office integration. A notable difference between ERP and CRM is that ERP can be implemented without CRM. However, CRM usually requires access to the back-office data that often happens through ERP-type integration. Without a connection to the ERP system, the customer-facing function will not be able to present details regarding things like order status and delivery date (Earls, 2002).

Yet, to gain competitive advantage, enterprise system developers have begun to provide solutions that link front-office and back-office. It has become evident that ERP systems also gain advantages by using market and customer information. It provides long-term thinking and a predicting capacity that enablea more efficient back-office operations (Persson, 2004)

Supply chain management (SCM)

Supply chain management (SCM) is a concept that has gained substantial support as managers have increasingly recognised the importance of logistics as the last cost-cutting frontier (Tarn et al., 2002). The supply chain represents the whole production process of goods, starting from supplier processes, raw materials, the manufacturing process to post production and product distribution. Min and Mentzer (2000) suggested three major objectives of implementing SCM:

- Reduce inventory investment in the chain.

- Increase customer service through increased stock availability and reduced order cycle time.

- Help build competitive advantage for the channel to create customer value.

To be effective in fierce competition, a firm needs to integrate its CRM activities with SCM. Now companies are trying to connect CRM activities and customer insight information with upstream operations in the supply chain (Xu et al., 2002).

On the other hand, Angeles and Nath (2000) argue that highly-integrated (SCM) and accompanying logistics services have now become the basis of competition in the increasingly electronic and web-driven marketplace. This integration will help sales force and front-line employees to have the right data in the supply chain.

Xu et al. (2002) also add that a salesperson, for example, is exposed to updated inventory and production data, so that he/she will be able to offer accurate information to customers when asked. Thus, by integrating CRM with SCM, companies will be able to deliver customer-configured products, as Dell does.

Rackham (2000) clarified why channel relationships are so important, because most experts now agree that you cannot choose channels for reaching customers; your customers will choose their channels for reaching you. And, most likely, they will want every single channel that your competitors could possibly offer them.

Knowledge management (KM)

Knowledge has been recognised as one of the main assets of organisations (Drucker, 1999). KM, in particular, has been defined as the process of capturing the collective expertise and intelligence in an organisation, and using them to foster innovation through continued organisational learning (Nonaka, 1991). According to Oracle, CRM is about knowing your customers better, and effectively using that knowledge to own their total experience with your business, and to drive revenue growth and profitability (Stefanou *et al.*, 2003).

On the other hand, Bradshaw and Brash (2001) define CRM as a management approach that involves identifying, attracting, developing and maintaining successful customer relationships over time in order to increase retention of profitable customers. CRM, as explained, is absolutely related to the discipline of knowledge management since all expertise and intelligence refer to customers. Thus, the existence of sufficient and continually updated customer knowledge is critical for an effective CRM system (Stefanou *et al.*, 2003) (Figure 2.10).

According to Stefanou *et al.* (2003), companies should explore and refine CRM knowledge management methods in order to get value-added knowledge for themselves and their customers, and to understand not only customer purchasing patterns and trends but attitudes and preferences as well.

Figure 2.10 Relation between data and knowledge

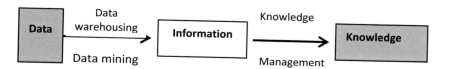

Source: Adopted from Ray (2003)

According to Gebert *et al.* (2003), knowledge flows in CRM processes can be classified into three categories:

- Knowledge for customers is required in CRM processes to satisfy customers' knowledge needs. Examples include knowledge on products, markets and suppliers.

- Knowledge about customers is accumulated to understand customers' motivations and to address them in a personalised way. This includes customer histories, connections, requirements, expectations and their purchasing activity.

- Knowledge from customers is customers' knowledge of products, suppliers and markets. Through interactions with customers, this knowledge can be gathered to sustain continuous improvement, e.g. service improvements or new product developments.

CRM technology

Silva and Rahimi (2003) identify three levels that characterise the complexity of CRM. The first level is the operative one. Its objective is to manage all points of contact with the customer (service, sales and marketing). The collaborative CRM is the second level. It offers customers a spectacular view of the organisation and enables the customer to complete some tasks, to communicate with the organisation, and to receive updated information through the different operational channels the organisation offers. The third level is the analytical CRM that contains technologies that analyse data received from interaction with the customer.

Furthermore, many practitioners and authors (e.g. Trepper, 2000; Dyché, 2002; Reynolds, 2002; Tie, 2003; Greenberg, 2004) support the fact that CRM technologies can be divided into these three functional categories.

Operational CRM

This category includes customer-facing applications that integrate front-office with back-office with the purpose of boosting the efficiency of customer interactions (Trepper, 2000; Greenberg, 2004). This involves automating business operations processes, such as order management, customer service, marketing automation, sales-force automation, and field service. In order to be successful, the firm has to choose skilled employees for this task, and must have a customer-centric focus (Persson, 2004). With the quick development of internet and communication technologies, operational CRM has evolved into two variants: e-CRM and m-CRM (Tie, 2003).

e-CRM

With the revolution of the internet, this term 'e-CRM' has emerged. Tie (2003) points out that it provides the ability to take care of customers via the web, or for customers to take care of themselves online. That is the main difference between CRM and e-CRM, which lies in the shift from client/server-based CRM to web-based CRM.

It was estimated that 59% of UK households would have internet access by 2006, compared with 21% at the beginning of 2000, and that the value of consumer transactions over the internet, fixed and mobile, would top $21 billion by 2005, compared with under $750 million in 2000 (Bradshaw and Brash, 2001).

Nowadays customers are equipped with more information than ever, so as to increase needs of obtaining personalised product and service; to address this trend CRM performing companies have to accomplish the challenging task of putting '*e*' into CRM. It is possible to argue that e-CRM is the future style of CRM; vendors who do not optimise their CRM applications for the web are the vendors who are likely to be out of business soon (Tie, 2003).

m-CRM

Another variant of CRM is m-CRM, which stands for Mobile CRM. According to Tie (2003), m-CRM can be considered as a future variant of e-CRM, since most CRM vendors are providing solutions to link e-CRM with wireless tools, such as mobile phones, PDAs or laptop computers. The aim of m-CRM is to enable two-way interactivity between the customer and the enterprise continuously, anywhere. It also can be seen as a means to make CRM more powerful with utilisation of advanced wireless communication tools.

Analytical CRM

In this category, we can use the data originating through operational CRM to enhance customer relationships (Dyché, 2002). These data are combined with other external data to measure customer satisfaction, customer loyalty, and customer profitability to support business decisions. Analytical CRM deals with strategic, effective and efficient use of data in order to provide management with good decision-making possibilities (Tie, 2003). Data warehousing and data mining are typical examples in this category.

Data warehousing

Data warehousing is a blend of technologies aimed at the effective integration of operational databases into an environment that enables the strategic use of data (Tie, 2003). Data warehouses extract, clean, transform, and manage large volumes of data from multiple, heterogeneous systems, creating a historical record of all customer interactions (Chen and Popovich, 2003).

In order to provide a complete customer profile, Dyché (2002) suggests that all data must be stored in a centralised cross-functional database. The database is called a data warehouse, where current and historic information moves in and out (Figure 2.11). The data can be collected from internal company sources, from the customer, and from third-party sources. A data warehouse can store large amounts of data, which enables a company to compare customer behaviour over time.

Figure 2.11 Integrated customer data on data warehouse

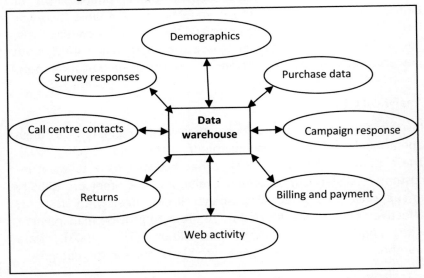

Source: Adopted from Dyché (2002)

Dyché (2002) further adds that the data warehouse constitutes an important part of CRM, since integrated data are necessary in order to make the right decisions about the customers. If the data are not integrated, the analysis of the customer relationships is based on a subset of the customer's actual interactions with the company, resulting in a false view of the customer. Chen and Popovich (2003) indicate that data warehousing technology makes CRM possible because it consolidates, correlates and transforms customer data into customer intelligence that can used to form a better understanding of customer behaviour.

Persson (2004) argues that data warehousing and analytical CRM are most effective when enterprise-wide; it allows the company to have a single view of the customer and of the business profitability. Tie (2003) also points out that CRM can not be practised in business without a major source of information, which, of course, is the data warehouse.

Thus, the data warehouse is vital for an organisation that adopts a CRM project. According to Chen and Popovich (2003), a survey conducted by Cap Gemini and International Data Corporation in 1999, found that 70% of US firms and 64% of European firms planned on building a data warehouse to support their CRM projects. According to Chen and Popovich (2003), a company can reap many benefits when applying such a technology including:

- Accurate and faster access to information to facilitate responses to customer questions.

- Data quality and filtering to eliminate bad and duplicate data.

- Extract, manipulate and drill-down data quickly for profitability analysis, customer profiling, and retention modelling.

- Advanced data consolidation and data analysis tools for higher level summary as well as detailed reports.

- Calculate total present value and estimate future value of each and every customer.

Data mining

Data mining is a new kind of business information analysis technique. It aims to find out unnoticed correlations among data by extracting, converting, analysing and modelling from a huge amount of transaction data in a business database. The goal of data mining is to create models for decision-making that predict future behaviour based on analyses of past activity (Tie, 2003).

Also, Persson (2004) states that the purpose of data mining is to identify significant patterns, rules and relationships from detailed data. He further adds that data mining can engender information about patterns without the analyst knowing about them before, and thus it is a great tool for acquiring new knowledge. Ahn *et al.* (2003) identify that a purpose of data mining/analysis in CRM is to extract the information necessary to provide efficient services to customers.

According to Persson (2004), data mining can be classified into three types:

- **Prediction analysis** involves determination of future behaviours by using historical data.

- **Sequence analysis** involves identification of combinations of activities that take place in a specific order. By performing such an analysis, a company can see whether customers are doing something in a certain order.

- **Association analysis** involves identifying groups of similar items or events. This kind of study is often performed to identify items or events that occur together, such as products often bought together.

Collaborative CRM

This category focuses on facilitating interaction between customers and companies (Trepper, 2000). Two-way dialogue between a company and its customers through a variety of channels has to be enhanced to facilitate and improve the quality of customer interactions, where customers get involved early with issues affecting their future purchase behaviour.

Greenberg (2004) points out that collaborative CRM involves any CRM function that provides a point of interaction between the customer and the supplier. Reynolds (2002) argues that collaborative CRM makes the interaction between a business, its channels, and its customers. It provides the means for the customers to contact the company, and enables collaboration between suppliers, partners and customers. It is a communication centre, a coordination network, aiming to provide the neural paths to the customers and suppliers (Tie, 2003).

References

Ahn, J. Y., Kim, S. K and Han K. S. (2003) On the design concepts for CRM system, *Industrial Management & Data Systems,* 103, 5, 324-31.

Al-Ajlan, M. and Zairi, M. (2005) Critical Success Factors in CRM implementation: Some Research Issues, *Quality in Services, Palermo 8th-9th September,* University of Palermo, Italy.

Al-Mudimigh, A. S. (2002) *Effective implementation of enterprise resource planning (ERP) software systems an empirical study of critical factors,* Ph.D. Thesis, University of Bradford.

Alohaly, M. (2004) Electronic Customer Relationship Management (eCRM) in The Saudi Banking Sector, *Computer Science,* King Saud University, Riyadh.

Ang, L. and F. A. Buttle (2002) ROI on CRM: a customer-journey approach, *IMP-conference,* Industrial Marketing & Purchasing, Perth, Australia.

Angeles, R. and Nath, R. (2000) An empirical study of EDT trading partner selection criteria in customer-supplier relationships, *Information & Management,* 37, 241.

Baumeister, H. (2002) Customer Relationship Management for SMEs, *proceedings from E2002.*

Bolton, M. (2004) Customer centric business processing, *International Journal of Productivity and Performance Management,* 53, 1.

Bolts, N. (2002) Five Critical Success Factors for Customer Loyalty, *CRMGuru.*

Bordoloi, C. (2000) *CRM Projects: A Framework for Success,* IQ4hire Inc. Chicago, Illinois,

Bose, R. (2002) Customer relationship management: key components for IT success, *Industrial Management & Amp,* 102, 2.

Brandon, G. (2005) Five Steps to a Successful CRM Implementation, *Elite Information Systems.*

Brendler, W. F. and Loyle, D. (2001) 8 Critical factors that make or break CRM, *Target Marketing; Philadelphia,* 24, 4, 57-61.

Buggy, D. J. (2001) A CRM strategy for distribution, *Industrial Distribution; New York,* 90, 3, 96.

Bull, C. (2003) Strategic issues in customer relationship management (CRM) implementation, *Business Process Management Journal,* 9, 5.

Buttle, F. (2004) *Customer relationship management concepts and tools*, Butterworth-Heinemann, Oxford.

Chase, P. (2001) Why CRM implementations fail and what to do about it, *CRM Knowledge Base*.

Chaudhry, R. (2002) Why CRM Projects Fail?, *Zen & Art of Client Server Computing, Inc.*

Chen, I. J. and Popovich, K. (2003) Understanding customer relationship management (CRM): People, process and technology, *Business Process Management Journal*, 9, 5.

Cho, Y., Im, I., Hiltz, S. and Fjermestad, J. (2002) An Analysis of Online Customer Complaint: Implication for Web Complaint Management, *The 35th International Conference on System Sciences, Hawaii*.

Corner, I. and Hinton, M. (2002) Customer relationship management systems: implementation risks and relationship dynamics, *Qualitative Market Research: An International Journal*, 5, 4.

Colvin, J. (2003) *CRM Success Factors, A Dozen Critical Lessons Learned*.

Crosby, L. A. (2002) Exploding some myths about customer relationship management, *Managing Service Quality*, 12, 5.

Cuthbertson, R. and Laine, A. (2004) The role of CRM within retail loyalty marketing, *Journal of Targeting, Measurement and Analysis for Marketing; London*, 12, 3, 290-304.

Dailey, N. and O'Brien, K. (2002) You Can't Have Effective CRM Without ERM (Employee Relationship Management), *CRM Today*.

Dravis, F. (2003) 3 Ways to maximize CRM systems, *Target Marketing; Philadelphia*, 26, 5, 59-61.

Drucker, P. (1999) Knowledge worker productivity - the biggest challenge, *California Management Review*, 41, 2, 79-94.

Dyché, J. (2002) *The CRM handbook a business guide to customer relationship management*, Addison Wesley, Boston.

Earls, A. (2002) Integrating ERP can overcome CRM Limits, *Software Magazine*, 22, 29-32.

Fjermestad, J. and Romano, N. C. Jr. (2003) Electronic customer relationship management: Revisiting the general principles of usability and resistance - an integrative implementation framework, *Business Process Management Journal*, 9, 5.

Fjermestad, J., and Romano, N. C. (2003) An Integrative Implementation Framework for Electronic Customer Relationship Management: Revisiting the General Principles of Usability and Resistance, *36th Annual Hawaii International Conference on System Sciences (HICSS'03), Hawaii.*

Fluss, D. (2005) Business Process Management Drives CRM Success, *CRMGuru.*

Galbreath, J. and Rogers, T. (1999) Customer relationship leadership: a leadership and motivation model for the twenty-first century business, *The TQM Magazine*, 11, 3.

Gartner Group (2003) Why CRM Fails, *Gartner Group.*

Gebert, H., Geib, M., Kolbe, L. and Brenner, W. (2003) Knowledge-enabled customer relationship management: Integrating customer relationship management and knowledge management concepts, *Journal of Knowledge Management; Kempston*, 7, 5, 107-123.

Gillies, C., Rigby, D. and Reichheld, F. (2002) The story behind successful customer relations management, *European Business Journal; London*, 14, 2, 73-77.

Girishankar, S. (2000) Companies Want CRM Tools to Manage Business Relationships, *Information Week*, 65.

Greenberg, P. (2004) *CRM at the speed of light essential customer strategies for the 21st century*, McGraw-Hill/Osborne, Berkeley, Calif.

Gurau, C. (2003) Tailoring e-service quality through CRM, *Managing Service Quality*, 13, 6.

Harvard Business School (2002) *Harvard business review on customer relationship management*, Harvard Business School Press, Boston.

Hendricks, K. B., Singhal, V. R. and Stratman, J. (2006) The impact of enterprise systems on corporate performance: A study of ERP, SCM, and CRM system implementations, *Journal of Operations Management*, 25, 65-82.

Interface Software (2005) Ensuring the Success of Your CRM Initiative, *Interface Software.*

Keen, P. (2000) ECRM: The new ERP, *Computerworld*, 34, 28.

King, P. (2004) *The Top 10 Reasons CRM Projects Fail*, CGI Group.

King, R. and Tang, T. (2002) E-CRM in the Post Dot-Com Age: Nine Critical Factors for Success, *Media and DM Review.*

Knox, S. (2003) *Customer relationship management perspectives from the market place*, Butterworth-Heinemann, Oxford.

Kotler, P. (1997) *Marketing management analysis, planning, implementation and control,* Prentice-Hall, Englewood Cliffs, NJ.

Kotorov, R. (2003) Customer relationship management: strategic lessons and future directions, *Business Process Management Journal,* 9, 5.

Kristoffersen, L. and Singh, S. (2004) Successful Application of A Customer Relationship Management Program in A Non-Profit Organisation, *Journal of Marketing Theory and Practice; Statesboro,* 12, 2, 28-42.

Lawler, J. (2006) Case Study of Customer Relationship Management (CRM) in the On-Line Affluent Financial Services Market, *Journal of Internet Commerce,* 4, 4, 153.

Lee, D. (2002) Four Steps to Success with CRM, *CRM Today.*

Lee, J. S. and Sohn, S. Y. (2006) Cost of ownership model for a CRM system, *Science of Computer Programming,* 60, 1, 68.

Lester, L. Y. (2003) CRM meets Wall Street, *Target Marketing; Philadelphia,* 26, 3, 50-61.

Light, B. (2001) A review of the issues associated with customer relationship management systems, *The 9th European Conference on Information Systems, June 2001.*

Light, B. (2003) CRM packaged software: a study of organisational experiences, *Business Process Management Journal,* 9, 5, 603-616.

Lindgreen, A., Palmer, R., Vanhamme, J. and Wouters, J. (2006) A relationship-management assessment tool: Questioning, identifying, and prioritizing critical aspects of customer relationships, *Industrial Marketing Management,* 35, 1, 57-71.

Lipscomb, D. (2004) Making the Case for Customer Relationship Management, *CRMGuru.*

Market Force (2000) Critical Steps to Successful Customer Relationship Management, *Market Force,* Arlington, TX.

Meltzer, M. (2004) Successful Customer Relationship Management Implementations Depend On Communications, *CRM Today.*

Min, S. and Mentzer, J. (2000) The role of marketing in supply chain management, *International Journal of Physical Distribution & Logistics Management,* 30, 9, 765-787.

Mohammad, A., Zairi, M. et al. (2002) *Customer Relationship Management (CRM) Implementation: A Best Practices Perspective and Proposed Model,* The

European Centre for Total Quality Management (ECTQM), University of Bradford.

Mohammad, A. B. (2001) CRM implementation an empirical study of best practice and a proposed model of implementation, *TQM*, Bradford.

Myron, D. (2003) 6 Barriers to CRM Success and How to Overcome Them, *CRM Magazine.*

Newell, F. (2003) *Why CRM doesn't work how to win by letting customers manage the relationship*, Kogan Page, London.

Nonaka, I. (1991) The knowledge-creating company, *Harvard Business Review; Boston*, November, 96-104.

Patton, S. (2002) Get the CRM you Need at the Price you Want, *CIO Magazine.*

Pavlin, T. (2004) *The 5 Phases of CRM Implementation: Planning Key to Successful Project*, Editor's Aide Inc.

Pawlowsiki, S. and Boudreau, M. (1999) Constraints and Flexibility in Enterprise Systems: A Dialectic of System and Job, *Proceedings of the Americans Conference on Information Systems (AMICS)*, Milwaukee, WI, USA.

Persson, P. (2004) Customer Relationship Management: How a CRM system can be used in the sales process. *Department of Business Administration and Social Science,* Lulea University of Technology, Stockholm.

Pinto, J. K. and Slevin, D. P. (1987) Critical Factors in Successful Project Implementation, *IEEE Transactions on Engineering Management; New York*, EM34, 1, 22.

Pushmann, T. and Alt, R. (2001) Customer Relationship Management in The Pharmaceutical Industry, *Proceedings of the 34th Hawaii International Conference on System Sciences*, Hawaii.

Rackham, N. (2000) Channel strategy: the next generation, *Sales & Marketing Management*, 152, 40-42.

Radcliffe, J. (2001) Eight Building Blocks of CRM: A Framework for Success, *Gartner Research*.

Ray, S. (2003) *Enterprise Applications: A Conceptual Look at ERP, CRM, and SCM*, Hill Associates Inc.

Rigby, D. K., Reichheld, F. F. and Schefter, P. (2002) Avoid the four perils of CRM, *Harvard Business Review; Boston,* 80, 2, 101-109.

Ryals, L. and Knox, S. (2001) Cross-functional issues in the implementation of relationship marketing through customer relationship management, *European Management Journal; London*, 19, 5, 534-542.

Sanchez, M. (2003) CRM: preparation and implementation, *Materials Management and Distribution; Toronto*, 48, 6.

Saviano, N. (2004) CRM Casualties Why Technology is the Cause of Most CRM Failures, *Office World News; Ft. Lauderdale*, 30, 6, 10-12.

Silva, R. D. and Rahimi, I. (2003) Issues in Implementing CRM: A Case Study, *Issues in Informing Science and Information Technology*, 1054-1064.

Simpson, L. (2002) The real reason why CRM initiatives fail, *Training; Minneapolis*, 39, 5, 50-56.

Starkey, M. and Woodcock, N. (2002) CRM systems: Necessary, but not sufficient. REAP the benefits of customer management, *The Journal of Database Marketing*, 9, 3, 267-275.

Stefanou, C. J., Sarmaniotis, C. and Stafyla, A. (2003) CRM and customer-centric knowledge management: an empirical research, *Business Process Management Journal*, 9, 5, 617-634.

Stewart, N. (2004) The Need for Change Management on CRM/Customer Engagement Journeys, *CRMGuru*.

Stimpson, J. (2003) CRM is hot! *The Practical Accountant; Boston*, 36, 1, 38-41.

Tanoury, D. (2002) Why CRM Projects Fail: Common Strategic & Tactical Mistakes, *CRM Knowledge Base*.

Tarn, M., Yen, D. and Beaumont, M. (2002) Exploring the rationales for ERP and SCM integration, *Industrial Management & Data Systems*, 102, 1, 26-34.

Teo, T. S. H. and Devadoss, P. and Pan, S. L. (2006) Towards a holistic perspective of customer relationship management (CRM) implementation: A case study of the Housing and Development Board, Singapore, *Decision Support Systems*, 42, 3, 1613-1627.

Tie, W. (2003) *Implementing CRM in SMEs: An Exploratory Study on the Viability of Using the ASP Model*, Masters Thesis in Accounting, Swedish School of Economics and Business Administration.

Trepper, C. (2000) Match your CRM tool to your business model, *Information Week*, 74.

Trestini, H. (2001) *Defining CRM for Business Success*.

Umashankar, V. (2001) E-CRM Issues of Semantics, Domain & Implementation, *Productivity*, 42, 1, 19-25.

Wells, D., Fuerst, L. and Choobineh, J. (1999) Managing information technology (IT) for one-to-one customer interaction, *Information & Management*, 35, 1, 53-62.

Xu, Y., Yen, D. C., Lin, B. and Chou, D. C. (2002) Adopting customer relationship management technology, *Industrial Management & Data Systems Management*, 102, 8, 442-452.

Chapter 3

Best practice CRM implementation and a proposed roadmap

Introduction

This report presents IDC's (2000) detailed analysis of two client case studies of CRM implementations. The focus of the study, as originally conducted, was:

- To identify what types of metrics companies have used to measure the success of their CRM initiative.

- To understand how organisations have been able to quantify the changes that have enabled them to successfully renew customers that they might otherwise have lost or identify areas in their customer service and support processes that allow them to gain a competitive advantage.

- To identify the organisational and cultural discipline needed to ensure that everyone in the organisation supports the CRM initiatives.

IDC believes that this type of review of real-life situations is essential to understanding how CRM is helping organisations develop closer relationships with their customers.

This chapter will therefore provide information that will support the strategic decisions e-CRM service providers are making in order to compete and lead in this dynamic and growing market.

Profiled clients

The information gathered in this report is based on one-on-one interviews and discussions with five clients conducted by IDC. The client companies that participated are as follows but only the first two are discussed in detail in this report:

- Robeco Private Banking
- A German Bank (Anonymous)
- Murphy's Brewery Ireland
- Philip Morris
- Global One

Case study 1: Robeco Private Banking

In 1999 Rabobank (Switzerland) Ltd, a relationship private bank, and Robeco Bank (Switzerland) Ltd, an offshore direct private bank, merged to form Rabo Robeco Bank (Switzerland) Ltd, a pan-European personal and private bank. At the end of 1999, the bank had 160 employees with 8 billion Swiss francs of assets under management.

However, the following case study is based primarily on the offshore 'direct' private banking operations of ex-Robeco Bank, which implemented a new client and prospect management system with Cambridge Technology Partners (Cambridge), between November 1998 and October 1999.

According to Robeco, offshore direct private banking means providing clients with services at a distance, i.e. acquiring and managing clients remotely. The product range included in-house funds and individual securities, fixed interest deposits and loans. The bank focused on cross-border marketing to wealthy individuals seeking high performance investments in mutual funds and individual securities.

The customer loyalty vision (Project Avanti)

In 1998, the bank made a decision to integrate a programme of change, which they christened 'Avanti'. This programme was designed to focus on proactive and segmented client management and addressed key aspects of the organisation, processes, systems and staffing, aimed at enabling client relationship managers to provide a much more comprehensive service and increase revenue and profit per client. The project was really driven from top management, with some initial resistance from the bottom.

One of the major initiatives within the Avanti programme was the implementation of a new client and prospect management system with Cambridge as the principal contractor. At the time the decision was made to go ahead with the implementation of a CRM solution, the bank was negotiating a merger with Rabobank. Initially, the bank had been spending large sums of money on client acquisition and needed to have a more integrated approach to client and prospect management.

With over 60,000 prospects and leads with a conversion rate of approximately 10% through mailings and individual contacts, the bank decided it needed to refocus its efforts on customer retention in addition to acquisition. The bank was providing its clients with a full range of offshore products, advice and assistance, transactions and interaction via phone, post, fax, email, internet services and branches, at a distance physically but not at a distance mentally. Building relationships at a distance is becoming more complex, according to Robeco. The bank believed it needed to refocus on existing clients in addition to acquisition, by improving:

- Client retention.

- Share of wallets (related to measuring customer loyalty).

- Client referrals.

The client management strategy that was enlisted can be seen in Figure 3.1 below.

Figure 3.1 Client management strategy in the Robeco Bank

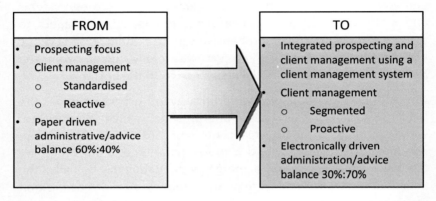

Source: IDC (2000)

Service provider selection

Robeco looked to external partners for guidance. The company spoke with a number of different players including PriceWaterhouseCoopers, who had earlier given advice on the entire direct business model in 1998, and Cambridge Technology Partners. At the time, Robeco wanted a more technology-oriented approach, so it decided to start with Cambridge. Additionally, it had a preference for Cambridge's fixed-time fixed-price approach.

Robeco decided on dual responsibility rather than giving full project management responsibility to Cambridge. The team included a senior and a junior project manager and two top IT people from Robeco's side and very senior project managers from Cambridge. Robeco felt it needed to be involved in the project management side and that the transfer of knowledge to internal IT people was essential.

The customer care solution

The CRM solution chosen as a base was Vantive Sales and Support version 8.0 and was designed, developed and implemented between November 1998 and October 1999. The main objectives to achieve better client service and improve the overall prospect base included the following:

- Clients
  - o Client profiling
  - o Client profitability/revenue analysis
  - o Contact management
  - o Service plans
  - o Proactive follow-up for marketing campaigns
  - o Correspondence, management letters, faxes, email
  - o Reminder management
  - o End-user queries and 'mini campaigns'
  - o Compliance alerts.
- Prospects
  - o Structured follow-up for prospecting
  - o Automated and personal follow-up.

The Vantive solution was an out-of-the-box cross-industry application, as at the time there was no application available specifically for the banking or private banking sector.

The solution did have some prospecting functionality, which was perceived to be applicable to the cross-business sector. However, the customer functionality had to be built into the Vantive product.

Transition from paper to electronic

Robeco decided to create a group called the client service department, which would be responsible for making sure everything became available online. Email response was considered to be the first functionality while providing clients with access to their accounts online, a separate project, was the second functionality. The whole approach to e-business was to focus on service and advice and not on transactions.

One of the critical things Robeco noticed was that it had to change the whole processing side of its operations since everything was moving online, letters and faxes were being scanned, and the inbox was flooded with emails which created a different kind of routine. One of its priorities was to improve the servicing side of the business, create easier account access and access by email in order to provide quick and timely responses.

Service segmentation

To further improve client service, types of clients were segmented according to separate levels of service, as illustrated in Figure 3.2.

Figure 3.2 Segmentation of services in Robeco Bank

Personal banking	Private banking

• Call centre approach enabled by Vantive
• Client management groups by language
• Oriented towards fund investments
• Reactive service excluding selected marketing campaigns
• 1,000 clients per relationship manager
	• Personal relationship manager
	• Segmentation by:
	  o Language/geography/ethnic group
	  o Asset management
	  o Advisory/discretionary
	• Fund and direct investments
	• Proactive service based on needs, wants and profitability
	• 250-300 clients per relationship manager

Clients were segmented based on transaction behaviour and the frequency of transactions. In the design phases the program also segmented people on the basis of their service needs – those that were more active had a different kind of service plan to those that had a more passive approach. To a great extent there was a mass marketing campaign approach, but micro campaigns involving each desk starting a campaign on its own client base were introduced in early 2000.

This type of segmentation led the bank to develop stronger relationships with clients and become more proactive with the most profitable segments in terms of advising and selling.

Customer-centric data warehouse

The bank developed its own customer-centric data warehouse solution in house. It was then able to segment its client base not only by the different levels of service but also combine this using information that was captured in the database, such as assets, revenue and the profitability of the Rabo clients after the merger. This information was vital in terms of mapping out a commercial direction for the bank.

Training

Project managers, product champions and business managers who could drive the business use of the project provided training to the end-users. Systems administrators took care of the training for the applications.

Measuring the benefits

Through the implementation of the Vantive solution the bank hoped to realise the benefits based on its initial assumptions as represented in Figure 3.3.

Figure 3.3 Cumulative costs and benefits of the Vantive solution in Robeco 1998-2003

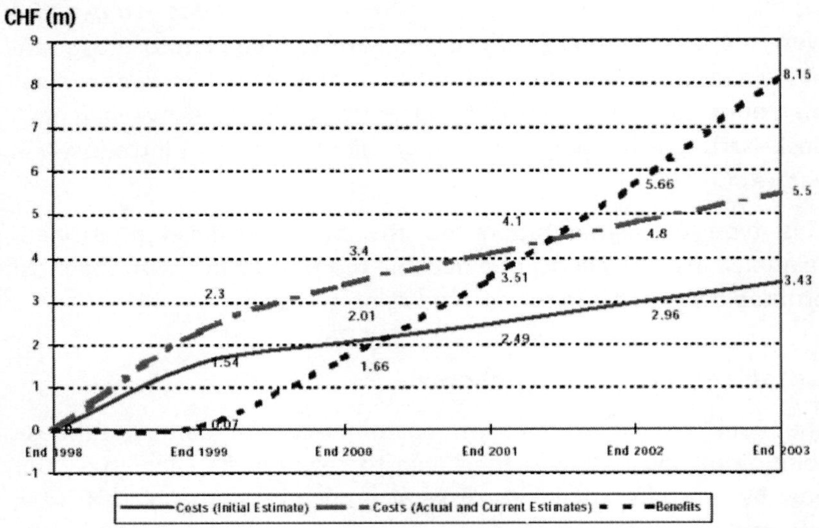

Source: IDC (2000)

According to Robeco, it already knew there was nothing available in the market place and whatever solution it chose would therefore be costly, as a lot of customisation would be required. Initially it thought the project would cost around CHF 1.5 million, and grow with ongoing costs to reach CHF 3.4 million over 5 years, but after implementation the costs reached CHF 2.3 million growing to CHF 5.5 million, as can be seen in Table 3.1.

The main reasons for the miscalculation in the budget were:

- Implementing while Robeco was merging with Rabobank, which brought further complications and delays.

- Underestimation of the online processing side, which became complex and had to be redesigned.

- The cost of customisation was not fully included since Robeco had selected Vantive, an out-of-the-box system, and it needed much more customisation.

Therefore, instead of the expected benefits being realised earlier, the payback reality was now from 2-3 years, due mainly to the merger. Based on this assumption, a benefits analysis was developed that projected the client loss rate. The benefits analysis information is depicted in Table 3.1 below:

Table 3.1 Robeco CRM project benefits analysis main assumptions 1999-2003

	End 1999	End 2000	End 2001	End 2002	End 2003
Incremental AUM (CHF M)	27	74	144	235	347
Increase in clients by:	163	314	516	731	960
• Retention	141	276	413	562	736
• New clients	22	38	104	169	234
Client loss rate	6.1%	5.6%	5.1%	4.6%	4.1%

Source: IDC (2000)

The client loss rate was calculated based on improved client intimacy. The bank expected that by having more contact with clients, and becoming proactive rather than reactive, it could then calculate the impact on a cumulative basis. An increase in clients, partially by retention and by client intimacy would also lead to referrals. The client loss rate was based on the total client base and the goal was to reduce the client loss rate of 6.5% in 1998 over a five-year period to 4.1%. Based on incremental figures adding up over a 5-year period, it expected to have found 960 more clients (about 736 by retention and 234 by referrals) by the end of 2003. The impact of improving the client loss rate from 6.1% to 4.1% over time on an incremental basis was estimated at CHF 350 million in assets under management (AUM) based on the impact over five years. By clearly recording and tracing the movements in customer acquisitions and retention on a periodical basis the bank was able to quantify customer and shareholder value. Although still a little early to measure the success of this project, all metrics have been put into place.

Robeco was also very concerned about user acceptance. It spent a lot of time with Cambridge to ensure it was building a system that would be usable in the future. At the design phase there was intensive participation from the (potential and future) users on the relationship management level, on campaign management and on the prospecting side. The company even let users sign off certain functionalities.

However, not all of the benefits have been through financial measurements, some have been accounted for by so-called 'soft' benefits such as better communication with customers. One of the initiatives of the Vantive solution was to route paper requests from clients to electronic, thereby improving processes and allowing for a better balance between 'advice and administration'.

First financial results

Within the first few months of implementing the Vantive solution, the bank already noticed some favourable results. Its negative cash flow from existing clients of CHF 86 million in 1998 turned into a positive cash flow of CHF 40 million in 1999. The strong involvement of the users in both the development and implementation phases of Vantive, lead to a much more 'existing client' focus throughout year and not just during the last months when Vantive was live. This explains the much better CHF 126 million cash flow realised compared with the originally assumed CHF 27 million incremental impact for 1999.

Critical milestones and learning

According to Robeco, keeping within the timeframe was critical to the success of this project in light of its merger with Rabobank. The time pressure on the organisation placed Cambridge at the forefront of its choice because of its fixed-time fixed-price approach. However, the project was delayed by two to three months, due to the merger.

The transferral of knowledge was another critical factor, especially on the IT side. As Robeco stated: 'going into a development project such as this is a very risky business. You have to bring the outside in to develop and when the developers are finished, if you do not have that transfer of knowledge in the IT department you get a real integration problem afterwards.'

After the project went 'live' it experienced numerous small problems and the project managers and IT team had to resolve these on a weekly basis. This ongoing work on small changes to make the project smooth was the reason for some of the additional costs.

Initially, Robeco had some resistance from users, but over time people became familiar with the system and its capabilities. The key is to keep the ongoing development as close to the users as possible and keep them continuously involved, according to Robeco.

Implementing the Vantive solution in the ex-Robeco bank was the first phase of this CRM initiative. In mid-2000, it rolled out Vantive to ex-Rabobank in Zurich and Geneva, integrating and developing a multi-channel system through which clients would have the choice of interacting through letter, fax, telephone, email and the internet.

Outstanding development work relates to giving clients access to their accounts via the internet, receiving online advice and ultimately achieving transactions online. The latter will be implemented more for the purpose of operational efficiency than in answer to demand from clients who prefer the service and advice functionality rather than online transactions.

Managing the organisational impact

Taking the business online was a very important step for Robeco, which virtually had to reengineer its processes and ways of working. This proved to be an extremely important element for merging the two organisations properly. Once people saw the commercial impact of the CRM system, management had to have a critical discussion on whether this was something it wanted to bring to the rest of the business. Further steps for the bank in Switzerland will be acquisitions. As many private banks are using this same bank engine it would be cost efficient, especially in terms of mergers, as it helps to strengthen the deal.

Summary

The changing need of clients and competitor investments has lead banks to place more effort on building client loyalty and retention rather than client acquisition. Customer satisfaction to foster loyalty remains a strategic point for European banks.

As the European banking market becomes more competitive, the demand for advanced banking solutions grows. Banking customers have become increasingly aware of the most convenient or attractive financial products and services currently available. In light of this increasing competition Robeco could be considered pioneers in terms of developing a CRM system in the private banking sector, well before the market even understood the potential of CRM. Its head start in this initiative has enabled it to extend its client access, over its competitors.

The partnership developed between Robeco and Cambridge provided the elements necessary for Robeco to successfully complete the project on time as well as helping to set the stage for bringing its online banking into the electronic future. The challenge posed to Robeco was the merger with Rabobank, which made the situation more complex.

Despite this, Robeco believes the project ran smoothly, although it did suggest that Cambridge should force its clients to look at the transfer of knowledge, as this is essential once the service provider completes the project. Additionally, Robeco felt that Cambridge was so focused on CRM that the whole issue of integration between web and back office did not seem to be at the top of its mind, i.e. too focused on the CRM functionality. According to Robeco, 'if you want to move your business online, CRM is just one element, integration and up-functionality is critical'. Despite this and the fact that CRM was in its infancy stage in early 1998, Robeco believes the partnership was a 'happy marriage'.

The open flexibility of the Vantive solution led Robeco to build a customised system, which ultimately required a lot of maintenance and was considered a long-term burden.

On the one hand it was good as it could model the solution to meet its needs, but on the other hand Robeco was not in the systems business. One of the other frustrating concerns of the bank is the fact that it now has a custom application which it believes is difficult to bring to market standard. The bank now has a prototype product, which it is willing to share with the marketplace, possibly through a service-level agreement (SLA) or by participating in future developments with the software providers.

However, the bank still owns the product, which has caused it to be more involved with the IT side than it would have ultimately preferred. In the long term the bank does not believe it has any value keeping a customised solution as it becomes too expensive. Ideally, a standard solution for the private banking sector would have been more appropriate, but unfortunately was not available at the time.

Organisational discipline is considered somewhat complex and it has become vital that any change initiative should be communicated and supported by everyone in the organisation. Although initially there was some resistance to the CRM initiative within Robeco, employees soon bought into this concept once they could see the benefits of the system. While the change process is slow, measuring a tangible return on relationships is not an easy task. However, Robeco implemented metrics that enabled it to justify customer and shareholder value, through the evaluation of customer retention and the number of customer referrals.

Case study 2: A German bank (anonymous)

This case study focuses on a German bank, which chose to remain anonymous. IDC felt this case would still be valuable to readers, however. The German bank is an international commercial bank for private and corporate customers, formed by mergers. The case study concerns the retail division of the bank.

Customer loyalty vision

The retail division of the bank has approximately 1.2 million customers and it decided to develop its CRM strategy by engaging in a database-marketing project for these customers. The database marketing system is based on data warehouse technology and primarily supports marketing operations for private and company customers. The bank was facing more competition and its margins were decreasing, it therefore needed to devise a marketing strategy based on solid data. Through this realisation the bank decided to enhance the central database marketing solution. Top management in the marketing division initiated the project.

At the time it had a centralised marketing division and needed to increase direct activities, such as mailings and call centre activities, and make this process much more efficient. At the same time it wanted to develop an interactive one-to-one relationship with its customers. The main objectives of the database-marketing project were:

- To gain a competitive edge.
- To better identify hidden client potential.
- To consolidate and strengthen market position.
- To create more efficiency.
- To implement faster response to changing market conditions.

At the time, costs were an issue, and the bank needed to reduce these and raise its earnings. It realised that it required a data mining solution to discover the affinities of its customers and discover its customers' needs and wants in order to adapt processes to fulfil such needs. It wanted to attract customers and build loyalty and it realised that it was good in doing mailings to a vast number of customers, but often with poor results and high mailing costs.

Initially, this was a regional rollout, as the retail customers were located in southwest Germany, but after the merger the bank realised it had direct and online banking activities, which enabled it to rollout across the whole of the country. The bank was operating its retail services through more than 200 branches, with classes of customers ranging from the average to the wealthy, including enterprises. However, its main focus was the B2C market, with specialisation in private customers.

Service provider selection

The bank recognised that it had some in-house IT skills available, but also realised that it required the help of external providers to take care of the more complex integration and database marketing skills. At the time it didn't have special database marketing skills and needed to employ someone with these skill sets. It had to put a process in place to help employees learn the dynamics of this type of activity and how to cross and up-sell product's functions that were made more efficient by the deployment of the data mining solution.

CSC provided system integration and IT support, but also gave support to project management, the requirement definition, business concept and database marketing skills. The data mining solution selected was from the SAS Institute, which was deployed by CSC. Prior to the data mining solution the bank also deployed SAS Reporter, a project controlling tool.

The customer care solution

The data-mining project was initiated in October/November 1999 on a relatively low scale. The bank believes that one of the problems it faced was the fact that the data sources were coming from different databases within the bank with different formats and structures. Customer information now resides in one warehouse database and analysis of customer profiles, based on types of products and services, such as credit cards, is simple. However, in April 2000, the first real activity or first analysis of customers took place. This identified the customers with investment funds and began profiling those that did not have such funds. It is now starting to make a network of activities this year, starting with its branches and now including call centres.

Through the data mining solution the bank could determine the percentage of customers buying bank products, such as accounts, investment funds and loans, prior to the merger. After the merger it gained additional customers from other banks coming from the same sector. However, to maximise the value of the data mining solution, the bank currently has three data miners, one internal and two from CSC. These data miners extract, segment and profile customer information, which is then bundled and sent through the intranet to the marketing and sales departments. Through this the bank is hoping to improve its knowledge of the customer and deepen its skills. The bank believes that the data miner market is currently very limited in Europe and that there are only approximately 200 data miners across Europe that have the skills for this type of activity.

The bank has deployed a multi-channel strategy through which its customers can interact with the institution via its branches, call centre, online banking, fax, internet, short message service (SMS) and mobile banking. However, most of these channels are not yet fully integrated. Internet connection to the call centre for real-time benefits or online support is not yet in place. Neither are web-based marketing capabilities, though these should be available by 2001. Further, the bank is also currently examining a campaign management tool, which it plans to integrate in the short term.

Training

CSC and SAS consultants largely provided training for the bank's employees. The bank sent a number of its employees to SAS to learn some of the techniques from both technical and soft skills perspectives.

Measuring the benefits

The bank does not yet measure the impact of customer loyalty through this system. However, in August 2000 the database was enlarged, capturing more data about customers and their accounts. Concepts of customer segmentation, life cycle analysis and customer values are now available, and will help the bank to gain more benefits from the system. In August a kickoff took place for another step of the project. This deals with database marketing quality management and aims to receive even more data about the customers and their contentment or dissatisfaction. The information will help to improve models about churn analysis and loyalty programmes. The first results are expected in 2001.

Critical milestones and learning

Initially, the bank found it difficult to understand what it was trying to achieve with the database marketing solution, for more than a year it felt it did nothing more than spend money. At the same time, the bank needed to determine whether the client was a long-term or short-term client, and by using the information that was being gathered in the database it could develop different scenarios to support its action plan.

One of the major concerns of the bank was the Y2K issue and the institution realised that it needed to upgrade its legacy system and buy new software. The system it had in place tracked and contained very poor data, which could not be analysed effectively. The bank believes that to start a project it is important to find a good integrator and an external partner as they can help to realise the bigger picture of the project and have a better knowledge of emerging technologies and business solutions.

Managing the organisational impact

The bank's employees have recognised that by filling in good data in the system they are able to gain valuable information on customers and develop better products and services that fit to the clients' needs. This process is a strong learning curve, which is slowly being implemented. However, one of the bank's major concerns is building key skills in data mining and finding professional data miners.

The project was initiated in the marketing department and learning to deal with the mentality of IT people was considered a difficult task. Gaining business value from the technology seemed to be a challenge to address at the IT level.

Future initiatives

The bank believes that creating multi-channel access will be significant for the retail business of its bank. Clients are changing; some use online banking today, but may prefer offline channels during their life cycle. For the broader scope of the CRM initiative, the bank is planning to implement a campaign management solution with the services of HP and the Epiphany solution. The bank believes that the Epiphany solution is the most innovative product on the market. It considers Epiphany to be a very open tool through which consultants can design campaigns.

It plans to use HP for the deployment of the solution. CSC will be responsible for the data delivery of the system and also for the integration of the distribution channels to close the customer loop. CSC has historical knowledge of the bank and is familiar with its data pool, which is one of the reasons it is still in the project, according to the bank.

Summary

The market environment has changed considerably over time and requires banks to create more customer-centric organisations and become more responsive to the individual needs of their customers in order to improve retention and increase business opportunities. Front-office solutions integrated with analytical tools enable a greater knowledge of customer needs.

Today, companies are beginning to recognise that customer analytics is critical to the success of CRM initiatives. For the past couple of years the market has seen an influx of call centre and sales force automation deployment, mostly as standalone implementations. However, these solutions alone are not enough to gain a thorough understanding and knowledge of a customer base. They need to be integrated with a customer-centric data warehouse through which valuable customer information can be captured, translated and leveraged as a strategic resource.

The bank approached its CRM initiative by first deploying a database marketing solution with which it could capture relevant customer information and develop better products and services for its customers. The fact that the market has a shortage of data miners has allowed CSC to position itself strategically in this project. CSC has two of its consultants working with the bank to help it analyse its customer data and become familiar with its data pool. However, developing a strong data warehouse infrastructure that allows for effective CRM analytics is a challenge – not only at a technology level but also at a business level where the business value of the solution needs to be recognised as a value added proposition.

IDC believes that as new technologies and markets emerge, companies will need to ensure that analytical solutions become a standard foundation of their CRM initiative. Moreover, accessing customer information in real time and developing strong customer knowledge management will become a commodity.

Figure 3.4 Benefits of calculating ROI in CRM

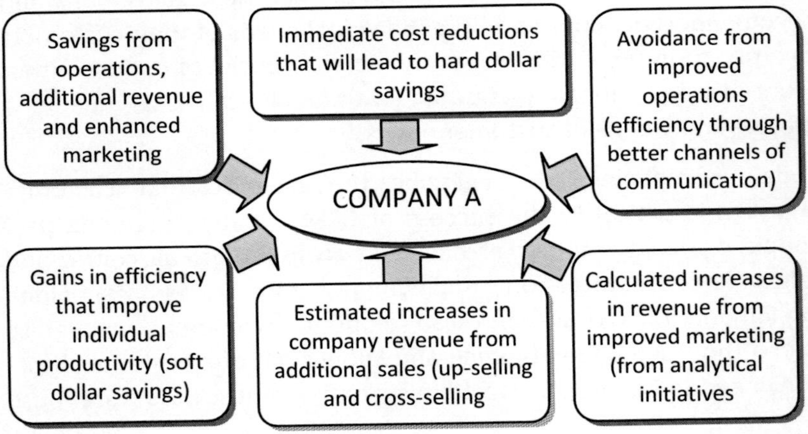

Savings from operations, additional revenue and enhanced marketing

Immediate cost reductions that will lead to hard dollar savings

Avoidance from improved operations (efficiency through better channels of communication)

COMPANY A

Gains in efficiency that improve individual productivity (soft dollar savings)

Estimated increases in company revenue from additional sales (up-selling and cross-selling

Calculated increases in revenue from improved marketing (from analytical initiatives

Source: IDC (2000)

Figure 3.4 shows the operational elements of CRM (contact centres, sales force automation and marketing automation) and identifies intelligent CRM as the focal point of the operational activities.

Generic analysis of best practice: 5 case studies

Table 3.2 is a generic analysis of 5 case studies adapted from IDC (2000), giving a one glance view of customer loyalty in 5 different organisations that have implemented CRM.

Table 3.2 Generic analysis of 5 case studies

Client	Service provider	Project goals	Industry	Performance management	Critical issues
Robeco Private Banking Switzerland	Cambridge Technology Partners	Initially, the bank spent large sums of money on client acquisition and needed to have a more integrated approach to client and prospect management. With over 60,000 prospects and leads with a conversion rate of approximately 10% through mailings and individual contacts, they decided to refocus efforts on customer retention in addition to acquisition.	Banking	Client loss-rate 6.1% to 4.1%, 5 years. Increased client retention. Share of wallet. Number of client referrals increased. Stronger client communication. End-user involvement from phase one.	Transfer of knowledge. On time, despite merge with Rabobank. Additional costs due to customisation and changes to make the service run smoothly.

German Bank	CSC	To reduce costs and raise earnings: the bank realised that it required a data mining solution to discover the affinities of its customers and customers' needs and wants in order to adapt processes to fulfil their needs. It wanted to attract customers and build loyalty.	Banking	Currently does not measure impact of customer loyalty through system. Enlarged database, concepts concerning customer segmentation, life cycle analysis and customer values now available, which will help it to gain more benefits from the system.	Unsure what it was trying to achieve from the database. Later realised it could use information gathered to develop different scenarios to support its action plan. Needs good integrator and an external partner: bank believes external partners have better knowledge of emerging technologies and business solutions. Major concerns in building key skills in data mining and finding professional data miners. Gaining business value from technology a challenge to address at the IT level.

Murphy's Brewery Ireland	Price Water-house Coopers	Restructure the sales organisation, create a customer service department, and establish a coordinating and planning department, restructuring packaged beer logistics.	Consumer goods	Sales of packaged beer increased 14% on last year Increased customer satisfaction Up to 10% of customer sales reps' time freed Orders delivered 99.8% on time in full	Implemented call centre and sales force automation (SFA) too quickly and in isolation, instead of reviewing the strategic requirements for an enterprise wide business solution. End-user involvement at phase one was key. Level of development and knowledge of Siebel application within service provider was limited at the time.
Philip Morris	Deloitte Consulting	Firstly, on the technical side, to investigate the potential of using a packaged application across each of the affiliates. Secondly, on the business side, to evaluate the fundamental role of the sales field	Consumer goods	Gained better insight of its customers. Increased sales revenue. Increased presence through Point of Sales. Project ran on time and	To identify a good percentage of common functions across the countries, in order to provide similar solutions to each affiliate. Needed a

		in the European region and to understand if there was any potential for synergy in the different countries.		within budget. The newly created central support group allows sharing costs of application support across all affiliates. The CSP, and the manner deployed, will allow all affiliates to easily take advantage of new functionality provided in future Siebel releases.	solution that would integrate with other systems such as SAP. Initial resistance from lower levels, overcome by involvement in project. PMI preferred to use Deloitte Consulting for overall project management, but looked for local integrators for the more technical aspects of the project.
Global One	Global One	To provide customers with the ability to monitor and analyse real time information on performance and status of services. To generate performance and traffic reports. To use external providers for bigger outlook of CRM strategy, targeting SMEs.	Telecom	Increased customer acquisition. Improved overall customer service. Customer Workstation improved workload for customer support centre staff.	Testing of product is critical at customer level. Performance through the internet is a challenge. Learned that it needs to build a portal to integrate all services it provides to its customers.

CRM implementation: a proposed roadmap

Headlines are abound with news of CRM application failures, with failure rates as high as 80% being reported. At the same time, technology application providers continue to sell CRM as the ultimate solution for business success. CRM, when approached correctly, has the potential to significantly improve business results. If approached incorrectly, it can result in spend of considerable sums of money on expensive technology applications without ever seeing any tangible benefits.

Figure 3.5 Proposed model of CRM implementation

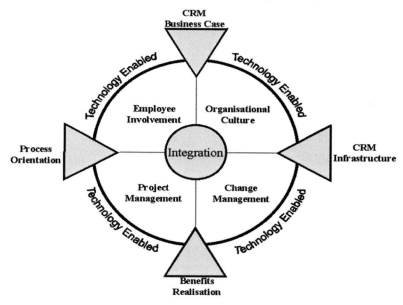

The following parameters will help ensure that even if the organisation's CRM initiatives don't amount to 'salvation', they will yield significant, positive impacts for the business. The following 10 parameters are selected after thorough and in-depth research study (careful comparison) of many different factors discussed and argued by many different experts and gurus in their publications, articles, white papers and journals regarding the successful implementation of CRM within different organisations.

Based on the case studies and the literature review, this study has revealed the above-mentioned model of CRM as shown in Figure 3.5.

Accurately assess the CRM needs

CRM is not right for every company. The management should begin by clearly defining its business issues and needs, and then determine whether CRM can and should be a part of the solution. CRM strategies that are clearly linked to business objectives have a much greater likelihood of success (Eberhardt, 2001).

Critical success factors

- **Understanding** what CRM is all about.
- Well **defined** CRM.
- Management's **accurate perception** of the process.
- **Defining** the market.
- Selecting an outside **consultant as a facilitator** to keep efforts on track.
- **Developing an implementation plan in collaboration with a consulting company** that is complete and specific in the assignment of responsibilities and deadlines.
- Defining and documenting **business goals and objectives.**
- **Define and document existing business processes.**
- Keep management committed.
- **Involve** the appropriate individuals and departments.
- Have **cross-functional teams.**
- Have **tools** in place to **analyse** collected scalability.
- Emphasise **business strategies** that focus on coddling the customer.
- Meeting **customer expectations.**

Put a stake in the ground

According to Jim Dickie, (1999), David Thomas from Pitney Bowes recently offered a great suggestion at a conference where they co-presented. In reviewing his company's recent successful CRM project, he pointed out that one of the first things Pitney Bowes did was write a mission statement. The statement was as follows:

> *'Deliver a world-class price quote and configure solution and related supporting processes that can be implemented to a cross-section of the sales force to increase our systems business and overall sales productivity.'*

The value of a simple statement like this is enormous. Forcing an organisation to agree up front on the expectations of the initiative will eliminate any misconceptions people have about the project's goal. It also becomes the roadmap for the project so that at any time in the future the management can pull it out and see if it is still on course. As one of America's great philosophers, Yogi Berra, is credited with saying: 'If you don't know where you are going, you'll probably end up somewhere else.' He also added that 'Frequently we have seen the goal of a project shift over time from getting a system out that solves problems, to getting a system out-period.'

Gather information

Fadia (2001) argues that it is critical to gain insights of various key stakeholders and decision-makers within the organisation. These insights can be acquired most effectively by holding one-on-one meetings. Fadia used an 'interview template' that consisted of more than 30 questions, which served as the foundation for framing initial discussions with their clients. Examples of questions that helped them gauge the health of the client's CRM included:

- How would you define CRM?

- What types of customer information is captured/tracked (acquisition/retention costs, churn, cost to serve, etc.)?
- What information would you like to know about your customers that you currently do not?

Given their more frequent and direct interactions with the customer, front-line personnel may know more about customer needs, preferences and concerns that may not have been communicated to the executive level. Further, these results are then used to determine how close these organisations are to meeting and exceeding their customers' expectations, and present the gaps between their current state of CRM and their desired state (Fadia, 2001).

Project planning and management

According to Foran (2001), successful selection and implementation projects begin with up-front planning. He strongly maintains that developing parameters for the project is important in maintaining schedules, managing scope and utilising resources. He further recommends the following four steps for successful project planning and management:

Define the project

It is important to create a clearly defined plan that is realistic, understood by all parties, and will serve as the roadmap to enhance communication and gain consensus. According to Foran, the initial planning stages provide a forum for determining the project scope and interviewing key programme participants, and can provide the following deliverables:

- A comprehensive programme budget.
- Measurements to compare actual performance to plan.
- Agreed upon methods of project communication.

- Approved issue logs.

- An organised review process.

Review current systems environment
Effective CRM solutions require a company to review existing practices and systems environments before attempting a change. Companies that forego this step expose themselves to the risk of automating 'bad' processes.

It is important to consider internal and external constraints such as organisational competencies, staffing levels and skill levels, and the specific retailer's unique elements. This will help decision-makers judge the level of CRM sophistication required. Once the assessment of current conditions is complete, it is critical to develop user requirements, plan the re-engineering of business processes, discuss platform options and determine high-level functionality.

Formulate grounds for evaluation
Building decision parameters is essential in the decision-making process. It is important for a company to evaluate and prioritise the criteria for the package selection to compliment their CRM strategy.

Develop recommended systems architecture
According to Foran, the decision to invest in a CRM software package must consider the technical logistics involved. The final decision-makers need a perspective and understanding of available systems architecture configurations. He suggests that planning activities leading up to the selection process are expected to produce documentation that describes the ultimate operating environment:

- Feature/function criteria.

- Interfaces.

- Operating structure and platforms.

Additionally, this documentation will describe required operating changes:

- Re-engineered management processes.

- Controls.

- Performance measurements.

Using these findings, it is then possible to perform a cost/benefit analysis to fully examine the advantages and disadvantages of all of the alternatives.

Engaging the right consultant is the best bet for a successful CRM implementation

Trailer (2000) states that for every successful CRM implementation that benefited from outside consulting services, there's at least one other that is a tale of woe. What should a company do when contemplating a consulting engagement to maximise its chances for a successful project?

For finding and dealing with consultants, perhaps the best advice comes from the horse's mouth. Liz Seckler of the CRM consulting firm, GettingThere, advises clients not to expect the moon from consultants. 'Consultants can't fix all their [client's] problems or make everything happen,' says Seckler.

'If the VP of sales talks of support but isn't involved in and committed to the project, a consultant can't fill that void.' Vague and unrealistic expectations are difficult for everyone. Instead, advises Seckler, you and your consultant should have an explicit mutual understanding of the project specifics, including roles and responsibilities (Trailer, 2000).

Once software is separated from process, CRM emerges as a customer-centric business strategy supported, not driven, by technology

According to Lee (2000), organisational development guru Bill Brendler, who specialises in rescuing technology implementations, strongly suggests that companies are racing to embrace CRM technology, but what they don't realise is they've got to redesign their company first. The real opportunity comes from taking the time to rethink their relationships with their customers, to figure out how to put them in charge of their company.

Brendler adds that software is the ultimate shortcut. So they try software first, and only start asking, 'What is CRM?' after they create misery and confusion. So let's forge a workable definition of CRM.

A working definition

CRM is: implementing customer-centric business strategies; which drives redefining of functional roles; which demands re-engineering work processes; which is supported, not driven, by CRM technology. This definition, expressed as four sequential steps, each driven by the step prior breaks through the technology clutter.

Lee (2000) suggests the following four-step process for CRM:

- Implementing customer-centric business strategies;

- ... which drives redefining of functional roles;

- ... which demands re-engineering work processes;

- ... which is supported, not driven, by CRM technology.

Implementing customer-centric business strategies
According to Lee (2000), this is how CRM starts, with customer-centric strategies adopted by top-level executive management. Middle managers, even functional heads, don't have the authority

to initiate enterprise-wide, customer-centric business strategies. When CRM starts at the middle management and staff levels it means one of two things: either the company is already customer-centric, which very few are yet, or it is headed down the tubes, at least with CRM.

Redefining functional roles and re-engineering work processes
Most companies have a marketing department, a sales department, a customer service department, an accounting department, a credit department, and maybe a product-engineering department, each with its own leader and staff, and turf. It is almost impossible to become customer-centric while maintaining this type of organisation.

Lee (2000) states that a CRM initiative that starts with customer-centricity requires huge changes in the organisation such as:

- Customer service should unchain itself from accounting and move from the back to the front office.

- Some sales and service functionality should shift to the internet, and other sales functionality should probably migrate to service.

- Order entry should move out to sales, along with product configuration.

- Product engineering may become a customer contact function, and not strictly internal.

- Product management will almost certainly scale back in importance, replaced by customer segment management.

- Manufacturing might schedule runs according to customer priorities, rather than strictly manufacturing efficiencies, which means they need sales data.

- Accounting will have to push transaction data to sales, instead of hoarding it.

- Legal will have to find accommodation with customers, rather than sticking odious contracts in customers' faces.

Lee further suggests that if the management takes step one and two carefully, process re-engineering will flow right out of redesigning functional activities, just as redesigning functional activities flows right out of developing customer-centric strategies.

Supporting work processes (not driving them) with CRM technology
Almost inevitably, newly defined CRM work processes require more structure and information management support than old ones. And odd as it may seem, organisation can make the CRM software support its work processes, not vice versa (Lee, August 2001).

Lee strongly recommends, first taking the control of the software buying process away from the software sellers (the best of the software companies actually encourage organisations to take the lead). Then clearly define the organisational needs and ask competing vendors to show the organisation how they're going to meet them. 'Proof of concept', this is called. And if a vendor asks for a contract before showing how their system will conform to the organisational needs, show them the door.

Lee further adds, to be sure to detail both organisational process control and information management support requirements one step at a time (this is step three driving step four). And don't forget to bring up seemingly minor issues, such as, 'Field reps need to work offline with full data and functionality' or 'Reps don't have access to telephone connections.' For example, if either of these crop up, you'll want to wash your hands of 'thin client' CRM solutions that relegate remote workers to accessing not only their data but their software functionality over the internet (or dial-up connection).

Don't view CRM as a technology initiative

CRM applications can be a viable component of a CRM strategy, but they are not the whole solution. Leading the CRM efforts with technology solutions is akin to allowing the tail to wag the dog. Understand the business requirements and design the right business processes to support relationship management, and allow technology to play the right role as an enabler (Eberhardt, 2001).

Critical success factors

- Perform **gap analysis.**
- **Define the technology requirements** based on the business methodology and priorities.
- **Start with technology** changes that have the greatest impact on reaching goals.
- Treat CRM as a **long-term journey.**
- See the CRM business model as an interactive one.
- **Build relationships** at every point of contact.
- CRM is about **strategy not technology.**
- **Build** a great customer relationship management strategy.
- **Employ technology wisely.**

CRM: strategy and implementation

CRM is a combination of organisation, processes and roles supported by systems and technologies. Many organisations make the mistake of choosing the systems and technologies and then trying to adapt their business operations around the result, usually with serious consequences and impacts on the business. It doesn't matter how efficient or inefficient the enterprise is now, it's the vision of where the enterprise needs to be positioned in its markets, how is it differentiated from competitors, and how it will achieve the vision that are the drivers for success (Emmerton, 2001).

People and processes make CRM work

Focusing on technology alone could be the problem. In most companies there are many process gaps. Process gaps occur when the customer wants one thing but the process produces something else.

Managers commonly believe that deploying CRM technology will bridge these gaps. But these gaps often exist because the processes that affect the customer are poorly designed. These poorly designed processes cause wait times between the steps a customer has to take to get what they want. Examples of these are:

- Processes that require too many managers' approval.

- Processes that don't add any value to the customer experience.

- Processes that cannot get done properly because of poor organisational culture (i.e. a culture that rewards individuals with information, chilling collaboration).

- Processes that are not done properly because individuals do not understand the goal of the organisation.

According to Brendler (2001) implementing CRM requires discipline and a commitment to closing gaps and removing resistance to change. It involves much more than just automating existing process. Automating processes just speeds up the 'old goat paths,' increasing the rate at which bad processes are performed.

The goal should be to close the process gaps to make it easier for the customer to do business with the company; the goal should not be installing CRM technology. The customer might want instant information, but the process takes too long to deliver it (Brendler, 2001).

Figure 3.6 Enabling architecture

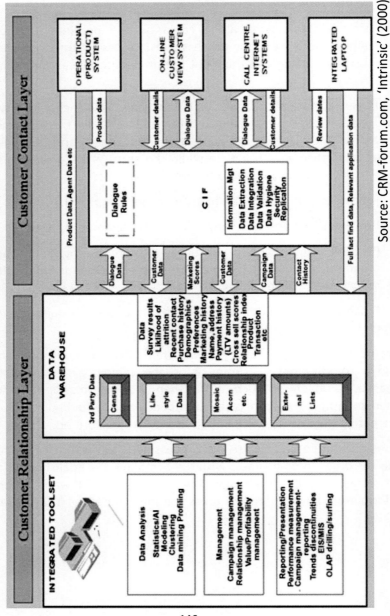

Source: CRM-forum.com, 'Intrinsic' (2000)

According to Steve Bell (2000), Professor Dr Reinhold Rapp, German CRM pundit (Managing Partner of CRM GmbH) rails against companies throwing technology at problems, insisting that customer segmentation should come first.

Professor Dr Reinhold Rapp defines CRM as 'a strategic concept to manage the assets of a company' and is adamant that those companies that view it only as a technology are doomed to failure. Technology is certainly a major part of the equation, but it should only be introduced after the strategy has been determined. And this should be built on the foundation of its assets, which in the final analysis are its customers. These should be segmented according to their profitability, and then strategy and tactics can be tailored according to the value of these customers to the company.

Bell (2000), states that Bob Shaw (a visiting professor of marketing at Cranfield University), points out that countless other factors influence financial results. 'To claim that [CRM] is the "be all and end all" of business is quite silly, although companies can certainly leverage value from CRM if they do it in a smart way.'

CRM requires a new management mindset

CRM depends on management commitment to customer care. In the past a day without customers calling was a good thing, it meant nobody had a problem. Whereas at present not receiving any customer complaint calls, raises the alarm bells of the company. Complaining customers show their expectation and loyalty towards the company, and if the management doesn't hear from their customers, they must ask whether their customers are still with them or have changed their loyalties.

The rate of customer turnover is particularly significant on the internet, where the opportunities for customer loss occur at a distorted speed. A recent McKinsey study (Agrawal *et al.*, 2001) found that 98.7% of online visitors do not become repeat customers, while another determined that most sites would lose 60% of their first-time customers in a six-week period.

As reported by Lowenstein (2006), offline, the numbers are just as striking. A study by KPMG about customer defections in the United Kingdom reported that 44% of UK customers had changed at least one of their key product or service suppliers (supermarkets, phone companies, etc.) in the past year.

According to Brendler (2001), it has recently been acknowledged that keeping existing customers is ultimately much more profitable than the conquering of new customers, especially in highly competitive markets. Research has shown that the retention of 5% of the existing customer base can have a profit impact up to as much as 125%.

Today, dealing with customers after the point of sale isn't just about answering questions. Instead it's about building relationships that transcend individual transactions and ensure customer satisfaction and repeat buying. What used to be simply customer care has become full blown CRM that hopes to improve service and reduce cost, give customers individual personalised attention and build long-term connections.

This is a mindset change for most executives. To manage complete customer relationships companies need to adopt a culture focused on much more than just problem solving. All the technology in the world that provides automated, profile-driven customer service will never replace human contact (Brendler, 2001).

Understand customer requirements

CRM initiatives are intended to drive better relationships with customers. And the relationships that are most important to a company are those that provide the greatest profit potential. To make intelligent decisions about CRM strategy and technology, it is critical that management understands its customer's value, needs, requirements and behaviours. This understanding allows the management to build systems and processes based on customer requirements and to allocate their CRM expenditures toward customer segments that are likely to yield the greatest returns (Eberhardt, 2001).

Critical success factors

- **Understanding the customers'** product/service and support requirements.
- **Understanding the competition.**
- **Enhancing** customer lifetime value.
- Customer **communication channel.**
- **Integrating customers** into enterprise strategy.

Integrating customers into enterprise strategy

The reason for company failure at CRM or making losses is that, for most companies, customers are simply not integrated into enterprise strategy. Listening to the voice of the customer, and taking action based on that input are two very different activities. Without a top-down mindset to include the customer in every decision, managers and customer care people quickly revert to inwardly focused decision making, which is basically a financial-only focus.

An enterprise with customers integrated into strategy behaves in different ways than one centred on efficiency, product or channel. A truly customer-centric organisation designs projects from the customer interaction backward and makes the customer experience inviolate in investment decisions. (Goldberg, 2001)

The 360-degree view (identifying customer segments)

The key to effective relationship management is crafting a comprehensive customer view. CRM requires that management adopt an enterprise-wide '360-degree customer view.' To adopt a 360-degree customer view, start by profiling the customers and determining how they are segmented. By breaking customers into groups that differ on behavioural, attitudinal, demographic and other relevant dimensions, organisations are able to optimise their product offerings, service and support systems, order processing, marketing communications and all other significant customer interactions, thereby gaining an ever greater 'share of customer' (Bibb and Gehm, 2001).

Quantify expected returns from CRM

The old adage 'You can't manage what you can't measure' remains true today. Part of the reason CRM has failed to prove its worth has been the inability to demonstrate measurable benefits. Don't be satisfied with intuitive CRM benefits alone. Ensure that the planned strategies and expenditures are clearly linked to measurable business impacts. And, leverage those measurable results to gain support and momentum for the organisations CRM efforts (Eberhardt, 2001).

Critical success factors

- **Monitor** customer retention rate.
- **Ensure** that the planned strategies and expenditures are clearly linked to measurable business impacts.
- **Leverage** measurable results.

Research reveals reasons for lost loyalty

According to Rodgers (2000) loyalty guru Frederick Reichheld, author of *The Loyalty Effect* and the creator of Bain & Co's loyalty practice, revealed the potential risks of making bad judgement calls when it comes to retaining the loyalty of regular customers and employees. Recent research has shown that a poor understanding of what drives customer loyalty, coupled with a failure to monitor retention rates, is resulting in businesses losing excessive numbers of customers and employees. According to him the average company loses 15 to 20 per cent of its customers each year, equivalent to around half its customer base over five years. The rate of attrition among employees is even higher, ranging from 15 to 30 per cent.

Figure 3.7 CRM continuum

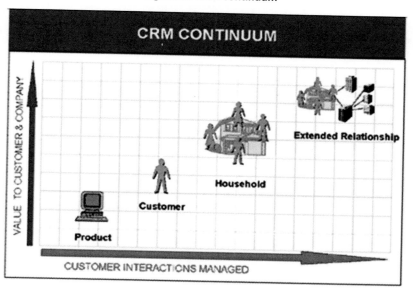

Pointing to research due to be published in June 2000 in the Harvard Business Review, Frederick Reichheld, demonstrated that a five point increase in customer retention leads to explosive improvements in cash flows over the course of a customer life cycle, with the most dramatic impact being felt in e-tailing. 'There is a real economic underlying loyalty,' he said. 'And loyalty is more relevant economically in the e-space.' Yet most businesses, he argued, fail to monitor customer churn (Rodgers, 2000).

Make CRM an enterprise-wide initiative

CRM efforts within an organisation are often championed by one functional area, and strategies are pursued in a functional vacuum. This approach fails to consider that almost all business processes involve more than one functional area within the company. The greater the level of integration among all functional areas, the better experience they will be able to deliver to their customers. (Eberhardt, 2001)

Critical success factors

- **Embed core values.**
- **Gain top management support and commitment.**
- **Leadership is critical** to any significant business change initiative.
- Active **involvement of executive** level management.
- **Involve all levels** in the existing process definition.
- Assign an **executive to be responsible** for enterprise business process development, enforcement and continuous improvement.
- **Assess** the company's ability to manage and adjust to change.
- Planning must include **adequate time for testing** and multiple **pilot sessions.**
- Ensure that **change management procedures** are clearly defined and followed.
- Sell to **sales force.**
- **Multi channel environment.**
- **Organise** project management team.

Getting CEOs onboard with the customers

Many chief executives must relearn competitive analysis to become customer-centric. Occasionally, studies are published that capture the percentage of time that the CEO of an organisation is involved in a CRM initiative; typically, it is less than 25 percent of the time. At the same time, the industry publishes initiative failure rates that approach 50 percent! Something is missing from this picture, and perhaps it is the CEO.

In reality, the involvement of the CEO should be 100 percent for those who want to be successful. Customer relationship management is not a bottom-up strategy. Although there are innumerable definitions of CRM and newly evolving definitions around some version of e-(add a favourite acronym), a customer-based focus is first and foremost a strategic business decision. Technology- and process-related initiatives are implemented to support the CRM strategic decision. Therefore, if the CRM strategy is real, the CEO must be at the forefront of the initiative (Petersen, 1999).

Leadership and management

The most important factor in the success of a CRM implementation is leadership buy-in. Management must sell the importance of the CRM initiative to the sales representatives on business, organisational, sales, customer service and personal levels. This way, sales reps will understand how the project affects them, their sales quotas and the overall organisation, and-'get on board.'

Time horizons

It is generally accepted that CEOs are expected to address issues that are associated with longer time horizons. Many systems fail because of lack of anticipation. While this can be due to monolithic customisation time frames, more often it is a lack of synchronisation with a vision for the future, or lack thereof. If a CRM system is to be implemented, it is very important to have 100 percent commitment of the CEOs, to make it a success (Petersen, 1999).

Organisation and people

Create and sustain an organisational and cultural environment that will support and adhere to the new business processes and systems. One of the keys to successfully implementing a CRM project is getting the users to buy into the idea, what Dickie calls 'Selling CRM Inside Your Company'. Many companies get so caught up in thinking about hardware and software that they forget they are eventually going to give all this technology to the people in sales, marketing and support, who will be the ultimate users of the CRM system (Dickie, 2000).

Once it is decided that change management is indeed important to the CRM initiative, having strong change management procedures in place to support this integration is critical, especially to CRM initiatives. Many CRM projects fail because most organisations do not pay attention to all the criteria needed to succeed. Companies alter processes and adopt new technologies, but do not prepare their people for these changes or reconfigure organisational factors to sustain the change (Wheeler and Uhlfelder, 2000).

Ensure integration across all distribution channels

Customers today demand the ability to do business through more than one channel of distribution, and they expect a seamless transition between channels. Consumers will never understand why a product bought online can't be returned to the local store. These consumer demands require management to track information about customers across all channels and to develop integrated systems, data and processes. That way the management will be able to project one view of the company to customers, and one view of the customer to all areas/channels within the organisation (Eberhardt, 2001).

Critical success factors

- **Integrate** systems.
- Ensure that the **re-engineered processes integrate** from department to department. Tear down the existing figurative walls that prevent inter-departmental cooperation.
- **Ensure that each process contributes** to reaching the company goals and objectives.
- **Review re-engineered business processes** and the integration between departments. Make sure that the engineered processes provide for the ability to accept and adapt to change.

Employees will make or break the CRM efforts

The best CRM strategies and applications don't stand a chance of succeeding without employee buy-in. Organisations have the choice between making their employees allies or dealing with them as adversaries. Leveraging employee input on CRM strategy development and application selection on the front-end will lead to greater buy-in post implementation. The efforts to ensure employee alignment should also include skill development, awards/incentives, tools to gather and address feedback, and ongoing communication strategies (Eberhardt, 2001).

Critical success factors

- **Leverage employee input** on CRM strategy development.
- **Employee buy-in.**
- **Selling IT investments to the board.**

Selling IT investments to the board

Finance directors must go beyond traditional cost/benefits analysis in convincing the board to invest in IT infrastructure. There is, however, evidence to suggest that board directors are not even discussing IT and e-commerce investments.

Research commissioned last year by the Institute of Directors showed that 50.5 percent of UK directors had never even had a technology briefing. This year, 'ClearCommerce', a vendor of e-commerce transaction software, conducted a survey that suggested that only 42 percent of strategic e-commerce decisions are made at board level.

In fact, Y2K was the first time IT was properly scrutinised by the board, as it became increasingly clear that getting Y2K risks ironed out was critical to the survival of the business.

Be willing to change the processes

Using new CRM technology to enable ineffective business processes is like putting pearls on swine. It is better to invest in designing or redesigning business processes to more efficiently and effectively manage customer relationships (Eberhardt, 2001).

Critical success factors

- **Invest in** designing or redesigning business processes.
- **Clearly define** the company's **CRM rules of engagement.**

Defining the company's CRM rules of engagement

To succeed at CRM, first develop guidelines for engaging different levels of the company. Companies need to develop guidelines for involvement, or rules of engagement for different levels in the organisation, so team members understand how and where their skills will be utilised and, more importantly, what issues they should resolve and what issues they need to raise to the next level of management.

With most CRM implementations these rules are not clearly defined. As a result, key strategic decisions are often made by the implementation team, those least equipped to make business decisions. A well-constructed implementation allows the people who best understand the issues to make the decisions. The CEO manages the inevitable trade-offs among strategic priorities. Top operating management is accountable for the operational/tactical trade-offs. The first-line managers and implementation teams make the detailed design and execution trade-offs (Brendler, 2000).

Build the right CRM infrastructure

There are a number of critical components to an effective relationship management system including: data warehouses, decisions support tools, links to operational systems, front-end applications, and staff to manage implementation and maintenance. Many companies spend considerable sums of money on CRM without achieving the anticipated results because they fail to address all of the basics of a strong CRM infrastructure (Eberhardt, 2001).

Migrating to a customer-centric model

Barry Goldberg (2001a) suggests that there are four fundamental disciplines in a framework for successful customer relationship management, in which a company must have some level of mastery in order to become a customer-centric enterprise. It is most useful to think of these as strategic capabilities. According to Goldberg this structure can also be applied to any enterprise change initiative; however, it is particularly useful for the construction of a maturity model and for enabling the transition to a customer-centred strategy.

Critical success factors

- **Selection** of technology solution(s) that best fit organisations' methodologies with the least amount of customisation (**best-of-breed**).
- **Leadership** and adoption.
- Customer **information**.
- Technology **delivery systems**.
- **Organisational effectiveness**.

The four fundamental disciplines are:

- Leadership and adoption: Cultural and strategic depth needed to execute any enterprise initiative and emotionally mature leadership in the executive suite.

- Customer information: An ability to capture, manage, interpret and exploit information about customers at a very granular level.

- Technology delivery systems: Technology architecture that makes customer information available in useful form both to planners and at the moment of truth with a customer.

- Organisational effectiveness: Alignment and measurement of people to remove conflict from consistently excellent performance with customers.

Each of these core disciplines has both strategic and tactical implications. At a strategic level, each is required to move through the maturity model. Understanding the role that each discipline plays, depending on the initiative that is been undertaken, is key to determining the upside potential and the level of risk to which the project is exposed. A CRM project that is laid over organisational, process and technology infrastructure that is still in the product or channel stage will invariably be expensive and risky. Even when successfully implemented, these initiates rarely see return on investment beyond simple productivity lift (Goldberg, 2001).

Implementing CRM: fully integrated or best-of-breed

Emmerton (2001) suggests that when choosing a new CRM solution, management must ask themselves whether they go with a fully integrated CRM package or choose best-of-breed components that fit each functional requirement but must be integrated with each other.

Emmerton suggests first to define CRM? According to him, customer relationship management (CRM) is comprised of complementary layers:

- It is a philosophy of caring for and nurturing your customers.

- It is the organisation and roles that deliver fulfilment of customer needs.

- It is a strategy for growth based on predicting and fulfilling customer needs.

- It is a set of best-practice business processes that support the strategy.

- It is the dialog and behaviour of all of your customer-facing personnel.

- It is a support application within the information systems infrastructure.

- It is the channels and information technologies that enable customer communications.

- It is the enterprise-wide information and data that provide you with the knowledge of the habits, preferences, and concerns of your customers.

Figure 3.8 Five steps for growth

Source: www.destinationcrm.com (2001)

When these components are successfully combined in a business operation, great synergy is introduced into the management of customer relationships. As depicted in Figure 3.8, the end result is the progression through a series of steps that leads to enhanced customer enthusiasm for the enterprise, products, and services. This, in turn, brings increased sales and profitability.

CRM: integrated or best of breed?

Emmerton (2001) poses the question: if the organisation has an unlimited budget for a CRM solution, how should it spend it? On the 'best software suite available' from a single vendor, or on 'best-of-breed applications' from multiple vendors that it would integrate to form one CRM support system? The scope of these choices across departments including the call centre, sales, support, and service is indicated in Figure 3.9.

Figure 3.9 CRM: Best of breed

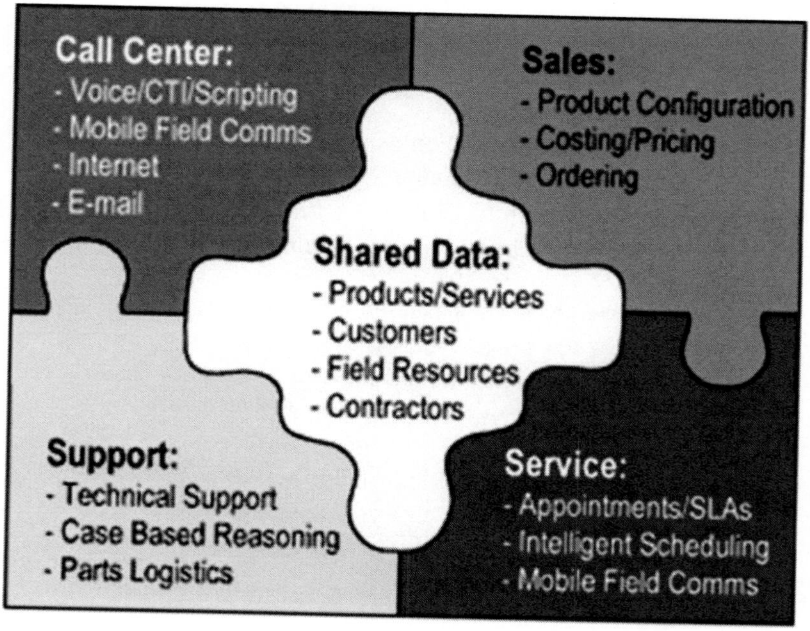

Source: www.destinationcrm.com (2001)

Emmerton (2001) suggests to first review the strengths and weaknesses of the single CRM application as summarised in Table 3.3, below (note that for each strength identified, the corresponding weakness is indicated).

Table 3.3 Single CRM application

Strength	Weakness
• Simplicity of choice • Fully integrated • Single vendor • Out-of-the-box CRM functionality • Assumes standard processes • Mobile communications technology • Incorporates rules-based scheduling	• Standard solution across the business • Lack of modular flexibility/upgrades • Lack of specialist expertise • Difficult to change/customise • Not necessarily best-practice processes • Locked into communications vendor/products • Inefficient service schedules

The issue here seems to be that one size does not fit all enterprises, in that out-of-the-box functionality does not fulfil their strategic needs or business operations. Table 3.4 looks at the challenge of integrating disparate, but best-of-breed applications.

Table 3.4 Integrating best-of-breed solutions

Strength	Weakness
• 'Best fit' for all customer service functions • Modules can change with the business • Multiple, specialist vendors • Business mapping enables best practices • Standard interfaces (APIs) available • Choice of communications channels • Can integrate intelligent scheduling	• Time to evaluate/select • Time to upgrade • Time to evaluate/select • Time to map processes • Time to integrate • Time to evaluate/select • Time to integrate

The key issues here are the time and cost related to selecting and integrating best-of-breed solutions versus the relatively poor fit and inflexibility of single CRM applications. More subtle weaknesses are the key risks involved in trying to force an out-of-the box CRM application into the business, together with the missed opportunities for introducing best-practice processes and lower-cost service delivery schedules.

US based publisher DestinationCRM.com recently conducted a poll on their website, which produced results that are surprising. They asked those polled to assume an unlimited budget for CRM, figuring that a vast majority of respondents would eschew the complexity of tying together various pieces of software for the relative ease of architecting a solution with software from one vendor whose separate parts all speak the same language. Matt Purdue, director of content, reported the following results:

- 42% were in favour of integrating best-of-breed applications.

- 38% opted for a single CRM package.

- 20% responded with 'don't know' or chose 'other solution.'

These results suggested a very important conclusion to him. 'No CRM vendor has yet developed a solution that fits the diverse requirements of a 21st century enterprise,' he commented. 'Despite the vendors' best attempts at throwing around buzzwords like end-to-end and fully integrated, many of our respondents cannot find or do not want such a solution.'

The internet poll, although not a fully scientific survey did indicate results that are consistent with the findings and conclusions discussed on the European seminar and conference circuits (i.e. integrating best-of-breed CRM components can fit businesses better than implementing single CRM applications) (Emmerton, 2001).

Recognise that CRM is a change effort

Enterprise-wide CRM can be all encompassing, consisting of people, processes and technology. Few companies are recognised for outstanding customer relationship management, as the road to CRM success is a long one. Successful companies view the path to CRM as an evolution and are willing to make mistakes, learn from them, and regroup to get closer to the goal. They treat CRM as a change effort, gain sponsorship of company leaders, establish success measures, recognise and reward successes, and establish processes to ensure continuous improvement. Allocate dedicated resources toward managing change and maintaining momentum for CRM efforts and the management will be much more likely to achieve success (Eberhardt, 2001).

Critical success factors

- **Win executive sponsorship.**
- **Executive sponsorship is key.**
- CRM: An **evolution process.**
- **Measure, measure, measure**.
- Treat CRM as a **change effort**, gain sponsorship of company leaders, establish **success measures**, **recognise and reward successes**, and establish processes to ensure continuous improvement.
- Create the **right environment**.
- **Integration is the watchword**.
- Have a **cross-functional perspective** on what is needed to change to a customer-centric organisation.

CRM works only if the right environment is created

To implement CRM successfully, management have to reorganise their customers and change their organisational mindset. The complexity of modern business and the need for quick responses to changing conditions do not allow employees to go through channels anymore. But many companies have a hard time combining information, action and interpretation across old structural boundaries. Often, the result is decisions so untimely as to be irrelevant, no matter how technically correct they are.

When CRM works, it helps to solve this problem by meshing everyone together and focusing the entire organisation on the customer. Often, people are forced to cross old organisational boundaries and to deal with others they barely knew before, collaborating to make decisions that affect the customer.

But Brendler (2001) strongly suggests that, if this process of integrating employees around the customer is not done well by the leaders of the organisation, the results can be explosive. Ideally, of course, the organisations are already integrated around the customers and see the advantages of working in cross-functional teams. If not, CRM will force those issues in ways that previous waves of business change, like total quality management (TQM) and re-engineering, never did. TQM and reengineering won't shut the business down, but losing customers will.

The new customer challenges demand dramatic changes in how organisations are organised. To ensure CRM is successful, integration is the watchword. And for some, this will require a large leap of faith. Barring the CEO, managers often don't have a cross-functional perspective on what is needed to change to a customer centric organisation. The fact is that, many managers are comfortable in their traditional, functional silos. Most were trained as functional specialists. In addition to that, many management systems further encourage and reinforce this functional specialisation.

This traditional, functional view optimises individual functions at the expense of customers and the whole business. This narrow scope, to which so many want to cling, leads decision-makers to attack symptoms in one function but miss the causes rooted in another.

This happens all the time in the silos – sales, marketing and customer service. Making CRM work often depends on the management's openness to change and their determination to reorganise teams around their customers. Today's losers are internally focused, functionally managed and management-centred (Brendler, 2001).

References

Agrawal, V., Arjona, L. D. and Lemmens, R. (2001) E-performance: The path to rational exuberance, *The McKinsey Quarterly*, February.

Bell, S. (2000) *Rapp: A CRM Strategy Beyond Technology*, Dec, available at http://www.destinationcrm.com.

Bibb, R, and Gehm, E. (2001) *The 360-Degree View*, June, available at http://www.destinationcrm.com

Brendler, W. F. (2000) *Defining Your Company's CRM Rules of Engagement*, Dec, available at http://www.destinationcrm.com.

Brendler, W. F. (2001) *People and Processes Make CRM Work*, Apr, available at http://www.destinationcrm.com.

Dickie, J. (2000) *Selling CRM Inside Your Company*, July, available at http://www.destinationcrm.com.

Eberhardt, C. (2001) *A CRM Starter Pack: Strategic Steps to Success*, D7 Consulting LLC, June, available at http://www.destinationcrm.com.

Emmerton, T. (2001) *Implementing CRM: Fully Integrated or Best-of-Breed?* May, available at http://www.destinationcrm.com.

Fadia, A. (2001) *Eight Steps to Developing a CRM Roadmap*, Oct, available at http://www.destinationcrm.com.

Foran, T. L. (2001) *A Structured Approach to Retail CRM*, Apr, available at http://www.destinationcrm.com.

Goldberg, I. B. (2001) *Part One: Integrating Customers into Enterprise Strategy*, Apr, available at http://www.destinationcrm.com.

Goldberg, I. B. (2001a) *Part Two: Migrating to a Customer-Centric Model*, Mar, available at http://www.destinationcrm.com.

IDC (Analyst – Rasika Versleijen Pradhan) (2000) *Measuring Customer Loyalty in the eBusiness Era: Five Real-Life Case Studies*. International Data Corporation.

Lee, D. (2000) *Self-guided CRM,* High-Yield Marketing Press.

Lee, D. (2000) *The Customer Relationship Management Survival Guide*, High-Yield Marketing Press.

Lee, D. (2001) *Why climb the CRM mountain?* Aug, available at http://www.crmguru.com.

Lowenstein, M. W. (2006) Second Lifetime Value: Customer Reincarnation Through WinBack, *The Harris Report*, 1, 2, Sept. Available at www.harrisinteractive.com.

Petersen, G. (1999) *The CEO and CRM: Only Leaders Need Apply,* Oct, available at http://www.destinationcrm.com

Rodgers, K. (2000) *Research Reveals Reasons for Lost Loyalty*, Aug, available at http://www.destinationcrm.com.

Trailer, B. (2000) *How to Evaluate CRM Consultants*, Apr, available at http://www.destinationcrm.com.

Wheeler, J. H. and Uhlfelder, H. (2000) *Making Change*, Jan, available at http://www.destinationcrm.com.

Chapter 4

CRM implementation – key factors: A benchmarking analysis report

Introduction

Secondary data comprise one of the elements in data collection. Information that has been published or is accessible indirectly can provide a fruitful source of data which can be obtained at a fraction of the cost, time and inconvenience associated with primary data collection (Remenyi *et al.*, 1998). Secondary case analysis is a reliable source of data that gives validity to the study and enhances confidence in the result across organisation sectors.

A CRM project is complex and not easy to implement if the organisation does not consider several critical factors that contribute directly or indirectly to success of its implementation. CRM implementation is not off-risk and needs a customer-focused organisation; it may also require re-engineering of the current business processes to support the implementation (Xu *et al.*, 2002; Bull 2003; Kotorov 2003; Bolton 2004).

The investigation of factors potentially affecting the success of CRM implementation is of great importance, since the CRM software market worldwide, according to a Gartner group prediction would reach $76.5 billion in 2005, up from $23.26 billion achieved in 2000 (Starkey and Woodcock, 2002). Consequently, understanding the critical factors of CRM project implementation will help to avoid failure in future implementation.

Generally, several critical factors of CRM implementation have been identified by a number of authors and practitioners, based on case studies, or empirical studies (Galbreath and Rogers, 1999;

Mohammad, 2001; Radcliffe, 2001; Ang and Buttle, 2002; Dyché, 2002; Bull, 2003; Gurau, 2003; Knox, 2003; Kotorov, 2003; Newell, 2003; Greenberg, 2004).

Even though the main critical factors of CRM project implementation have been presented in the literature, the emphasis on aspects has varied. None seems to share the same set of critical factors; most of these studies have not covered all aspects of CRM implementation. For instance, Radcliffe (2001) and Kotorov (2003) mentioned the critical success factors (CSFs) of CRM implementation from strategic and tactical perspectives, but have not cited the level of project implementation. Chen and Popovich (2003) depicted a CRM implementation model that aligns people, process and technology together, but did not consider the importance of project plan or integration in the implementation.

This study provides a complete analysis of case studies of CRM project implementations of 81 organisations presented in the literature, in order to demonstrate the most critical factors of CRM project implementation.

Case studies: background

These case studies were collected from different sources, the literature and CRM vendor success case study stories published online through their websites (see Table 4.1 for full list of organisations). The main objective of this study is to verify the most critical factors of CRM project implementation based on best practice perspectives of CRM implementation. All case studies used were success stories, therefore support the main objectives of this study.

Table 4.1 Case studies

	Sector	Bull (2003) / UK / Manu-facturing / ELMS	Rigby et al. (2002) / US / Manu-facturing / Square D	Rigby et al. (2002) / US / Service / BMC	Corner and Hinton (2002) / UK / Service / EES
1	System integration	X		X	
2	Data and information	X			X
3	Client consultation	X			
4	Software selection	X			
5	Resistance to change	X		X	
6	Understanding customer			X	X
7	Resources and budget			X	X
8	Business processes	X	X		
9	Holistic approach	X			
10	Segmentation and targeting	X	X		
11	Project vision	X			
12	Project planning and management	X			
13	Business justification				
14	Organisational change	X	X	X	
15	Communication			X	X
16	Executive sponsorship	X	X	X	X
17	Developing customer- centric strategy		X		

Company	Source	Country	Sector	1	2	3	4	5	6	7	8	9	10	11	12	13	14	15	16	17
FAW-Volkswagen	SAP success story	China	Manufacturing	X	X															X
Orange	Knox *et al.* (2003)	UK	Service												X		X	X	X	X
Britannia Building Society	Knox *et al.* (2003)	UK	Service	X	X				X				X	X			X	X		X
Brother International	Rigby & Ledingham (2004)	US	Manufacturing		X				X				X							
Goods Co	Light (2003)	US	Manufacturing	X	X															X
Dow	CRM guru	US	Manufacturing	X	X				X			X				X	X			
Software AG	Robinson (2002) CRM guru	Germany	Service						X											X
3Dfacto	Siebel Success Story	Denmark	IT	X															X	

Company	Sector	Country	Source	1	2	3	4	5	6	7	8	9	10	11	12	13	14	15	16	17
Boehringer Ingelheim's	Pharma-ceutical	US	Siebel Success Story								x			x	x				x	x
Alaska Airlines	Service	US	Siebel Success Story	x	x				x					x		x				
Erdgas Südsachsen	Energy	Germany	Siebel Success Story	x		x									x				x	
Unilever	Con-sumer Goods	UK	Siebel Success Story		x				x						x			x	x	
Tata Motors	Auto-motive	India	Siebel Success Story			x	x				x				x				x	x
Swiss Post	Logistics	Switzer-land	Siebel Success Story	x			x				x						x			
Sun Micro-systems	IT	US	Siebel Success Story				x		x		x						x		x	

Company	Sector	Country	Source	1	2	3	4	5	6	7	8	9	10	11	12	13	14	15	16	17
Saab	Automotive	US	Siebel Success Story	X	X											X				X
Virgin Mobile	Communications	US	Siebel Success Story	X										X					X	X
WestStar Bank	Financial services	Colorado	Siebel Success Story			X										X	X	X	X	X
Wisconsin Retirement System	Public Sector	US	Siebel Success Story	X			X								X				X	
YORK International	Manufacturing	UK	Siebel Success Story				X												X	
Aviall	Aerospace	US	Siebel Success Story	X			X				X				X				X	
Bayer Crop Science	Chemicals	Germany	Siebel Success Story						X						X		X		X	X

Company	Source	Country	Sector	1	2	3	4	5	6	7	8	9	10	11	12	13	14	15	16	17
Binda	Siebel Success Story	Italy	Consumer Goods	×											×		×			×
Deloitte	Siebel Success Story	US	Service	×							×		×							
ELDIM	Siebel Success Story	France	Manufacturing	×											×		×	×	×	×
Fujitsu Siemens	Siebel Success Story	Germany	IT	×	×						×						×	×	×	
Southwest Airlines	Cannon (2002) CRM guru	US	Service	×	×				×				×							
Harrah's Entertainment	Swift, (2003) CRM guru	US	Service		×				×				×							
Fair Isaac Corporation	Rigley (2003) CRM guru	US	Service				×		×		×	×	×				×			

Company	Sector	Country	Source	1	2	3	4	5	6	7	8	9	10	11	12	13	14	15	16	17
EMAAR Properties	Service	Dubai	Peppers & Rogers Group		x		x							x					x	x
Hewlett-Packard (HP)	IT	US	Peppers & Rogers Group						x		x				x					x
Jaguar Cars	Manufacturing	UK	Peppers & Rogers Group		x					x				x	x					x
Animal health	Pharmaceutical	US	Peppers & Rogers Group						x						x	x				x
United States Postal Service (USPS)	Service	US	Peppers & Rogers Group		x		x	x	x				x							
Circuit City	Electronics	US	www.cio.com		x				x				x				x		x	x
Best Buy	Electronics	US	www.cio.com																	x

Company	Source	Country	Sector	1	2	3	4	5	6	7	8	9	10	11	12	13	14	15	16	17
Emerson Process Management	CRM Today	US	Service		x				x											x
Sealing Devices	CRM Today	US	IT				x	x											x	
Red Letter Day	CRM Today	UK	Hospital-ity	x		x								x						x
Aventail	CRM Magazine May 2005	US	Network-ing						x		x		x		x			x		
Adams Harkness Bank	CRM Magazine May 2005	US	Service	x			x											x		x
Blue Cross BlueShield of Tennessee	CRM Magazine May 2005	US	Service	x														x		
Farm Credit Services of America	CRM Magazine May 2005	US	Agri-cultural Bank	x	x	x														x

Company	Sector	Country	Source	1	2	3	4	5	6	7	8	9	10	11	12	13	14	15	16	17
FedEx	Service	US	CRM Magazine Feb 2003	X	X		X		X	X	X			X	X					X
Marriott International	Hospitality	US	ICMR CASE CATALOG 2005				X					X				X	X		X	
Mahindra & Mahindra	Diversified	India	ICMR CASE CATALOG 2005	X												X	X		X	X
HP	IT	US	Siebel Success Story						X		X						X			X
Irish Life & Permanent	Service	Ireland	Siebel Success Story			X	X								X				X	
Malaysia National Insurance	Insurance	Malaysia	Siebel Success Story		X		X	X									X			X
Manitoba Telecom	Communications	Canada	Siebel Success Story	X	X		X										X		X	

Company	Sector	Country	Source	1	2	3	4	5	6	7	8	9	10	11	12	13	14	15	16	17
OCBC Bank	Service	Singapore	Siebel Success Story						X		X						X		X	X
Robeco Bank	Service	Belgium	Siebel Success Story	X		X							X						X	
Swiss Post	Logistics	Switzerland	Siebel Success Story	X				X			X				X					X
Boise Office	IT	US	C. Millike (2002) CIO Magazine	X			X		X								X		X	
CIMCO	Communications	US	Jay Curry, (2004) CRM guru						X	X				X			X		X	X
T-Mobile	Mobile	UK	Teri Robinson, (2004) CRM guru		X								X							X
The MAPFRE Group	Insurance	Spain	SAS Success Story						X					X						X

Company	1	2	3	4	5	6	7	8	9	10	11	12	13	14	15	16	17	Sector	Country	Source
Bank of New York			x											x			x	Banking	US	http://www.bnet.com
Telekurs Multipay AG	x	x																Financial Services	Switzerland	SAP Success Story
U. Austria State Government		x		x				x										Public Sector	Austria	SAP Success Story
Audi AG	x	x				x									x		x	Automotive	Germany	SAP Success Story
Avid Technology,				x		x										x		IT	US	SAP Success Story
Capstone Turbine Corporation,														x			x	Manufacturing	US	SAP Success Story
Eczacıbaşı Group,	x					x		x										Consumer Goods	Turkey	SAP Success Story
Schwan's Food Service,	x			x		x												Consumer Goods	US	SAP Success Story

Company	Source	Country	Sector	1	2	3	4	5	6	7	8	9	10	11	12	13	14	15	16	17
Canada Post Corporation	SAP Success Story	Canada	Service	X	X				X					X						X
CenTrade	SAP Success Story	Czech	Retailing		X				X						X				X	
Charles Schwab	ICMR CASE CATALOG 2005	US	Financial Services			X					X								X	X
IBM	ICMR CASE CATALOG 2005	US	IT	X	X				X								X			X
1-800-FLOWERS.COM	SAP Success Story	US	Flowers		X		X		X		X									
The AA's	SAS Success Story	UK	Motoring	X	X		X			X										X
HFC Bank	SAS Success Story	UK	Banking		X		X													X
Hjemmet Mortensen	SAS Success Story	Norway	Service	X	X								X					X		

181

Company	Sector	Country	Source	1	2	3	4	5	6	7	8	9	10	11	12	13	14	15	16	17
CSL	Communications	Hong Kong	SAS Success Story		x	x													x	x
JCB Co	Service	Japan	SAS Success Story		x								x							
Allianz Elementar	Service	Austria	SAS Success Story	x			x													
The Arena International Group	Water wear	Italy	SAS Success Story	x	x				x										x	x

182

All factors were indentified and classified according to the conceptual framework of CRM project implementation methodology (see Figure 4.1), and their degree of criticality was analysed by using a content analysis approach (the number of times the case authors mentioned the factor were coded). The main reason for using the conceptual framework of CRM project implementation is the fact that it has been created through a comprehensive study of the relevant literature. The selection of cases for analysis was based on the availability of information.

Figure 4.1 CRM conceptual model

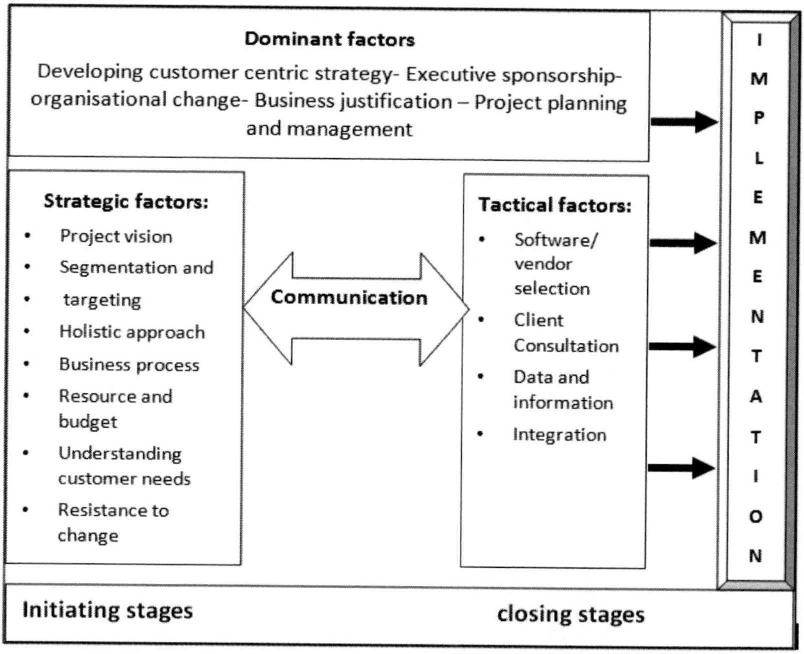

Source: Al-Ajlan and Zairi (2005)

Key findings

The results of the 81 studies revealed a number of critical factors that influence the implementation of a CRM project. All factors are related to people, process and technology and they are highly interdependent. Moreover, it is critical to address all these factors at the same time of implementation. In essence, failure in one factor can affect the overall CRM project implementation. Also, the analysis results brought out clear evidence that CRM projects are applicable to all types of organisations regardless of the organisation's size or sector.

General results of CRM implementation

The 81 case studies analysed covered many sectors and services. As Figure 4.2 reveals, CRM is appropriate to all sectors. The result shows that the CRM project is more attractive to the services sector with 73%.

Figure 4.2 Organisation sector

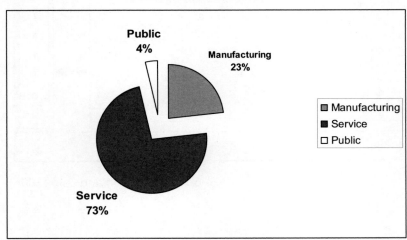

On the other hand, 23% of these organisations were from the manufacturing sector, which means that the CRM project has a bright future to expand over this sector. In addition, the figure shows that only 4% of organisations came from the public sector, which enhances the ability to apply such projects at non-profit organisations.

Figure 4.3 shows the region of these organisations. They have been categorised according to continent (Asia, Europe and USA). It can be observed that most of these organisations came from the USA 48% whereas Europe rated second with 38%; Asia and other countries made up 10% and 4% respectively.

Figure 4.3 Organisation location

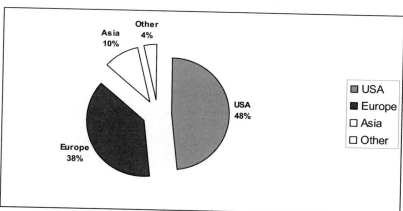

Critical factors of CRM implementation

Analysis of the case studies shows many critical factors that affect the implementation of CRM projects. All factors hypothesised to play a prominent role in the implementation of CRM projects (refer to Figure 4.1), including the six dominant factors, were identified as critical factors of CRM project implementation in the cases analysed. Also, all strategic and tactical factors were presented too.

However, the results confirm that most CRM project implementations fail because the organisation fails to adopt a clear strategy and fails to make appropriate changes to its business processes (Crosby, 2002; Xu *et al.* 2002; Bolton, 2004).

Overall, the percentage of each factor is presented in Figure 4.4. The figure shows that the most critical factor in successful CRM project implementation that stands out over all others is strategy. CRM does better in organisations that are already customer-centric (Ang and Buttle, 2002; Harvard Business School, 2002). The following section analyses all other critical success factors of CRM project implementation.

Figure 4.4 Overall case studies

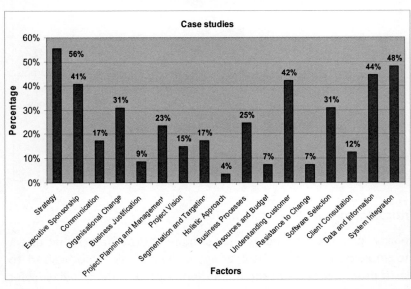

Dominant factors

The dominant factors have to be recognised throughout the implementation phases, as they have a big impact on the process of implementation. As can be observed in Figure 4.5, 56% of case studies identified that developing customer-centric strategy is a critical factor for their successful implementation of the CRM project. Not surprisingly, one key point that managers should understand is that although CRM depends on, and is driven by cutting edge technology, it works only when supported by the corporate culture that embraces customer-focused aims (Xu *et al.* 2002).

Figure 4.5 Dominant factors

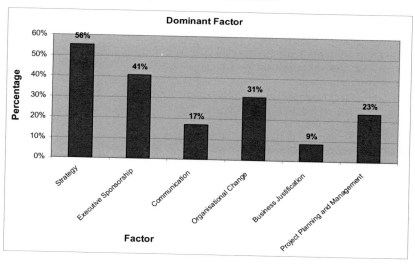

The second important aspect in the dominant factor category is executive sponsorship with 41%. Bull (2003) emphasised that the role of leaders is of importance, and because leaders monitor the external environments of an organisation they are often the best placed to set the vision or strategic direction for CRM projects.

In addition, Figure 4.5 shows that organisational change is found to be the third most critical factor with 31%, whereas project planning and management and communication come next with 23% and 17% respectively. One surprising result is that business justification comes at the end with 9%. However, the literature reviewed emphasised that the project leader must start by crafting a valid business case for CRM before selecting a vendor, upgrading software, or launching a new project (Myron, 2003; Greenberg, 2004; Knox, 2003; Tie 2003; Xu *et al.* 2002).

Strategic factors

According to Ang and Buttle (2002), at a strategic level, CRM is seen as a core business strategy, which is combined with technology to effectively manage the complete customer lifecycle. Consequently, the decisions regarding CRM implementation have to be considered at this level.

Figure 4.6 shows all critical success factors at the strategic level. Understanding customer needs and requirements is the first most important critical factor in CRM project implementation at this level with 42%. Also, 25% of these organisations believe that business process management is a critical factor in CRM implementation, whereas segmentation and targeting and project vision come next with 17% and 15% of case studies.

In addition, resistance to change and resource and budget were found to be less important factors with 7% for each. Finally, only 4% of these organisations succeeded because their CRM project involved the entire organisation and reached into so many potential parts of their businesses.

Figure 4.6 Strategic factors

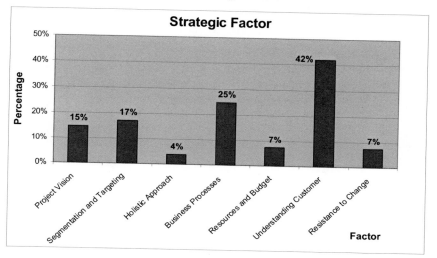

Tactical factors

At the tactical level where the decision regarding CRM implementation is made, several critical success factors emerged. Figure 4.7 shows that 48% of case studies regarded system integration as a critical factor in their CRM implementation. This was supported by Umashankar (2001), where 47% of firms said the ability to access all relevant customer information is the biggest challenge in implementing CRM. Moreover, this factor was the second important factor after customer-centric strategy.

It can also be observed that 44% of organisations deem data and information to be important factors in CRM implementation, while software selection and client consultation came next with 31% and 12% respectively.

Figure 4.7 Tactical factors

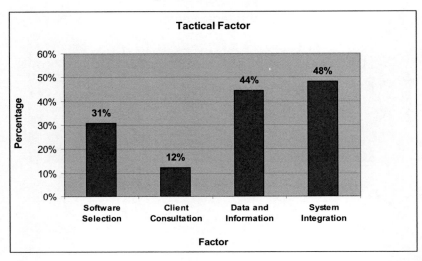

Limitations of study

This study was not without limitations, as in any study based on secondary source data. The limitations include:

- misinterpretation, whether by the author of this study or by the case studies' authors;

- case studies provided by software vendors or consultant agencies may be unreliable or exaggerated.

However, the purpose of this study was to tackle all critical factors of CRM project implementation as viewed by authors and practitioners, whether directly or indirectly mentioned. In essence, the critical factors revealed by this study have been found to agree with the framework of CRM project implementation methodology (see Figure 4.1). Furthermore, and in general, having considered a large number and a wide range of cases from many sources, it is believed that the overall conclusions drawn are representative of the issues faced in a general real-life situation.

Conclusion

To have successful CRM project implementation, an organisation has to learn several critical factors.

This study identified seventeen critical factors. The factor that stands out above all others as the most critical factor in CRM project implementation is developing a customer-centric strategy. Next in importance is system integration. In addition, the following factors were also found to be critical: executive sponsorship, communication, organisational change, business justification, project planning and management, project vision, segmentation and targeting, holistic approach, business process, resource and budget, understanding customer needs, resistance to change, software selection, client consultation and data and information. Table 4.2 shows the degree of criticality in CRM implementation. The ranking of these factors stemmed from the analysis of these case studies and the number of times the case authors mentioned the factors.

Table 4.2 Critical factors in descending order of importance

Factor	Percentage
1 - Strategy	56%
2 - System integration	48%
3 - Data and information	44%
4 - Understanding customer needs	42%
5 - Executive sponsorship	41%
6 - Organisational change	31%
7 - Software selection	31%
8 - Business process	25%
9 - Project planning and management	23%
10 - Communication	17%
11 - Segmentation and targeting	17%
12 - Project vision	15%
13 - Client consultation	12%
14 - Business justification	9%
15 - Resource and budget	7%
16 - Resistance to change	7%

References

Al-Ajlan, M. and Zairi, M. (2005) Critical Success Factors in CRM implementation: Some Research Issues, *Quality in Services, Palermo 8th-9th September,* University of Palermo, Italy.

Ang, L. and F. A. Buttle (2002) ROI on CRM: a customer-journey approach, *IMP-conference,* Industrial Marketing & Purchasing, Perth, Australia.

Bolton, M. (2004) Customer centric business processing, *International Journal of Productivity and Performance Management,* 53, 1.

Bull, C. (2003) Strategic issues in customer relationship management (CRM) implementation, *Business Process Management Journal,* 9, 5.

Chen, I. J. and Popovich, K. (2003) Understanding customer relationship management (CRM): People, process and technology, *Business Process Management Journal,* 9, 5.

Corner, I. and Hinton, M. (2002) Customer relationship management systems: implementation risks and relationship dynamics, *Qualitative Market Research: An International Journal,* 5, 4.

Crosby, L. A. (2002) Exploding some myths about customer relationship management, *Managing Service Quality,* 12, 5.

Dyché, J. (2002) *The CRM handbook a business guide to customer relationship management,* Addison Wesley, Boston.

Galbreath, J. and Rogers, T. (1999) Customer relationship leadership: a leadership and motivation model for the twenty-first century business, *The TQM Magazine,* 11, 3.

Greenberg, P. (2004) *CRM at the speed of light essential customer strategies for the 21st century,* McGraw-Hill/Osborne, Berkeley, Calif.

Gurau, C. (2003) Tailoring e-service quality through CRM, *Managing Service Quality,* 13, 6.

Harvard Business School (2002) *Harvard business review on customer relationship management,* Harvard Business School Press, Boston.

Knox, S. (2003) *Customer relationship management perspectives from the market place,* Butterworth-Heinemann, Oxford.

Kotorov, R. (2003) Customer relationship management: strategic lessons and future directions, *Business Process Management Journal,* 9, 5.

Light, B. (2003) CRM packaged software: a study of organisational experiences, *Business Process Management Journal*, 9, 5, 603-616.

Mohammad, A. B. (2001) CRM implementation an empirical study of best practice and a proposed model of implementation, *TQM*, Bradford.

Myron, D. (2003) 6 Barriers to CRM Success and How to Overcome Them, *CRM Magazine*.

Newell, F. (2003) *Why CRM doesn't work how to win by letting customers manage the relationship*, Kogan Page, London.

Radcliffe, J. (2001) Eight Building Blocks of CRM: A Framework for Success, *Gartner Research*.

Remenyi, D., Williams, B., Money, A. and Swartz, E. (1998) *Doing research in business and management an introduction to process and method*, Sage, London.

Rigby, D. K. and Ledingham, D. (2004) CRM Done Right, *Harvard Business Review; Boston*, 82, 11, 118-129.

Rigby, D. K., Reichheld, F. F. and Schefter, P. (2002) Avoid the four perils of CRM, *Harvard Business Review; Boston,* 80, 2, 101-109.

Starkey, M. and Woodcock, N. (2002) CRM systems: Necessary, but not sufficient. REAP the benefits of customer management, *The Journal of Database Marketing*, 9, 3, 267-275.

Tie, W. (2003) *Implementing CRM in SMEs: An Exploratory Study on the Viability of Using the ASP Model*, Masters Thesis in Accounting, Swedish School of Economics and Business Administration.

Umashankar, V. (2001) E-CRM Issues of Semantics, Domain & Implementation, *Productivity*, 42, 1, 19-25.

Xu, Y., Yen, D. C., Lin, B. and Chou, D. C. (2002) Adopting customer relationship management technology, *Industrial Management & Data Systems Management,* 102, 8, 442-452.

Internet resources

http://www.sas.com/success/solution.html#CustomerRelationshipManagement

http://www.crmguru.com/

http://www.siebel.com/resource-library/

http://www.peppersandrogers.com/View.aspx?ItemID=539

www.cio.com

http://www.crm2day.com/

http://www.destinationcrm.com/

http://www.icmrindia.org/

http://www.sap.com/solutions/business-suite/crm/customersuccess/index.epx

Chapter 5

CEM: The 'right brain' of customer focus

Introduction

Strategic management has focused on a number of areas over time. In the 1970s, the major focus seemed to be on quality improvement, this later turned into focus on brand in the 1990s, and in the 2000s, the focus shifted to services and service orientation (Mascarenhas *et al.*, 2006). More recently (mid 2000s), this trend shifted to the 'emotional attachment' of the customer to the firm or the brand (Mascarenhas *et al.*, 2006). One of the major areas being explored to achieve this is in ensuring that customers have positive experiences with the firm (Macmillan and McGrath, 1997; Carbone, 1998; Pine and Gilmore, 1998, 1999; Rowley, 1999; Wyner, 2000; Berry, 2000; Berry *et al.*, 2002; Gilmore and Pine, 2002, Mascarenhas *et al.*, 2006, Berry and Carbone, 2007). It is believed that companies need to understand the complete 'journey' of a customer with a product/service starting at advertising through post sales, and to learn about customer expectations (Berry *et al.*, 2002). This helps managers to design good 'experiences' for the customer. The concept of managing experiences is referred to as customer experience management, and has been embraced by numerous organisations around the globe (Verhoef *et al.*, 2009).

Customer experience management (CEM) is considered by some to be an extension of customer relationship management (CRM) strategy (Thompson, 2006). While CRM focuses on gathering data about the customer, CEM focuses on the customer's emotion and importance is given to the experience of consuming a product or service (Thompson, 2006). Others argue that CEM is different from CRM and needs to be looked at from a different perspective (Schmitt, 2003). Either way, the focus is on enhancing the customer experience. Stuart and Tax (2004) believe that companies need to design their systems in order to 'encourage greater active customer participation and/or to make the environment more conducive to customer absorption.' In CEM, the experience of a customer is derived from numerous interactions with the firm, and the resulting experience is one which is a sum of all these little interactions (Voss and Zomerdijk, 2007). Watching a TV advertisement, calling up customer services, waiting in line at a supermarket, asking a sales person questions are all examples of these interactions.

Having exceptional experiences with a firm not only makes the customer think positively about that firm, but also increases loyalty to that firm (Stuart and Tax, 2004). Companies that are able to do this, use 'tools' of customer experience management, which enable them to build strategic advantages over competitors that are often difficult to replicate (Berry *et al.*, 2002). Examples of companies that seem to be good at CEM include those in the leisure and entertainment industries (Voss and Zomerdijk, 2007). These firms have been 'experience' focused from their inception, and understand the demands of their customers which allow them to develop great experiences for their customers. Examples include, theme parks and cinemas (Voss and Zomerdijk, 2007). A customer can watch a movie at home, however the cinemas are no longer focusing on selling the 'movie' as a product, rather, they focus on the 'experience' of going to the cinema. Other types of firms are also putting greater emphasis on CEM. For example, HP not only attaches great importance to CEM, but also has a department for total customer experience (TCE) (Thompson, 2006).

Despite the adoption of CEM, many companies are still struggling to understand customers and approach them in an appropriate manner (Strativity, 2006). A recent study showed that many companies were still unable to understand the type of customer experience their customers expected (Thompson, 2006). As Figure 5.1, shows, there is a large discrepancy between a customer's view of excellent customer experience and what the companies perceive.

Figure 5.1 Companies struggle to cope with customer expectations

Companies provide an excellent customer experience?

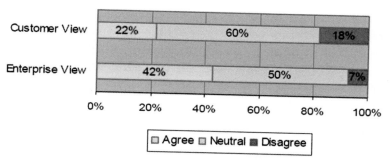

Source: Thompson (2006)

The more companies focus on customer experience management, the worse they seem to be fairing. Data from 2003 to 2005 shows that, overall, companies are not much better off than before in understanding their customers' needs (see Figure 5.2). Some areas have shown a great decline, including customer commitment.

Figure 5.2 Companies lack focus on the customer

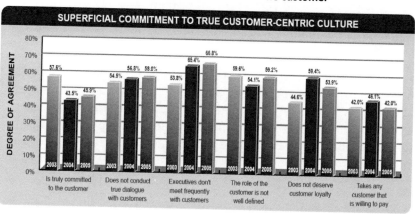

Source: Strativity (2006)

While many companies are struggling to understand their customers, managers and researchers point to the success stories. Examples of success stories are found in all types of sectors and industries (Voss and Zomerdijk, 2007) and need to be learned from. The rest of this chapter will consider CEM in detail and will examine the tools that companies can use to implement CEM in order to develop a successful experience management system for their customers.

What exactly is customer experience management?

Customer experience management as a strategy has been defined in a number of ways by various researchers. Most of these definitions are quite similar, and focus on similar aspects. The main focus of these is on the interaction that a customer has with a company, and improving that interaction. Berry *et al.* (2002) have described these interactions as an 'experience clue':

> *Anything that can be perceived or sensed — or recognized by its absence — is an experience clue. Thus the product or service for sale gives off one set of clues, the physical setting offers more clues, and the employees — through their gestures, comments, dress and tones of voice — still more clues.*

Schmitt (2003) has described these interactions as 'touchpoints'. According to Thompson (2006), an interaction covers a wide variety of elements 'from viewing a marketing message to the actual use of a product or service to a post-purchase service/support activity to solve a problem.' All of these elements and more are part of the interactions/touchpoints/clues that a customer has with a firm.

No matter what term we use to refer to these interactions, researchers agree that CEM needs to manage these. Hence, Schmitt (2003) says that CEM is, 'the process of strategically managing a customer's entire experience with a product or a company.' CEM is a customer-centric strategy, which is concerned with 'seeing your business through the eyes of the customer' (Procops, 2005). Not only is the business trying to see through the eyes of the customer but more specifically it is trying to understand the 'customer's perception of interactions with a brand' (Thompson, 2006).

Moreover, it is believed that companies need to adopt an 'integrative approach' by not only focusing on the customer, but also looking within the organisation in order to build pleasing customer experiences (Schmitt, 2003). Alperin (2005) presents another definition, which seems quite similar to earlier concepts:

Customer Experience Management (CEM) is the process of managing the events and personal interactions that make up a customer's experience.

Another definition of CEM comes from a managerial background. Rance, a customer experience expert believes that:

Customer Experience Management attempts to define how all the customer management capabilities within an organization, such as the brand, marketing, business rules, processes, decision-making authority, training, employee engagement customer data and metrics, etc. combine to influence the customer experience (Thompson, 2006).

Researchers and managers have argued that organisations now need to focus on building these positive experiences for their customers. Management focus has shifted from product orientation to service orientation and more recently to experience management, or as, Voss and Zomerdijk (2007) call it experiential services. Experiential services are services where the focus is on experiences of customers. Another variation to customer experience management is the total customer experience (TCE) strategy, propagated by Mascarenhas *et al.* (2006). According to them total customer experience is:

> *... a totally positive, engaging, enduring, and socially fulfilling physical and emotional customer experience across all major levels of one's consumption chain and one that is brought about by a distinct market offering that calls for active interaction between consumers and providers.*

Mascarenhas *et al.* (2006) described six 'principles' of a total customer experience, using case studies. These include:

- **Anticipating and fulfilling customer needs and wants better than competitors:** All five providers that Mascarenhas *et al.* studied anticipated and understood the specific needs, wants and desires of their target customers and fulfilled them uniquely and way beyond the normal call of duty.

- **Providing real consumer experiences:** Again, all five firms provided customers with real experiences that competitors did not.

- **Providing real emotional experience:** All five products/services generated customer experiences beyond physical attributes such as quality, quantity, delivery, price-product bundling, safety, security and privacy. They also triggered an emotional experience of meaning, value, entertainment, friendly and caring service, belongingness,

- **Experiences as distinct market offerings:** All cases offered experiences that were distinct economic offerings.

- **Experiences as interactions:** These experiences arose from the value-adding interactions of customer involvement and producer participation.

- **Experiences as engaging memories:** These experiences engage customers to create memories within them.

Whether we look at experience management as CEM or TCE, the focus is on the experience of customers. Research has discovered that managing this experience can result in numerous benefits to organisations.

Benefits of CEM to organisations

There are many different types of economic benefits to organisations that practice CEM effectively (Pine and Gilmore, 1999). CEM helps in adding value to a firm (Schmitt, 2003). It is not only valuable in business to customer types of businesses, but also in business to business sectors (Thompson, 2006). Research points to improved business performance for those firms that rank high on the CEM scale (Thompson, 2006). Figure 5.3 shows that those companies that were better off in CEM were much better in terms of business performance than others. One of the most important benefits that a company can achieve through the use of effective CEM is to achieve greater levels of customer loyalty. CEM allows companies to do just that.

Figure 5.3 Economic benefits of CEM

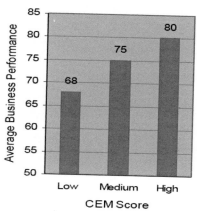

Source: Thompson (2006)

203

Building loyalty through CEM

Research has found that both a good service quality and high levels of customer satisfaction don't always lead to customer loyalty (Stuart and Tax, 2004). CEM, however is one such tool that has shown to build loyalty among its customers (Alperin, 2005). CEM is able to build loyalty among customers through the high level of experience it provides to the customers at every step. Schmitt says that, 'before and even after the sale, CEM provides value to customers by delivering information, service, and interactions that result in compelling experiences. It thus builds loyalty with customers and adds value to the firm' (Schmitt, 2003).

For example a report by the IBM corporation reveals that 'customer experience [is] a key factor for companies to use in building loyalty to brands, channels and services' (Badgett *et al.*, 2007). Research has also shown the importance of interactions with a firm as one of the most important variables (see Figure 5.4).

Figure 5.4 Factors in earning loyalty

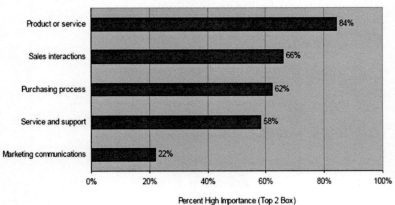

How important is the quality of each of these activities in earning your loyalty?

Percent High Importance (Top 2 Box)

Source: Thompson (2006)

When asked about the importance of various factors in earning loyalty, customers responded by saying that sales interactions were the second most important after the product/service itself. This research links with other research in the industry, which points to companies earning loyalty through the use of CEM.

Figure 5.5 Loyalty drivers by industry

To earn your loyalty in this industry, how important are these factors?

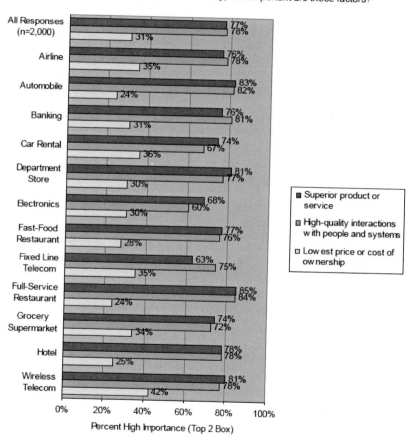

Percent High Importance (Top 2 Box)

Source: Thompson (2006)

This research is not limited to one industry, rather it spans across industries. Interestingly the industry average shows that interactions with people and systems (the focus of CEM) edged past the product or service itself (see Figure 5.5). The findings also suggest that companies need not take their concentration off the main product/service, but need to give equal importance to customer experiences, in order to win the loyalty of customers (Thompson, 2006).

Some researchers have said that not only do companies need to provide high levels of 'good' customer experiences, but they need to go beyond and offer 'compelling' customer experiences. This will lead to repeat purchases, positive word of mouth, and eventually customer loyalty (Voss and Zomerdijk, 2007). More recently research has also focused on emotional connections of customers with firms. Berry and Carbone (2007) believe that 'maintaining an emotional connection requires systematic management of the customers' experience with an organisation and its offerings from the customers' perspectives.'

Customer experience management has a number of financial benefits to offer firms. The importance of CEM can be seen through recent customer surveys, where customers in many industries have ranked experiences greater than the product itself. Effective implementation of CEM will lead to the ultimate benefit of all, customer loyalty. As discussed earlier, many organisations have failed to implement CEM properly. These organisations, as a result, have been unable to reap the benefits of CEM.

References

Alperin, B. (2005) *Customer Experience Management: Competing Successfully in Higher Education*, Aramark Education, Philadelphia, PA.

Badgett, M., Kleinberger, H. and Boyce, M. S. (2007) *Turning shoppers into advocates: The customer focused retail enterprise*, IBM Institute for Business Value - Quick Read: IBM Global Business.

Berry, L. (2000) Cultivating Service Brand Equity, *Journal of Academy of Marketing Science*, 28, 128-137.

Berry, L. L. & Carbone, L. P. (2007) Build loyalty through experience management, *Quality Progress*, 40, 26-32.

Berry, L. L., Carbone, L. P. & Haeckel, S. H. (2002) Managing the total customer experience, *Sloan Management Review*, 43, 85-90.

Carbone, L. P. (1998) Total customer experience drives value, *Management Review*, 87, 62.

Gilmore, J. H. & Pine, J. B. I. (2002) Customer experience places: the new offering frontier, *Strategy and Leadership*, 30, 4-11.

MacMillan, I. C. & McGrath, R. G. (1997) Discovering new points of differentiation, *Harvard Business Review*, 75, 133-142.

Mascarenhas, O. A., Kesavan, R. & Bernacchi, M. (2006) Lasting customer loyalty: a total customer experience approach, *Journal of Consumer Marketing*, 23, 397-405.

Pine, B. J. & Gilmore, J. H. (1998) Welcome to the experience economy, *Harvard Business Review*, 76, 97-105.

Pine, B. J. & Gilmore, J. H. (1999) *The experience economy*, Harvard Business School Press, Boston, MA.

Procops, T. (2005) Managing the customer experience with logging and monitoring solutions, *Customer Inter@action Solutions*, 24, 58-60.

Rowley, J. (1999) Measuring total customer experience in museums, *International Journal of Contemporary Hospitality Management*, 11, 303-310.

Schmitt, B. H. (2003) *Customer Experience Management*, John Wiley & Sons Inc. Hoboken, NJ.

Strativity (2006) 2005 Customer Experience Management Study: No Money, No Love At most companies, it's still "show me the money", *Strativity Group*, Parsippany, NJ.

Stuart, F. I. & Tax, S. (2004) Toward an integrative approach to designing service experiences: Lessons learned from the theatre, *Journal of Operations Management*, 22, 609-627.

Thompson, B. (2006) Customer Experience Management: Accelerating Business Performance, *Right Now Technologies*, Customer Think Corp.

Verhoef, P. C., Lemon, K. N., Parasuraman, A., Roggeveen, A., Tsiros, M. & Schlesinger, L. A. (2009) Customer Experience Creation: Determinants, Dynamics and Management Strategies, *Journal of Retailing*, 85, 1, 31-41.

Voss, C. & Zomerdijk, L. (2007) Innovation in Experiential Services – An Empirical View, *In* DTI (Ed.) *Innovation in Services*, DTI, London.

Wyner, G. (2000) The customer's burden, *Marketing Management*, 9, 1, 6-7.

Chapter 6

CEM implementation: The key factors

Implementing CEM effectively is crucial to achieving the desired results, i.e. business performance. Researchers and managers have looked at a number of different models for implementing CEM effectively. Table 6.1 summarises some of these concepts.

The Mascarenhas *et al.* model

The first model presented here is one by Mascarenhas *et al.* (2006). Their model focuses on four major aspects of the customer experience (searching, finding, using and post-usage). Each of these stages has been sub-divided according to the physical moments, emotional involvement moments and the value chain moments.

The searching stage consists of the actual search for the product. This stage reflects the various types of advertising that the customer comes in contact with. The managers need to ensure that each of the value chain moments that relate to this stage, are taken into consideration when designing the experiences for customers. For instance, making sure the customer receives the right advice. The second stage is about finding the product, which relates to looking at the availability of the product, seeing/testing the product physically, as well as interactions with sales persons. The final two stages where improvements are sought include the usage and the post usage. It includes factors such as warranties, finance, etc. Table 6.2, summarises these four stages.

Table 6.1 Various strategies for implementing CEM

Mascarenhas et al., 2006	Schmitt, 2003	Voss and Zomerdijk, 2007	Alperin, 2005	Berry and Carbone, 2007	Stuart, 2006	Thompson, 2006
Searching Finding Using Post-usage	Analysing the experiential world of the customer Building the experiential platform Designing the brand experience Structure the customer interface Engaging in continuous innovation	Innovations in physical environment Service employees Service delivery process Fellow customers Back office support	Inventory: Determine the touchpoints Input: Current service delivery effectiveness Improve: Enrich the experience Integrate: Integrate functions for a unified operation Ingrain: Implement customer service and leadership training Inform and influence: Communicate the experience and develop the brand Innovate: Stay ahead of the competition	Identify emotions that evoke customer commitment Establish and experience motif Inventory and evaluate experience clues Determine the experience gap Close the experience gap and monitor execution	Stay narrowly focused Communicate and share the service vision extensively Consistency in the service/ product Integrate (technical, performance, and business) Create a spirit of experimentation and innovation for all service employees Training and rehearsals Facilitate, do not direct	Developing a customer experience strategy Setting goals and defining measurements Aligning the organisation Redesigning the customer experience Improving customer experience with technology

Table 6.2 Capturing the customer experience process

Experience stage	Physical moments	Emotional involvements	Value chain moments The right.....
Searching	Print media search	What do I dream?	...motivation
	Audio visual media	Seeking information via ads	...product
	Website search	Viewing radio, TV, internet	...advice
	Place in-store	Seeking advice and direction	...shop/location
Finding	Availability	Salesperson interaction	...price
	The product	Touch, feel, see, believe	...package
	The brand	Colour, shape, texture, material	...solution
	The solution	Perceived problem solution	...financing
Using	Delivery	Excitement, surprise, curiosity	...use-experience
	Brand community	Personal satisfaction/delight	...social visibility
	Maintenance	Visibility, prestige, status	...community
	Support service	Brand community belonging	...warranty
Post-usage	Complaints	Satisfaction/dissatisfaction	...feedback
	Referral	Displeasure, anger, rage	...complaint
	Replacement	Positive or negative referrals	...re-purchase
	Repeat buy	Commitment, lifetime loyalty	...lifetime brand

Source: Mascarenhas *et al.* (2006)

Schmitt's model

The next framework is one which has been presented by Schmitt, (2003). In this framework, Schmitt proposes five steps that need to be undertaken by organisations. The first step is to 'analyse the experiential world of the customer.' Analysing the experiential world involves conducting a detailed audit of the 'sociocultural context in which consumers operate including their experiential needs and wants, as well as their lifestyles' (Schmitt, 2003). By doing this, the organisation will be able to identify the critical points within the experience journey of a customer with an organisation.

The next step is to develop an experience platform. In this step, the company needs to take what it has learned from the first stage, and then create a map of what the customer can expect from the service or product with the firm. It includes 'a dynamic, multisensory, multidimensional depiction of the desired experience' (Schmitt, 2003). Once a company has developed this experience platform, it needs to be followed by a brand which portrays that experience.

The customer expectations will need to be highlighted within the brand experience. This will include factors such as the experience related features, aesthetics of the product or service, etc. These features will also need to be embedded within the 'look and feel' aspects of the brand, and will include things such as the brand colours, logos, websites, slogans, signs, packaging, etc. Besides the brand, the experiential expectations need to be embedded in the 'structure and the customer interface.' These are all of the dynamic contact points the customer has with the firm. These could be face-to-face with a sales person, over the phone, or interactions with technology like ATM points, or a website. Schmitt says that it 'is important to structure the content and style of this dynamic interaction to give the customer the desired information and service in the right interactive manner' (Schmitt, 2003).

Improvements should not stop at this point, and should continue through innovation. Innovation is the final step in this framework. Schmitt says that the company needs to innovate both in terms of the product/service as well as in the customers' personal life aspects. Creative advertising and PR campaigns are also considered a part of this innovation process.

Voss and Zomerdijk's model

Voss and Zomerdijk's (2007) model is one which starts from the thought process and ends with recommendations to others. They believe that the process is cyclical, and one of these processes leads to another process (Voss and Zomerdijk, 2007). This process has been outlined in Figure 6.1 with reference to an example of Walt Disney World.

Figure 6.1 The service journey cycle

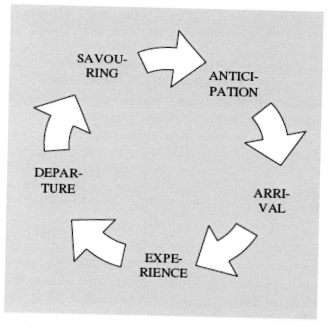

Source: Walt Disney World in Voss and Zomerdijk (2007)

During this cycle, the customer goes through a journey and the experience is built over time. Voss and Zomerdijk also believe that the journey consists of a number of touchpoints, which need to be managed by the company. Moreover, according to them the innovation can come not just at company level, but at the level of each touchpoint (Voss and Zomerdijk, 2007). They outlined five distinct areas that managers need to work on to develop an effective CEM programme.

The first of these is the physical environment, which is the place where the experience is created (Voss and Zomerdijk, 2007). The physical settings are considered very important in the delivery of the service. For example many restaurants charge higher prices, not because of the quality of their food, but because of the attractiveness of their physical settings. Companies such as Waterstones (a UK book seller), have been able to create pleasing atmospheres by providing sofas and chairs for customers to sit on, as a part of efforts to improve the physical environment within their retail outlets. The physical environment of a retail outlet or a service setting is an important factor for a customer, and can influence the way customers spend with a particular brand. It has been researched from a number of different angles (Voss and Zomerdijk, 2007), including environmental psychology (Mehrabian and Russell, 1974), servicescapes (Bitner, 1992), as well as atmospherics in the retail setting (Kotler, 1973; Turley and Milliman, 2000).

According to Voss and Zomerdijk, there are two areas where innovations can take place within the physical environment; design of the journey and sensory design. Things such as ease of moving around a store, getting inside and outside of the premises, crowding, etc. are all part of the design of the journey. Companies have been working on improving these areas, making sure that customers have a comfortable time. The second area includes sensory stimuli which appeal to our senses. An appropriate level of lighting, using the right colours, playing pleasing music, and even making sure that the physical settings smell nice are just examples of these.

Employees of an organisation are the second important factor that needs attention for effective deployment of CEM. The interaction between employees can have a significant impact on the perceptions of customers. Voss and Zomerdijk outlined two main areas where innovations can take place: engaging with the customers and managing the employee experience. Their study revealed that it was important that employees work on developing emotional connections with their customers, which makes the 'experience more personal, more positive and more memorable' (Voss and Zomerdijk, 2007). Their research also revealed that the employee experience was as imperative as the experience of customers. Satisfied employees helped to produce greater quality customer services.

Besides the employees, it was found that the service delivery process was an important aspect for CEM. Areas of improvement or innovation were to be found in managing the start, end and peaks of the service delivery process (Voss and Zomerdijk, 2007). If companies can concentrate on these three aspects, they can make the service delivery experience more pleasurable, and memorable.

A fourth area for improvement related to socialising with other customers. Fellow customers can have a great impact on the experience of customers. Socialising with other customers can make the experience a better one (Voss and Zomerdijk, 2007). There are numerous examples of settings where other customers are present during the service delivery process, such as airline travel. Companies are using the internet to create social communities for their customers, allowing them to discuss their products or services.

The final step in the CEM process is the back office support, according to Voss and Zomerdijk. The back office provides support to the front end employees in delivering a product or service to customers. Companies believe that it is best if the whole organisation works together in order to improve the customer experience. Hence the back office is the final area of concern for implementing CEM.

Lee's model

According to Lee (2006) the factors that companies need to consider for effective implementation of CEM include the customers, business strategy, people, processes and technology. Lee says that companies need to understand their customers and their experience expectations. Companies need that information to develop a strategy, which needs to be implemented through the use of trained and motivated employees. This has to be topped up with the right processes along with the use of appropriate technology (Lee, 2006). Figure 6.2 shows a diagrammatic representation of this system. It is a continuous process, which repeats itself. Different stages feed into and are linked to one another.

Figure 6.2 Implementation sequence

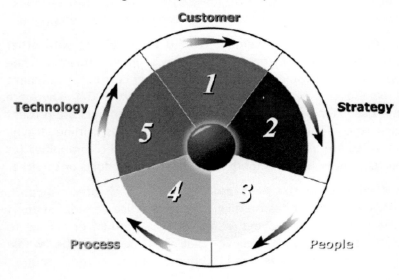

Source: Lee (2006)

Thompson's model

Thompson (2006) has come up with five steps for CEM based on research. Thompson identified problem areas in providing excellent customer experiences (see Figure 6.3) and based on those problem areas devised five steps that companies can take to provide effective CEM. The first step is to start with a customer experience map. Mapping the customers' experience points allows a company to see what and where the touchpoints are within the experience journey. For example Figure 6.4, shows a sample customer experience map of a customer's visit to Starbucks coffee shop. Thompson says that 'mapping is tracking all the points in which customers interact with your company' (Thompson, 2006).

Figure 6.3 Obstacles in providing excellent customer experiences

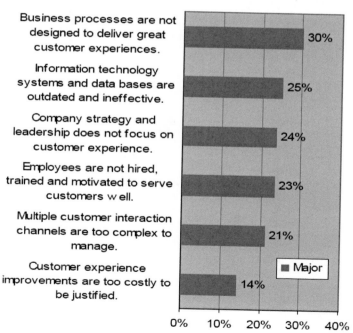

Source: Thompson (2006)

Figure 6.4 A sample customer experience map: Visit to Starbucks

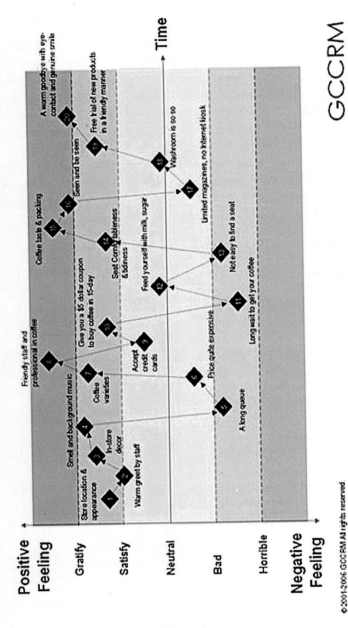

GCCRM

Source: Thompson (2006)

Once the organisation has done the experience mapping, it can then move to the next step, which is to set goals. An organisation needs to set goals for the various stages within the experience map. The experience map should have identified areas that the organisation is doing good, as well as trouble areas. Moreover, critical moments would also have been identified in this map. Hence, companies need to set goals that will help the organisation to work towards higher levels of performance in each of the experience touchpoints.

The next step is to align the organisation to the goals. The most important of these elements are the employees. Employees need to be not only well trained and helpful, but also friendly and caring. Employees that are well trained and follow a customer centric philosophy will be able to provide a high quality of customer services, which is the third factor in Thompson's plan. However, Thompson believes that extra attention should be provided to the 'loyal' customers, who should be recognised personally.

The fourth step involves the redesigning of the whole customer experience in order to differentiate the organisation. Furthermore, providing good customer services is not good enough if the product or service being sold is not up to customer expectations. Hence companies must focus on providing high quality of goods and services.

Finally, like Lee, Thompson too believes that technology needs to back up the rest of the processes within the firm. For instance the use of CRM systems can help companies to improve their strategies by focusing on the right customers, or having the right strategies for various customers. Thompson says that 'you don't necessarily need technology to establish a good customer experience management programme. But good technology supporting a good strategy can be a powerful combination' (Thompson, 2006).

Alperin's model

The next model presented here is one developed by Alperin (2005). The Alperin model has seven stages or steps. The first is called inventory, and is exactly the same as the Thompson model, which calls for developing an experience map. Instead of creating a map, Alperin calls for finding out the touchpoints with the customer. Next, it is required that the company should access its current service delivery effectiveness. In this stage, the company should find out from its customers what they think about the quality of the experiences. This data should help the company into the next step, which aims to try to improve the experience. Here, Alperin calls for improving problem areas, and trying to eliminate 'the points of frustration' (Alperin, 2005). This stage is followed by integration of the various functions. The goal is to have the whole organisation work towards a unified goal, i.e. improving the customer experience.

Employee training is also called for by Alperin. Not only customer service training, but also leadership training, needs to be given in order to 'align' the culture towards implementing CEM within the organisation. The next stage relates to communicating the experience to the target audience. This stage's emphasis is on advertising and marketing communications and is similar to Schmitt's third phase. Finally, in the same way that many of the other researchers have called for innovation, so too has Alperin. Innovation is required in order to 'stay ahead of the competition [so that you] don't rest on your laurels' (Alperin, 2005). Companies need to continuously improve their experience to make sure that they have a distinct advantage, and so that competition can not catch up.

Berry and Carbone's model

Berry and Carbone's model also consists of five steps, however it is slightly different from the preceding models. Instead of first developing an experience map, they have called for 'identifying the emotions that evoke customer commitment' (Berry and Carbone, 2007). This calls for asking the customers what sort of an experience they are interested in having with an organisation or a brand. This step is then to be followed by developing an experience map, or as Berry and Carbone call it, the experience motif. In this stage the feelings that customers' desire are recorded, giving the managers a visual representation of what the experience journey is like. Next they call for doing an inventory of and evaluating the 'experience clues.' This means that the organisation should look at the existing experience from the point of view of a customer. In the fourth step they look at the first few steps and compare these against each other to figure out where the discrepancies lie between what is and what is expected. The final step is to close the experience gap, and then to monitor the execution of this process. The Berry and Carbone model, in comparison to the other models seems to concentrate heavily on the research part of the process with less emphasis being laid on the implementation parts.

Stuart's model

The final model in the list is one which focuses not only on experience, but on creating memorable experience (Stuart, 2006). The term memorable experience has gained popularity after the publications of Pine and Gilmore (1998, 1999). Memorable experiences are those experiences which 'invoke emotions, commitment, and stronger relationship ties, service firms that offer them will achieve higher levels of loyalty' (Stuart, 2006). It is because of the intense reactions that memorable experiences invoke that research is slowly shifting away from simply designing experiences that meet customer expectations towards something extraordinary (Pine and Gilmore, 1999; Gilmore and Pine, 2000; Berry, 2000; Berry and Bendapudi, 2003; Fitzsimmons and Fitzsimmons, 2004; Stuart and Tax, 2004).

Stuart's model is derived from research into the theatre. Based on the research a seven step model is presented:

- Stay narrowly focused and within your defined resource capabilities.

- Communicate and share the service vision extensively, particularly with those with management responsibilities.

- Be ever vigilant to ensure consistency and authenticity in all aspects of the service product, from the largest to smallest detail.

- Integrate across all elements (including technical, performance, and business), using structured and unstructured communication mechanisms.

- Create a spirit of experimentation and innovation for all service employees by encouraging everyone's involvement in the creative process.

- Strive for total role and performance immersion from all front line service providers through extensive training and rehearsals.

- Facilitate, do not direct. Integrate

(Stuart, 2006)

Reinforcing the various models

Besides complete models, other researchers have agreed with a number of different elements that need to be pursued in order to develop effective CEM. For instance, Berry *et al.* (2002) called for using an 'experience audit,' which is similar to an experience map or an experience motif. They called for using various techniques such as video recording the customer to analyse body language and facial expressions when going through a particular experience journey within a firm to better understand the customer's emotions. This method reconfirms previous calls by other researchers to record the experience of customers.

Similarly, a Strativity report emphasises the importance of the employee experience as an important variable in developing CEM within a firm (Strativity, 2006). Sengupta *et al.* (1997) referred to the example of Marriott hotel and resorts. They talked about how the salary of employees is linked with their 'ability to bring creativity to the relationship-building process with the customer and 'move the relationship along' (Sengupta *et al.*, 1997).

A unified CEM implementation strategy

Based on the models presented above a new strategy for effective implementation of CEM is devised.

- **Step 1: Experience mapping:** Creating an experience map of what is the first thing that a company ought to do (Alperin, 2005). This will help to identify all of the various points of interaction a customer has with a firm. It may also be prudent to find out what the customer thinks of the current level of service being delivered for each of the experience points.

- **Step 2: Find out customer expectations:** Finding out what the customer expects should be one of the starting points in the customer experience management process (Schmitt, 2003; Berry and Carbone, 2007). This will help the organisation to understand what the customer desires, and what is of importance to the customer. Often companies find it difficult to develop effective CEM strategies because they are unable to understand the requirements of their customers (Strativity, 2006).

- **Step 3: Examine the competition:** Interestingly, not many of the models have talked about looking at what the competition is offering. A company cannot work in isolation. Knowing what the competition is offering will only help an organisation to set goals and targets where they can meet and exceed the competition. Customers will always compare a company with others, and hence it becomes imperative that the company know what its competition is up to.

- **Step 4: Analyse and plan:** Once a company knows what level of service it is providing, the level that customers expect, and the level that the competition is providing, it should be ready to develop its own plan. After analysing the three types of data, it should be easy for companies to devise their own plans and set levels of 'quality' that each experience should deliver to the customer. If the company is looking to provide memorable experiences (Stuart, 2006), then the company should try to set high goals, where the standards in critical functions exceed both customer expectations as well as competitors. This is similar to the delight concept (Kumar *et al.*, 2001) for customer satisfaction.

- **Step 5: Communicate the brand experience:** Before a customer actually comes in contact with a firm, the customer gets to experience the communications about the brand (Schmitt, 2003; Mascarenhas *et al.*, 2006; Stuart, 2006). Hence it is imperative that the various marketing communications media should reflect the brand experience that the company wants its customers to have. It is important that not everything is given away in the advertising (Schmitt, 2003), as this may lessen the impact of the surprise elements within the experience framework. However, all of the different communications media, including advertising, commercials, websites and public relations activities reflect the brand experience that the company wants to portray to the customers. If this first level of experience is good, the customer will be attracted to continue to the next stages.

- **Step 6: High quality product/service:** The experience is of little use if the actual product or service is not of the high quality, (Stuart, 2006). It is imperative that companies work to make sure that the product/service on offer meets the customer's expectations. No level of customer experience can help sell a poor product.

- **Step 7: Motivated employees:** Numerous researchers have called for having motivated and or satisfied employees (Mills *et al.*, 1983; Hoffman and Ingram, 1991; Kelley, 1992; Clarke and Payne, 1993; Loveman, 1998; Henning-Thurau, 2004). The first step is to hire the right employees and then to train them so that they are highly committed to providing the level of customer experience that the organisation expects of them. Making sure that the employees are satisfied and motivated will ensure that in the long run the customer receives a good experience and this can eventually lead to customer loyalty (Loveman, 1998).

- **Step 8: Customer interface:** The customer interface needs to embed the planned level of experiences. This includes the physical aspects of the customer's interactions and should appeal to the five senses of customers (Voss and Zomerdijk, 2007). Focusing on the right décor, the appropriate music, colour schemes, the design of the equipment etc. will help customers to feel comfortable and make the experience an enjoyable one. Technological aspects of the experience can also be included in this step. This would include things such as ATMs, payment points, automated call centres, and websites.

- **Step 9: Senior management focus:** Like other areas of management, senior management's commitment to and focus on the desired strategy is imperative for its success. Hence, for CEM too, the senior manager's commitment is imperative. Senior managers can not only set examples for the rest of the employees, but will also be more focused in the whole CEM process.

- **Step 10: Integrate functions:** It is important that the whole organisation is working towards providing a high quality experience for their customers. The back office as well as the front end employees need to work together (Voss and Zomerdijk, 2007) so that the customer can have the best possible experience. Companies have been cutting back costs by shifting some of their back office work overseas to lower cost centres. However, many of these have not been able to provide the right level of customer experience as desired by customers (Jaiswal, 2008). Although this may result in short term savings in cost, in the long run it results in customer defections. Hence, it is imperative that companies make sure that all operations are working towards the same goal.

- **Step 11: Post usage:** The customer needs to have great post usage experience. This can include things such as after sales service, warranties, upgrading or installations (Mascarenhas *et al.*, 2006). Good after sales service is a way of reminding the customer, long after he/she has used the product or service that the experience with the firm was great. This encourages the customer to return to the firm and to recommend it to others.

- **Step 12: Continuous innovations:** Continuously innovating and improving the experiences is one of the ways that the company can make sure that it stays ahead of competition (Alperin, 2005). It is also one of the ways that will help the firm to make sure that the customer receives the best possible experiences, and perhaps even help to design memorable experiences.

Links to orientations

Customer experience management is linked to a number of different strategic orientations. First, it is linked to the service orientation concept (Berry and Carbone, 2007). Organisations are no longer considered to be commodity businesses, rather each company is focused on the service. For example, the food retailing market is one that is based on commodities. However many successful food retailers have incorporated service orientation concepts and differentiated their businesses by providing great experiences (Berry and Carbone, 2007).

Next the CEM concept is deeply rooted in the customer orientation concepts (Mascarenhas *et al.*, 2006). The focus of CEM is the customer. It is all about customer experience and customer expectations. According to Mascarenhas *et al.* (2006) 'customer orientation as a strategy is a necessary but not a sufficient condition for total customer experience and lasting customer loyalty'.

CEM also has some roots in the market orientation concept. Market orientation consists of three main factors: customer orientation, competitor orientation and inter-functional coordination (Narver and Slater, 1990). Numerous researchers have discussed the importance of inter-functional coordination for effective CEM (Stuart and Tax, 2004; Alperin, 2005; Stuart, 2006). Similarly customer orientation, as discussed above, is a central concept of CEM. Competitor orientation is not as strongly exhibited in CEM as in the market orientation strategy. However, researchers have discussed the competition, and talked about staying ahead of the competition in designing CEM strategies (Berry *et al.*, 2002; Alperin, 2005; Mascarenhas *et al.*, 2006).

CEM is also linked to the quality orientation philosophy. The focus is no long on the quality of the produce or the service, it now includes the quality of the experience (Berry and Carbone, 2007). For instance, according to Berry and Carbone the focus is now on functional, mechanic and humanic clues. The functional clues relate to the technical quality, or the 'what' part of the experience. This refers to the reliability of the product or service (Berry and Carbone, 2007). The mechanic clues represent the physical settings in an intangible service. This would include furniture, sounds, colours, smells, etc. The humanic clues represent the employees, and their attitudes toward the customer. It is the behaviour of the service providers, their body language, etc. which need to be considered when thinking of quality within the CEM framework.

Brand orientation, too plays a role in the CEM process. Each brand has its own identity and a different message to convey to its customers. CEM takes the focus away from the product to an experience. The brand is thus no longer something which portrays a product, rather an experience. Hence, the brand orientation concept is linked to CEM to some degree.

These five strategic orientations have some type of link with CEM. The link may be a very evident one, as in the case of customer orientation, or one which has been modified to a degree, as is the case with quality orientation. CEM may give more importance to some compared to others. Nevertheless, each of the five orientations is linked to CEM in one way or another.

References

Alperin, B. (2005) *Customer Experience Management: Competing Successfully in Higher Education*, Aramark Education, Philadelphia, PA.

Berry, L. (2000) Cultivating Service Brand Equity, *Journal of Academy of Marketing Science*, 28, 128-137.

Berry, L. & Bendapudi, N. (2003) *Clueing in Customers*, Harvard Business School Press, Cambridge, MA.

Berry, L. L. & Carbone, L. P. (2007) Build loyalty through experience management, *Quality Progress*, 40, 26-32.

Berry, L. L., Carbone, L. P. & Haeckel, S. H. (2002) Managing the total customer experience, *Sloan Management Review*, 43, 85-90.

Bitner, M. J. (1992) Servicescapes: The Impact of Physical Surroundings on Customers and Employees, *Journal of Marketing*, 56, 57-71.

Clarke, M. & Payne, A. F. T. (1993) Customer retention: does employee retention hold the key to success, *Marketing education group conference*, Loughborough.

Fitzsimmons, J. A. & Fitzsimmons, M. (2004) *New Service Development – Creating Memorable Experiences*, Sage Publications, Thousand Oaks, CA.

Gilmore, J. H. & Pine, B. J. (2000) *Markets of One: Creating Customer unique Value through Mass Customization*, Harvard Business School Press, Boston, MA.

Henning-Thurau, T. (2004) Customer orientation of service employees, *International Journal of Service Industry Management*, 15.

Hoffman, K. D. & Ingram, T. N. (1991) Creating customer-oriented employees: the case in home health care, *Journal of Health Care Marketing*, 11, 24-32.

Jaiswal, A. K. (2008) Customer satisfaction and service quality measurement in Indian call centres, *Managing Service Quality*, 18, 405-416.

Kelley, S. W. (1992) Developing customer orientation among service employees, *Journal of Academy of Marketing Science*, 20, 27-36.

Kotler, P. (1973) Atmospherics as a Marketing Tool, *Journal of Retailing*, 49, 48-64.

Kumar, A., Olshavsky, R. W. & King, M. F. (2001) Exploring alternative antecedents of customer delight, *Journal of Consumer Satisfaction, Dissatisfaction and Complaining Behavior*, 14, 14.

Lee, S. (2006) Customer Management Framework, *CRM Body Check*, GCCRM.

Loveman, G. W. (1998) Employee satisfaction, customer loyalty, and financial performance: An empirical examination of the service profit chain in retail banking, *Journal of Service Research,* 1, 18-31.

Mascarenhas, O. A., Kesavan, R. & Bernacchi, M. (2006) Lasting customer loyalty: a total customer experience approach, *Journal of Consumer Marketing,* 23, 397-405.

Mehrabian, A. & Russell, J. A. (1974) *An Approach to Environmental Psychology,* The MIT Press, Cambridge, MA.

Mills, P., Chase, R. & Margulies, N. (1983) Motivating the client/employee system as a service production strategy, *Academy of Management Review,* 8, 301-310.

Narver, J. C. & Slater, S. F. (1990) The Effect of a Market Orientation on Business Performance, *Journal of Marketing,* 54, 20-35.

Pine, B. J. & Gilmore, J. H. (1998) Welcome to the experience economy, *Harvard Business Review,* 76, 97-105.

Pine, B. J. & Gilmore, J. H. (1999) *The experience economy,* Harvard Business School Press, Boston, MA.

Schmitt, B. H. (2003) *Customer Experience Management,* John Wiley & Sons Inc. Hoboken, NJ.

Sengupta, S., Krapfel, R. E. & Pusateri, M. A. (1997) The Marriott experience, *Marketing Management,* 6, 33.

Strativity (2006) 2005 Customer Experience Management Study: No Money, No Love At most companies, it's still "show me the money", *Strativity Group,* Parsippany, NJ.

Stuart, F. I. (2006) Designing and executing memorable service experiences: Lights, camera, experiment, integrate, action! *Business Horizons,* 49, 149-159.

Stuart, F. I. & Tax, S. (2004) Toward an integrative approach to designing service experiences: Lessons learned from the theatre, *Journal of Operations Management,* 22, 609-627.

Thompson, B. (2006) Customer Experience Management: Accelerating Business Performance, *Right Now Technologies,* Customer Think Corp.

Turley, L. W. & Milliman, R. E. (2000) Atmospheric Effects on Shopping Behavior: A Review of the Experimental Evidence, *Journal of Business Research,* 49, 193-211.

Voss, C. & Zomerdijk, L. (2007) Innovation in Experiential Services – An Empirical View, *In* DTI (Ed.) *Innovation in Services,* DTI, London.

Chapter 7

Best practice online customer experiences

Amazon: Simplicity is key

Amazon.com is the global leader in e-commerce and a Fortune 500 company, offering wide range of products from books and electronics to tennis rackets and diamond jewellery. Amazon.com operates sites in addition to the USA in the United Kingdom, Germany, France, Japan, Canada, and China (Joyo.com) and maintains over 25 fulfilment centres around the world.

When it was established by Jeff Bezos in 1995 in Seattle, USA, Jeff was ambitious to produce a large scale phenomenon like the Amazon river. His ambition proved rational 8 years later when Amazon passed the $5 billion sales mark that took Wal-Mart 20 years to achieve.

Amazon.com describes its vision as:

> Relentlessly focus on customer experience by offering our customers low prices, convenience, and a wide selection of merchandise.

Amazon has three sets of customers; buying customers with over 76 million accounts, 1.3 million active seller customers and developer customers who use Amazon web services and technology infrastructure to develop and host their own web services. The company has launched several loyalty programmes including Amazon Prime, a fee-based membership programme in which members receive free or discounted express shipping, in the United States, the United Kingdom, Germany and Japan.

In 2008, Amazon announced that it has over 76 million active customer accounts and order fulfilment to more than 200 countries and approximately 17,000 full-time and part-time employees.

Customer experience in Amazon.com

Although Amazon.com is heavily driven by technological innovations, it focuses on offering unique customer experience through diversified types of products, convenience, lower prices, personalised shopping experiences, and community features like Listmania and Wish Lists.

Amazon.com stresses that to earn repeat purchases customers should enjoy their shopping experience through key features that include:

- **Easy-to-use functionality** through 1-Click technology; image uploads; a search engine for the website as well as the internet; easy browsing; the ability to view selected interior pages and citations, and the ability to search the entire contents of many of the books through 'Look Inside the Book' and 'Search Inside the Book' features.

- **Fast and reliable fulfilment:** presentation of latest inventory availability information, delivery date estimates, and options for expedited delivery, as well as delivery shipment notifications and update facilities.

- **Website rich content** through editorial and customer reviews; manufacturer product information; web pages tailored to individual preference such as recommendations and notifications.

- **User-generated content** where Amazon communities of online customers create feature-rich content, including product reviews, online recommendation lists, wish lists, buying guides, and wedding and baby registries.

- **Trusted transaction environment** through secure payment systems.

- **Low prices** for the most popular products and higher prices, as well as greater margins for Amazon, with less popular products. Amazon uses free shipping offers to encourage increase in basket size as customers have to spend over a certain amount to receive free shipping, which is critical to Amazon profitability.

Amazon.com believes that its most effective marketing communication tool is a consequence of focusing on continuously improving the customer experience, where customers' word-of-mouth is effective in acquiring new customers and encouraging repeat customer visits.

Figure 7.1 Ratings and Listmania! on Amazon.com

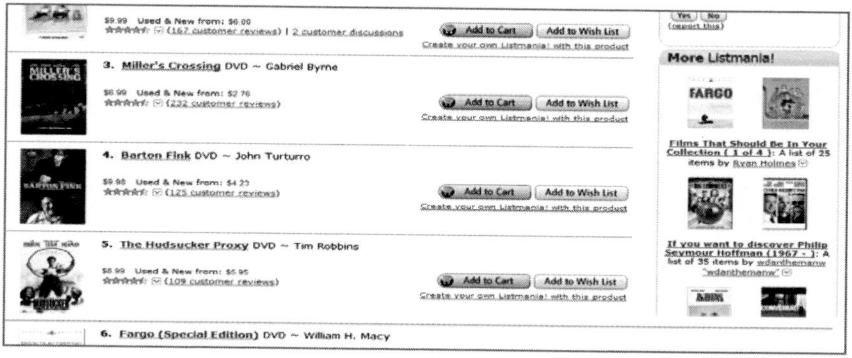

Customer engagement for a unique customer experience

When the sixth book of the hugely popular Harry Potter series was being released – in the same week Amazon was celebrating its 10th anniversary – Amazon.com created a unique and pleasantly surprising experience to engage its customers in both important events and to keep them hooked to the website. Amazon.com did all the things a physical bookstore would do, but the company's genius realised that it could and should do many other things conventional shops will not do. Some of its strategies included:

- Creating Amazon's first-ever Harry Potter Kids Review Panel where fans under the age of 18 sent 'audition videos' to Amazon explaining why they believe should be selected as Amazon's Harry Potter experts.

- Implementing a special delivery programme where famous celebrities like Harrison Ford and Anna Kournikova delivered Amazon orders to surprised customers. Videos of the special delivery were then captured in short videos for customers to view on the Amazon website.

- An Amazon 10th Anniversary Concert featuring performances by Bob Dylan and Norah Jones was viewable live on the Amazon website.

The culture of metrics in Amazon

The success of Amazon today is owed to the use of a measured approach to all aspects of the business, beyond the finance. Since 1997, Amazon CEO, Jeff Bezos, has stressed the importance of establishing a culture of metrics, utilising by that the web-based technologies that have given Amazon a unique window into human behaviour through generated data about customers' made every visit, every click and mouse twitch.

Data in Amazon is the king, every page viewed, every search and every purchase is recorded. Amazon relies on acquiring and crunching this massive amount of data. The technology used in Amazon allows for many data driven automations in order to improve customer experience, such as customer channel preferences; personalisation of content to different users including new releases and top-sellers, recommending related products and promotions such as Amazon signature (Customers Who Bought X, also bought Y) and even advertising through paid search.

Amazon realised that it has the tools to draw all sorts of conclusions about its customers, considering itself a repository of facts, and not only a mere store. Amazon uses its data to gauge its customer centricity and to emphasise customer enjoyment and ecstasy.

One of the metrics that is important to Amazon.com is the 'Contact Per Order' measure, which fits with the Amazon philosophy of 'The best service is no service'. The measure emphasises simplicity of 'during purchase' experience and aims at minimising and eliminating unneeded and unwanted contact with customer service staff. Analysing results of this measure allows Amazon to conduct root cause contact analysis and therefore improve the transaction experience.

Along with the culture of metrics, Amazon enjoys a culture of experimentation, where options and scenarios related to the site such as the home page design, moving features around the page, different algorithms for recommendations, changing search relevance rankings, etc. are tested against a range or parameters such as units sold and revenue over a limited time of a few days or a week. The site's new features are usually launched if the desired metrics are statistically significantly better. Tests are usually repeated to account for changing customer tastes and evolving needs.

Amazon.com technology

Amazon has been able to achieve its competitive advantage through a significant investment in technology that was internally developed or licensed from third parties. The main outcome of the technology was to simplify and improve the customer shopping experience. Amazon states in this regard:

> We use a set of applications for accepting and validating customer orders, placing and tracking orders with suppliers, managing and assigning inventory to customer orders, and

235

ensuring proper shipment of products to customers. Our transaction-processing systems handle millions of items, a number of different status inquiries, multiple shipping addresses, gift-wrapping requests, and multiple shipment methods. These systems allow the customer to choose whether to receive single or several shipments based on availability and to track the progress of each order. These applications also manage the process of accepting, authorizing, and charging customer credit cards.

Zappos.com: How shoes sell online

Zappos.com is an e-commerce retailer which started by selling shoes and expanded to a wider variety of products including bags, clothing and accessories. It has built a strong online brand that continues to succeed one year after the other; a fact that is proven by gross revenue growth from $1.6M in 2000 to $370M in 2005.

Zappos winning formula depends on acquiring customers through cost effective means such as search engine marketing (SEM) and offering a unique experience that keeps customers happy and coming back.

In brief, the business model of Zappos helped a lot in its success. Zappos sold other well known brands and therefore had the benefit of pre-established trust of customers. Furthermore, shoes are a product with a high ticket and good margins which allowed Zappos to invest in SEM and attract traffic to its site. It also relied heavily on affiliations and established 17,000 affiliates driving traffic and shoe sales to its site.

Zappos was established by Nick Swinmurn and Tony Hsieh in 1999 despite the constant reluctance from the business community, because no one believed at the time that shoes would be a good product to sell online. Nevertheless, and backed by the fact that shoes are a $40B market in the USA, out of which $2B are sold via mail order catalogues, the founders stuck to their guns and were proved later to be right.

In addition to its cost effective marketing strategy, Zappos success is also owed to the adaptability of its strategy. Zappos.com started as ShoeSite.com and aimed at offering the greatest selection of shoes. However, when the company found out that not all shoe manufacturers were willing to cooperate with an online small selling company; the team decided to focus its efforts on customer service and providing customers with a unique customer experience and therefore re-launched as Zappos.com.

Unique customer experience

According to Zappos' estimates, approximately 50% of orders are made by existing customers; another 20% is by new customers who have been referred by existing customers. Customers keep coming back and referring the site to others because of a great customer experience that has the following key features:

- After realising that Zappos competes with offline shoe retailers, Zappos decided to surprise its valued and returning customers with next day air shipment which shortens the delivery time from 5-7 days to 1 or 2 days for free. This small gesture made a great impression on customers and strongly impacted return purchases.

- In order to ease consumer apprehension around buying shoes online, Zappos offered free return shipping for a 365 day.

- It is an extremely simple and fast site. Zappos' site is almost stripped down with no ads, and nothing moves. Things are placed on the site based on one condition, which makes it easier for customers to move from here to there. Zappos' website was the fastest site among the top 50 internet retailers for broadband customers in September 2006.

- Sending personalised communications to customers, such as letting them know when their favourite brand introduces a new shoe.

- Providing smart and easy to use search options where customers can search shoes by shoe size.

- Offering a unique 24/7 customer service, with a number that is displaced in almost every page in the site. Customer calls are not measured against duration only but helpfulness of the customer service rep. Staff were allowed go the extra mile and direct customers to alternative stores if shoes were unavailable.

- Creating discussion forums and blogs for customers where they can discuss their favourite brands and what they like about their shoes.

Figure 7.2 Zappos blog

Dell: A case for customer engagement

Dell was founded in 1984 by Michael Dell with a simple concept: selling computer systems directly to customers; a direct customer model with new distribution channels that reach commercial and individual customers more effectively and efficiently.

Dell today is the number one PC provider in the US and number two worldwide. Dell offers a broad range of product categories, which includes desktop computers, servers, storage and networking products, software and peripherals and IT infrastructure services for large organisations.

Emphasis on customer experience has been affirmed in Dell's vision which states:

> ... strive to provide the best possible customer experience by offering superior value; high-quality, relevant technology; customized systems; superior service and support; and differentiated products and services that are easy to buy and use.

Dell chose several strategies to continuously create a unique experience for its individual and business clients. The company aims at emphasising 'customer intimacy' through developing strong relationships and simplifying the information that helps customers manage their hardware and software. Dell also offers a lot of promotions to emphasise affordability. This includes free shipping, free upgrades and accessories, money off discounts and service upgrades.

More importantly, Dell focuses on customers' engagement which allows customers to purchase custom-built products and custom-tailored services that fit exactly their needs through the build-to-order manufacturing model. This model reduces Dell's inventory levels, and helps bring the latest technology to customers.

In the online environment, Dell utilised the participative nature of Web 2.0 to listen more to customers' feedback and suggestions. Dell established several online blogs and encouraged the formation of customer communities. Dell IdeaStorm for instance provides flow of communication that improves customer experience on one hand but also gives Dell a unique opportunity to refine its products and target new ones.

On the company website, individual customers can place their ratings and reviews, or use support features like 'Help me choose' to receive customised advice.

There are more than 55,000 customer ratings and reviews on Dell.com and 9,100 ideas on IdeaStorm that have been promoted more than 617,000 times. Customer feedback and reviews received though the company websites and blog are treated seriously for product refinement and development.

Figure 7.3 Participation site of Dell

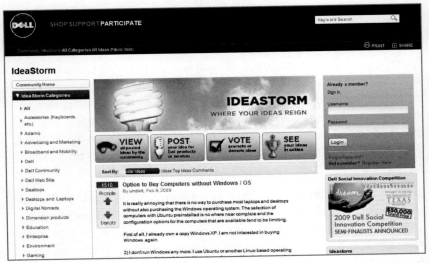

For large business and institutional customers, Dell dedicates account teams comprised of engineers and consultants to provide a single source of assistance and to specifically tailor solutions for these customers' unique needs.

For a better online experience, and to emphasise saving customers' money and time, Dell offers Premier (http://premier.dell.com) to its business customers; this is a secure, customisable procurement and support site or extranet designed for Dell's large business clients. The portal allows for:

- Easy order through a custom online store that ensures access to all products and their prices.

- Easy tracking which allows the customer to view real-time order status, purchase history details and online invoices.

- Easy control which includes custom access groups that allow customers to define what they see within the portal.

Figure 7.4 Dell Premier for corporate customers

TESCO: The loyalty ladder

TESCO is the UK's largest grocer and the third largest grocery retailer in the world. In 2008, TESCO was operating in 12 international markets, with 3,728 stores and 440,000 people worldwide. Its group sales reached $ 51.8 bn by serving millions of customers every week.

TESCO operates a balanced scorecard approach to managing its business which is known within the group as the 'Steering Wheel'. Earning lifetime customer loyalty is their ultimate customer objective.

Figure 7.5 Tesco steering wheel

Tesco launched its internet grocery business Tesco.com in 2000 and is now recognised as the world's largest online grocer. By the end of 2008, TESCO reported that it had over one million active online customers with a 20% increase on the previous year and an annual turnover of £1 billion online in the UK.

Product ranges at Tesco.com include food items and various non-food ranges such as books, DVDs, electrical appliances, Tesco Personal Finance, telecom products and other services that are offered in cooperation with specialist partners such as music downloads, DVD rentals, dieting clubs, flights and holidays, gas, electricity, etc.

Online customer engagement

Tesco.com is one of the most visited shopping sites in the UK. In addition to the variety of 20,000 available products, it includes a wealth of information that aims at informing and empowering customers to lead greener and healthier lives. For instance, Tesco diets.com is the UK's biggest online dieting and healthy eating service. It offers a range of 16 different personalised types of diets for customers who just want a healthier diet or a very specific health-based plan, such as diabetes or 'heart smart'. Tescocompare was also a site published by Tesco to encourage customers to compare product prices.

Tesco.com offers customers the option of bag-less deliveries which encourages more care for the environment with more than 40% of the online community requesting it.

Figure 7.6 Talking Tesco site

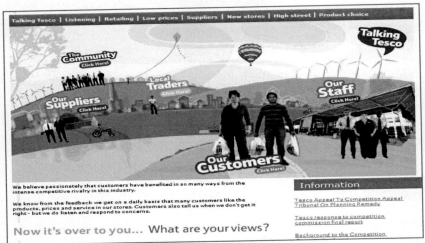

Loyalty ladder at TESCO

Humby and Hunt (2003) reported that Tesco.com uses a 'commitment-based segmentation' or 'loyalty ladder' to identify 6 life cycle categories of customers based on how recent their purchase was, frequency of their purchase and value of purchase. Tesco uses an automated event-triggered messaging system that is used to send targeted communication messages to customers to encourage continued purchase. The six life cycle segments are used as a basis for targeted communication. The life cycle segments are:

- Logged-on

- Cautionary

- Developing

- Established

- Dedicated

- Logged-off.

Tesco sends a series of follow-up communications that trigger after different customer events and according to the customer life cycle.

An example is provided below to illustrate how event-based communication can be used to convert a site visitor with little experience with Tesco.com to action.

Table 7.1 Targeted online marketing for better online experience

Customer experience event	Tesco reaction: auto response (AR)
Trigger event 1: Customer first registers on site but does not buy	(AR) 1-2 days after registration: email is sent offering phone assistance and £5 discount off first purchase to encourage trial.
Trigger event 2: Customer first purchases online	AR2: Immediate order confirmation.
	AR3: 5 days after purchase: email is sent with link to online customer satisfaction survey asking about quality of service from driver and picker (e.g. item quality and substitutions).
	AR4: 2 weeks after first purchase: direct mail offering tips on how to use service and £5 discount on next purchase to encourage re-use.
	AR5: Generic monthly e-newsletter with online exclusive offers encouraging cross-selling
	AR6: Bi-weekly alert with personalised offers for customer.
	AR7: After 2 months: £5 discount for next shop
	AR8: Quarterly mailing of coupons encouraging repeat sales and cross-sales
Trigger event 3: Customer does not purchase for an extended period	AR1: Dormancy detected: Reactivation email with survey of how the customer is finding the service (to identify any problems) and a £5 incentive.
	AR2: A further discount incentive is used to encourage continued usage after the first shop after a break.

As reported by Laura Wade-Gery, CEO of Tesco.com, the company has done several things to enhance customer online experience. Starting with product range development as a key area by adding more intangible offerings, such as e-diets and music downloads. It also reduced the time customers need to complete their first order, decreasing it from an average of over an hour to 35 minutes through site revisions.

Fiskars Craft: A case of customer empowerment

Fiskars is one of the oldest companies in the world. It began as an ironworks in the small village of Fiskars, Finland in 1649. Fiskars Brands Inc., one of the company's corporate subsidiaries is divided into four unique consumer product divisions: craft, garden, housewares and outdoor recreation.

Fiskars Craft started as an original scissors manufacturer and now makes an extensive line of ergonomically-designed speciality scissors, embossing tools, scrap booking supplies, paper trimmers, stencils, punches, and several more high-quality products.

Fiskars Crafts found itself in recent years losing market share to commoditised and cheaper rivals. Fiskars also realised that customers have no emotional connection to their tools such as scissors and crafting knives.

After conducting a few focus groups to understand customers and their needs, the company realised that it needed to create brand ambassadors to help revive Fiskars and connect to the crafting community. Fiskars.com was then revamped to include more creativity and to account for socialisation within the customer community.

The company sent out a national call looking for four customers who may be interested in a part-time paid job as a Fiskars ambassador or Fiskateer. The Fiskateers did not need to be crafting gurus but they needed to be passionate and engaging communicators.

Figure 7.7 Fiskars Crafts

Figure 7.8 The Fiskateers

Upon selection, the Fiskateers were given intense training using a tailored curriculum which emphasised that ambassadors should be transparent with customers and should not act as sales persons. The Fiskateers were educated and empowered. They were responsible for uniting the community of customers through the company blog which was considered to be a blog for crafters, online chats and other store activities. The Fiskateers were empowered to share their own experiences, write something about their lives and to build relationships with the community of customers.

Fiskars customers or potential customers could only join the Fiskateers community, if they were invited by one of the Fiskateers. This smart strategy made customers believe they were important to the company by providing an exclusivity feeling. Emotional connection to the brand increased substantially upon the launch of the Fiskateers campaign where customers were engaged in an active community and felt listened to.

Conversations on the Fiskateers blog were treated seriously and with a lot of attention. One of the examples reported by Fiskars outlines: 'a woman complained about paper (from Fiskars sub-brand Heidi Grace) that had a glitter coating , saying that the paper was curling when she mounted it on a harder stock paper, and also curled up when she left it in her car. It turned out that heat was causing the paper to curl. Heidi Grace changed the manufacture of the paper before a huge amount of it was printed – saving potentially thousands of dollars in printing costs'.

The blog also provided feedback on newly introduced products and help redesign or refine some of the products according to the feedback received.

Fiskars today has a community of 5,000 members in the Fiskateers community and five lead Fiskateers who are empowered customers with a predefined role, which aims at enhancing the emotional connection of customers to the brand.

References

Humby, C. and Hunt, T. (2003) *Scoring points. How Tesco is Winning Customer Loyalty.* Kogan Page, London, UK

Marcus, J. (2004) *Amazonia. Five years at the epicenter of the dot-com juggernaut,* The New Press, New York, NY.

Internet sources

www.amazon.com

http://www.customerthink.com/blog/beyond_customer_centricity_next_frontier

http://www.davechaffey.com/E-commerce-Internet-marketing-case-studies/Amazon-case-study/

http://econsultancy.com/blog/3578-amazon-pushes-2008-ecommerce-results

www.Zappos.com

http://www.startup-review.com/blog/zapposcom-case-study-why-shoes-are-great-for-e-commerce-%E2%80%A6-yes-really.php

http://www.cioinsight.com/c/a/Case-Studies/Zapposcom-Succcess-Through-Simplicity/

http://www.ideastorm.com/

www.dell.com

http://premier.dell.com/

http://www.davechaffey.com/E-commerce-Internet-marketing-case-studies/Dell-E-commerce-case-study

http://www.tescocorporate.com/

http://www.tescoreports.com/areview08/downloads/tesco_annual_review_08.pdf

http://www.davechaffey.com/E-commerce-Internet-marketing-case-studies/Tesco.com-case-study/

http://www.fiskars.com

http://www.whatsnextblog.com/archives/2008/10/fiskateers_how_a_social_community_became_a_veritable_sales_force.asp

http://www.womma.org/casestudy/examples/create-an-evangelism-program/fiskars-brands-creating-a-long/

Chapter 8

How to woo and create an emotional attachment: Lessons from the best

Introduction

Some companies have achieved remarkable success through implementing great CEM strategies. Others have not fared so well. There are a number of companies that have succeeded. As managers, our goal is to find out what makes great organisations great and then try to adopt those factors or models within our own organisations. Apple, Harley Davidson, IKEA, Singapore Airlines, Walt Disney and Zara are all examples of companies that have succeeded in developing exceptional and memorable experiences for their customers. Each company is unique and offers varying products and/or services. Apple sells consumer electronics and computers, Harley Davison sells motorcycles, IKEA sells home furnishings, Singapore Airlines provides transportation services, Walt Disney is involved in the entertainment industry and Zara sells clothing. Each of these companies has gone beyond selling their basic services or products. They are no longer selling mere products and services. These companies are now in the business of offering their customers a particular lifestyle consisting of a number of experiences. By focusing on selling experiences these companies have taken a step ahead of competition and created strategic competitive advantages which their competition are finding to catch up to. What can we learn from these great giants? In the following pages we discuss each of these case studies in detail and then come up with a model for implementing great customer experience management within our own firms.

Case study 1: Apple Inc.

Introduction

Apple Inc. started to sell computers out of a garage in 1976 (Nonaka and Kenney, 1991). It was one of the first companies to sell personal computers and since then has introduced many innovations within the consumer electronics market. Initially Apple started off as a successful company, with its Apple II computer, released in 1977, becoming a big hit in the marketplace. However, in the 1980s, due to increased competition from Microsoft Windows based PCs, Apple started to decline. Steve Jobs, one of the original founders of the company, who had left, rejoined the firm in 1996 thus starting a turnaround of the firm. Currently Apple ranks as the most admired firm, second year in a row, by Fortune Magazine (Fortune, 2009a). Not only is it the most admired company in the world, it's customers are very loyal to the brand (Fortune, 2009b).

Apple Computers has been one of the leading companies when it comes to consumer electronics. According to its annual report, 'the Company is committed to bringing the best personal computing, portable digital music and mobile communication experience to consumers, students, educators, businesses, and government agencies through its innovative hardware, software, peripherals, services, and Internet offerings' (Apple, 2008). It has succeeded, to a great extent, in achieving these goals. The company has made amazing progress in the last decade. It has established itself not just as a consumer electronics firm, but more importantly as an 'innovative lifestyle brand' (Davis, 2006).

Currently Apple sells everything from personal computers (Mac), mobile phones (iPhone), MP3 players (iPod), to software (such as the Mac OS). More recently the company started selling various products online, such as music (iTunes) and applications for its phones. The company has started a unique strategy by opening its own retail outlets and selling direct to the consumer. By the end of the 2008 financial year, Apple had 247 retail stores around the world (Apple, 2008).

Apple truly is a success story. It is a company that has focused on the customer and providing the customer with an excellent customer experience at every step of the consumption process. The next few sections look at some of the techniques that Apple uses to achieve this level of success.

Innovation

Innovation is at the heart of the company. Currently Apple ranks as the leading innovator in its industry (Fortune, 2009b). Apple has introduced to the world a number of exciting innovations and continues to focus on innovations within all aspects of its products and services. Recent innovations can be found in the personal computers, consumer electronics, and digital content distribution fields. Some of these include, but are not limited to, 'innovations, such as the iPod, iPhone, iTunes Store, and Apple TV' (Apple, 2008). The innovations are not only limited to the products, but are also found in its management style.

Although these markets are highly competitive and are undergoing aggressive pricing wars, Apple feels that it is vital for it to be an innovator in order to succeed. For this purpose Apple invests heavily in its research and development wing. The 2008 annual report of Apple states that 'the company believes continual investment in research and development is critical to the development and enhancement of innovative products and technologies' (Apple, 2008). For instance, currently the company is spending about $1.1 billion on research, up from $712 million in 2006.

Part of the innovation process involves anticipating customer's future needs. Apple is looks at the needs of its customers and accordingly develops new products and services. The Apple iPod and the iTunes is one such example. The iPod, an MP3 player, and the iTunes, a site selling music were brought out together to facilitate the customer in their music needs. Customers purchasing music online could easily transfer the music to their music players. This innovatory approach has helped to create a positive experience for its customers. While products from other companies pose connectivity problems for customers, Apple's one platform allows a customer to transfer data from various devices with ease. For instance a customer can take pictures with their iPhone, transfer it to their Mac personal computer, and download music onto the iPod without many complications. On other platforms, customers would be required to install software, find appropriate cables, and then accomplish the same task. Apple has created a good experience in a wide spectrum for its customers.

Customer focus

Innovation is not the only factor for success for the company. The innovation is driven in the right direction, i.e. customer. Companies come out with innovations that are hard to use, and difficult to set up. Apple ensures that the products and services they use are user friendly and easy to use while at the same time being powerful. A recent survey by Forester Research shows that Apple outscores its PC rivals by a large margin in terms of customer experience. Apple's score was 80% where as Compaq, HP and Gateway had between 63 and 66 percent satisfaction (Elmer-DeWitt, 2009a). Dell computers ranked even lower at 58%. This shows that Apple has its customers in mind when developing its products and services. Furthermore, Fortune also ranked it as number one in its industry in terms of the quality of its products and services (Fortune, 2009b).

Other examples where Apple beats its competition to developing customer friendly products include its operating system and the iPod. As compared to Windows operating system its operating system has been ranked as a more user friendly one (Davis, 2006;

Barsch, 2005). Another recent example, which has been outlined in recent Apple TV commercials is the issue of computer viruses, (Apple, 2009). Windows based PCs are prone to computer viruses and need heavy duty virus protection. This anti-virus software often slows a user's PC down, and needs constant updating, making the experience not so great. On the other hand the Mac operating system does not suffer from this problem, hence making the experience an enjoyable one.

Much praise has also been given to the iPod. According to Barsch the 'small ear-bud headphones that could be considered the best on the market, the iPod is far and away not only the market leader but also the market favorite' (Barsch, 2005). As discussed earlier, the consumer electronics marketplace is highly competitive. Moreover technology is often easy to replicate. However, analysts believe that Apple will continue to beat competition, simply because of its customer focus. 'While competitive devices swarm into the marketplace, Apple will keep winning in the marketplace because the iPod captures our imagination. It brings the universality of music into a compact device that's so easy to use – the owner's manual can be thrown in the trash' (Barsch, 2005).

Apple has been consistently good at finding out what the customer wants. In the current scenario it is easy to use, powerful and stylish products and services. Apple has done much research and continues to make sure that the customer experience is an enjoyable one with the firm.

Total customer experience

Apple is a unique technology firm in terms of its supply chain management. As a computer firm, it is the only company that produces the hardware, the operating system as well as most of the software for its computers. This strategy has helped it to maximise the use of various resources to give the customer the best experience using its computers. Apple has taken the same strategy to the selling of its products and services.

Apple operates its own retail outlets (both online and brick-and-mortar), one of the few companies to sell its products direct to the consumer without a middle man. 'By operating its own stores and locating them in desirable high-traffic locations, the company is better positioned to control the customer buying experience and attract new customers' (Apple, 2008).

The experience of the customer starts with the design of the stores. The stores are designed in an attractive manner with sleek and simple designs, which complement the presentation of its products. Furthermore, buying electronic products can be an unpleasant experience for many consumers. The main reason being, the high degree of uncertainty attached to purchasing hi-tech products. Most consumers don't have the level of knowledge to compare various models in the market. Apple has found a solution to this problem. It has trained its employees to provide a high level of support to customers. 'The Company believes a high-quality buying experience with knowledgeable salespersons who can convey the value of the Company's products and services greatly enhances its ability to attract and retain customers' (Apple, 2008). Salespeople can give advice, and guide people about various products and services. Apple has most of its products on display, which customers can use. Salespeople even give demonstrations of these products to customers in order to help them to make the right purchasing decision.

Apple also helps out some of the third party retailers by providing them with Apple Sales Consultants. These sales consultants work at the selected third-party reseller locations, providing assistance to customers and the other employees. Moreover, Apple also invests into its after sales service. The consumer's experience does not stop after the product has been purchased. Hence, Apple has developed AppleCare, a body that deals with customers' after sales problems and issues. AppleCare is able to offer customers assistance on product installation, product use, technical assistance, providing product information as well as other technical support. Apple works on providing the highest possible sales and after sales experience to the customer, to make sure that the customer remains loyal to the firm.

Through these steps, Apple has converted an unpleasant experience into a positive one. Since Apple controls nearly every aspect of the supply chain, they are able to make sure that the quality of the products and services are up to a standard level. Furthermore, all employees are working towards the same goal, i.e. providing the customer with great experiences.

Branding

Apple is working hard to create a positive image of the brand through its branding strategies. For example the current PC campaign focuses on the differences between Apple and Windows based computers. The campaign is centred on two individuals. One of whom is a young, stylish movie actor, who is representing MAC. The other is a middle aged, overweight man, representing Windows based PCs. There are a number of different commercials, all focused on showing the Apple lifestyle. Various commercials show the different facets of Apple's lifestyle and customer experience. These include the high technology of Apple products, the style associated with its machines, the ease of use with which its devices can be operated, as well as the power that is available in the computers. The commercials have become very popular among the masses and can be found online at Apple's website as well as on You Tube. A strong branding effort has enabled Apple to convey to its customers the message of the Apple lifestyle. The high quality of the branding has helped to raise awareness and to build a better brand image.

Reaping the rewards of effective CEM

Through its unique customer experiences, Apple has reaped many rewards. One of the most important of which is a high levels of customer loyalty. Apple's customers are not only loyal to the brand, but they are passionate about it (Mininni, 2006). Apple's culture has been strengthened by its devoted customers, some of whom have a cult-like following for the brand. The recent success of the iPod, which has a 92.7% of the US market share, according to NPD group (Barsch, 2005), has seen the number of loyal customers grow even larger.

Apple has benefited much financially. A look at their recent Annual Report shows some of these figures. Net sales for the firm arose to £32.4 billion in 2008, up from $8.2 billion 4 years earlier (Apple, 2008).

Table 8.1 Apple's financial status over the last four years

	2008	2007	2006	2005	2004
Net sales	$ 32,479	$ 24,006	$ 19,315	$ 13,931	$ 8,279
Net income	$ 4,834	$ 3,496	$ 1,989	$ 1,328	$ 266
Earnings per common share:					
Basic	$ 5.48	$ 4.04	$ 2.36	$ 1.64	$ 0.36
Diluted	$ 5.36	$ 3.93	$ 2.27	$ 1.55	$ 0.34
Cash dividends declared per common share	$ —	$ —	$ —	$ —	$ —
Shares used in computing earnings per share:					
Basic	881,592	864,595	844,058	808,439	743,180
Diluted	902,139	889,292	877,526	856,878	774,776
Cash, cash equivalents, and short-term investments	$ 24,490	$ 15,386	$ 10,110	$ 8,261	$ 5,464
Total assets	$ 39,572	$ 25,347	$ 17,205	$ 11,516	$ 8,039
Long-term debt	$ —	$ —	$ —	$ —	$ —
Total liabilities	$ 18,542	$ 10,815	$ 7,221	$ 4,088	$ 2,976
Shareholders' equity	$ 21,030	$ 14,532	$ 9,984	$ 7,428	$ 5,063

Source: Apple (2008)

Table 8.1 shows that net income for the firm grew from $266 million in 2004 to an amazing $4.8 billion in 2008. In addition to this the brand equity of the company also increased immensely. The brand equity of the company grew to $8 billion by the year 2005 (Davis, 2006). The total sales of the company rose by about 36% over the last year (see Table 8.2). While Apple controls over 90% of the MP3 player marketplace in the US, it is fast expanding into other related areas. Its online music store did remarkably well by hitting 1 billion downloads in just nine months (Elmer-DeWitt, 2009b).

Financially, Apple is doing extremely well. Despite an economic recession, Apple is still managing to sell products and services to its customers. It seems to be doing much better than its competition, and is expected to continue its growth well into the future.

Table 8.2 Apples sales

	2008	Change	2007	Change	2006
Net Sales by Operating Segment:					
Americas net sales	$ 14,573	26%	$ 11,596	23%	$ 9,415
Europe net sales	7,622	40%	5,460	33%	4,096
Japan net sales	1,509	39%	1,082	(11)%	1,211
Retail net sales	6,315	53%	4,115	27%	3,246
Other Segments net sales (a)	2,460	40%	1,753	30%	1,347
Total net sales	$ 32,479	35%	$ 24,006	24%	$ 19,315
Unit Sales by Operating Segment:					
Americas Mac unit sales	3,980	32%	3,019	24%	2,432
Europe Mac unit sales	2,519	39%	1,816	35%	1,346
Japan Mac unit sales	389	29%	302	(1)%	304
Retail Mac unit sales	2,034	47%	1,386	56%	886
Other Segments Mac unit sales (a)	793	50%	528	58%	335
Total Mac unit sales	9,715	38%	7,051	33%	5,303
Net Sales by Product:					
Desktops (b)	$ 5,603	39%	$ 4,020	21%	$ 3,319
Portables (c)	8,673	38%	6,294	55%	4,056
Total Mac net sales	14,276	38%	10,314	40%	7,375
iPod	9,153	10%	8,305	8%	7,676
Other music related products and services (d)	3,340	34%	2,496	32%	1,885
iPhone and related products and services (e)	1,844	NM	123	NM	—
Peripherals and other hardware (f)	1,659	32%	1,260	15%	1,100
Software, service, and other sales (g)	2,207	46%	1,508	18%	1,279
Total net sales	$ 32,479	35%	$ 24,006	24%	$ 19,315
Unit Sales by Product:					
Desktops (b)	3,712	37%	2,714	12%	2,434
Portables (c)	6,003	38%	4,337	51%	2,869
Total Mac unit sales	9,715	38%	7,051	33%	5,303
Net sales per Mac unit sold (h)	$ 1,469	—%	$ 1,463	5%	$ 1,391
iPod unit sales	54,828	6%	51,630	31%	39,409

Source: Apple (2008)

Conclusion

Apple has made an amazing turnaround in the past decade. It is has released one hit product after another. One of the main reasons for the success of the firm is its ability to create a great experience for its customers. Apple seems to be doing this by focusing on innovations, its customers and through the use of creative branding. Apple is working to create a total customer experience, making sure that the customers get a high quality experience at every touchpoint. This has resulted in an increase in its market share, and a growth in its passionately loyal customers.

Case study 2: Harley-Davidson

Introduction

Harley-Davidson (HD) is perhaps the world's most famous motorcycle brand. Not only is Harley-Davidson a manufacturer of top quality motorcycles, it is one of the best examples of a how a company builds customer experiences. The following statement found on Harley-Davidson's annual report says it all:

> *Harley-Davidson, Inc. is a global leader in fulfilling dreams and providing extraordinary customer experiences through mutually beneficial relationships with our stakeholders.*
> (Harley-Davidson, 2008)

Harley-Davidson has recognised, through its past experiences, that in order to survive and to prosper it needs to concentrate on providing its customers with extraordinary experiences. It has transformed its identity from being just a motorcycle to being 'a way of life, a global family, it's a whole culture, it is the archetypal brand' (Rodger, 2008). In following this strategy, HD has been able to create a large following of loyal customers (McAlexander *et al.*, 2002), and prosper financially at the same time (Harley-Davidson, 2008).

Harley-Davidson wasn't as profitable throughout its history. In fact, not too long ago its business was facing the possibility of becoming bankrupt. How did HD turn itself around and reach this status? How has HD been able to start with just three bikes in 1903 to over 300,000 in 2008 with a turnover of over $5.5 billion? (Rodger, 2008) This case study looks Harley-Davidson's history and evaluates its secret to success.

The history

Harley-Davidson started off as a partnership between William S. Harley and Arthur Davidson in 1903 (Harley-Davidson, 2009). By the 1960's it had a massive market share of 70% in the United States (Hartley, 2004). However with the introduction of Japanese motorcycle companies, specifically the Honda, its market share started to decline. With their lightweight motorcycles, Honda was able to take away much of the market share from HD, resulting in a 65% drop in Harley-Davidson's share within a span of a few years (Hartley, 2004). One of the key factors in the success of Honda, and the failure of HD was the quality of the products. Honda was producing higher quality products, while HD had rested on its laurels and was producing lower quality products. This was remedied in part by the efforts of Vaughan Beals, who purchased a stake in HD. Beals introduced quality control measures as one of the means to turn around HD. The most important, perhaps, steps that he took were to start the Harley-Davidson Owners Group (HOG). These efforts later resulted in the final turnaround of the company. The development of the HOG as well as improvements in quality has resulted in a remarkable loyalty level of 92% (Hartley, 2004).

The next sections discuss in detail the steps that HD took in order to turn around its company and to develop an exceptional experience for its customers.

CEM at Harley-Davidson: The Harley way of life

Perhaps the most important moment in Harley-Davidson's life was to take a revolutionary step by creating the Harley Owners Group (HOG). According to an old saying, necessity is the mother of invention. It was in the darkest hours of HD, when they had no money available for advertising that they went out and created an owners group (Lowenstein, 2005). HOG was a community of owners who were given a chance to interact with one another and share experiences with one another through the use of the Harley-Davidson products. Initially this group started with only 50 members in the first chapter. Through its years, the HOG has used various means to keep in touch with customers and to create a unique community of users such as no other company has been able to achieve. Within two years of forming the HOG, the number of members had grown to 60,000 (Lowenstein, 2005), and currently there are over a million members of this group (Harley-Davidson, 2009).

The Harley Owners Group is a unique brand community, which has been set as a benchmark by many other organisations. A brand community is defined as, 'a specialized, non-geographically bound community, based on a structured set of social relationships among users of a brand' (Muniz and O'Guinn, 2001). The HOG is a unique entity that HD has used to ensure that the customer's experience does not end with the purchase of the bike. In fact the experience enhances post purchase and continues throughout the life of the customer. For Harley-Davidson users, the bike has become a way of life (Harley-Davidson, 2009), and hence the relationship never stops.

Initially HD pays its customers' first year of membership fees (Berry, 1995). Membership to the group allows group members to take benefit from a host of services offered by HOG. For instance HOG organises and sponsors events, rallies, training sessions, weekend rallies, etc. (Harley-Davidson, 2009; Berry, 1995). Owners are given among other things a magazine, roadside assistance, touring handbooks, and access to exclusive events (Harley-Davidson, 2009). What the HOG does is to promote a sense of brotherhood among its group members (Pugliese and Cagan, 2002). They try to reemphasize the HD lifestyle, which is a sense of a 'rebellious spirit' and 'natural freedom' through the HOG.

When HD says that it is a way of life, they really mean it and back it up with the desired actions. For example, members of the HOG can get help in taking special vacations that are focused around the bike. Members can get help transporting their bikes, getting breakdown assistance, and the chance to interact with other people who have similar passions. Through this community, HD has transformed this from a mere motorcycle to incorporate it into every aspect of a customer's life. The customers in return hold the company, its brand and the motorcycle with 'great respect and distinction' (Pugliese and Cagan, 2002). Not many brands can boast that their customers will go through the pain of having the logo tattooed on their body parts (Rodger, 2008). The HOG not only includes the stereotypical rebellious outlaw type of a customer. Instead now it includes people from every facet of life, including CEO's and senior executives from different organisations (D'Souza, 2004).

It is through this community that Harley-Davidson has transformed the product from a mode of transportation to recreation as well as a symbol of status (Pugliese and Cagan, 2002). The HOG allows owners to enhance their experience with the product. It allows them to tap into potential unrealised benefits of the product, and to enhance that experience with interactions with others, including company employees. At the various functions and rallies, it is not only the owners of the bikes that come and participate, but also employees of HD as well as senior members of management. Even the CEO of HD rides a Harley-Davidson. This allows the company to get a unique insight into the lives of their customers, in a way that perhaps no other brand has been able to achieve.

Other critical factors

Besides creating an exciting experience for its customers, HD has done a number of other things to help it build a strong organisation. A great leadership has been one of these factors. The leaders at HD have taken a hands-on approach to doing business. They have worked by setting examples for others to follow (Hartley, 2004). Moreover, HD has focused on innovation. They have been one of the industry leaders in terms of innovation with the product and innovation in other aspects of the business. HD has also focused on its employees, and encouraged them to be creative. Furthermore, they have invested much time and effort in improving the quality of their products and services. HD learned its lesson from the Honda fiasco. HD now practices continuous quality improvement techniques in their business.

Reaping the rewards

Creating an owners community has benefited Harley-Davidson through the years. Recently the CEO of Harley-Davidson, James Zimmer, said that they had achieved a 217% increase in sales as compared to a decade ago (Harley-Davidson, 2008). An investment in HD out grows a similar one in the Stand & Poor's 500 (see Figure 8.1). This shows that the company is financially strong, and has not only recovered from its darkest point in the early 1980s, it has become a growing firm.

Between 1984 and 1996 Harley-Davidson spent not a single penny on advertising (Lowenstein, 2005). Even after this period the amount spend on advertising was very small compared to competitors. It was the community, through its network and through word-of-mouth that Harley-Davidson was able to achieve this growth without spending on advertising.

Figure 8.1 Investment in Harley-Davidson vs. Standard & Poor's 500

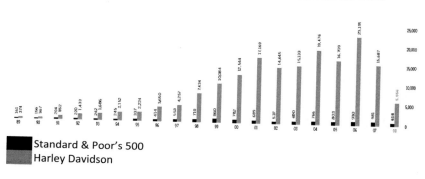

Standard & Poor's 500
Harley Davidson

20 year comparison of year end value of $100 invested Dec 31 1988. Assumes for both HD and S&P that all dividends are reinvested.

Source: Harley-Davidson, 2008)

Since Harley-Davidson has been able to offer 'a cohesive, beneficial, and motivating brand experience' (D'Souza, 2004) they have earned the loyalties of their customers. Harley-Davidson currently has a large percentage of loyal customers (McAlexander *et al.*, 2002). These loyal customers consider the company as a 'God's gift' (Rodger, 2008) and thus spend heavily with the company. The bikes can cost as much as £20,000 or more. Customers not only spend money buying the bikes, but also spend on upgrading their bikes, adding accessories to the bikes, and spending money on gear such as jackets, boots, etc. This ensures multiple revenue streams for Harley-Davidson coming at regular intervals from a constantly loyal group of customers.

An additional benefit to HD is that they are able to find out about their customers more intimately than any other marketing research tool. According to an estimate, nearly half of the owners of Harley-Davidson motorcycles participate in rallies or events (D'Souza, 2004). This means that Harley-Davidson has access to and can observe the lifestyles of nearly 50% of their customer base. This, coupled with the company's policy to be close the customer allows them to study and understand their customers. HD is able to get important feedback and can monitor new trends. The community gives them feedback, even if they don't ask for it, they get the feedback (D'Souza, 2004). It is this continuous feedback that allows Harley-Davidson to keep on developing high quality products and services.

According the Berry (1995), there are numerous other benefits for cultivating communities based around brands. There is positive word-of-mouth (references), hence customers act as brand missionaries (Berry, 1995). This explains why HD was able to increase its sales by not advertising for such an extended period of time. Moreover, these customers seem to be more forgiving of failures than others. In many cases, HD owners have come up with innovations that the company has adopted. 'Customers who are highly integrated in the brand community are emotionally invested in the welfare of the company and desire to contribute to its success' (McAlexander *et al.*, 2002).

Conclusion

Harley-Davidson had an impressive start, which was halted with the introduction of competition from Honda. With a decline in sales, market share and quality, Harley-Davidson revived itself to come back from the ashes to being one of the most successful motorcycle companies in the world. Though strong leadership, improved quality management, a focus on innovation and by building owner communities, Harley-Davidson has been able to revive the company and has become a market leader. It has created an exceptional and unique experience for their customer which is an envy of all.

Case study 3: IKEA

Introduction

IKEA is the largest furniture manufacturer in the world (Anonymous, 2006; Arnold, 2002). It is also, perhaps the most famous Swedish company, with revenues well above $30 billion (IKEA, 2008; Strand, 2009). IKEA is considered to be one of the best examples of a market oriented firm, which adopts an innovative style to its business (Tarnovskaya *et al.*, 2008). It is a firm that values customer relationships (Kumar *et al.*, 2000), and has built a strong brand, recognized the world over (Tarnovskaya *et al.*, 2008). Overall, IKEA offers its customers 'immediate satisfaction and a pleasurable shopping experience' (Arnold, 2002).

Figure 8.2 IKEA sales

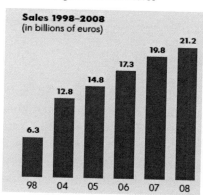

Source: IKEA (2009)

IKEA was started up by Ingvar Kamprad and started selling its products in 1958. While attending an exhibition that sold furniture, Ingvar got an idea, to sell quality furniture at reasonable prices. Since then IKEA has been working hard to provide great quality products at prices which are lower than competition. IKEA's philosophy is to produce well designed, quality products while at the same time being hardworking and innovative in the business (Tarnovskaya *et al.*, 2008). Currently IKEA is the leading global retailer of furniture and furnishings and has over 250 stores in 35 countries and gets an amazing 565 million visitors a year (IKEA, 2009).

The next few sections will look into and discuss the critical factors that have enabled it to create a successful business focused around 'pleasurable shopping experiences.'

Brand orientation

One of the ways that IKEA has been able to succeed is through its brand orientation. Currently the IKEA brand is recognised the world over as a leading brand, and it regularly wins recognition from the industry such as Business Week's most value brands (Tarnovskaya *et al.*, 2008). IKEA's brand is based on a vision of 'creating a better everyday life for the many people' (IKEA, 2009). They do this by offering innovative, fashionable, and quality furnishings at affordable prices. However, IKEA has worked hard to communicate this message to the world. Traditionally most consumers were not used to this strategy and IKEA faced an uphill task in many of the countries it operated in. Hence as a part of the branding strategy one of the first tasks for IKEA was to educate the customer about its brand, and to help them modify their priorities in purchasing furniture.

IKEA has been able to create this awareness through a number of different means. The primary of these is advertising in the mass media. For example in the UK marketplace, where customers were accustomed to furnishings with flowery designs, it was a challenge to change consumer preferences about IKEA, which provides modern looking furniture. St Luke's advertising agency was hired for this task to 'undertake a radical change in IKEA's image in the UK' (Edvardsson *et al.*, 2006). Their campaign worked and the IKEA brand in the UK marketplace was seen by the public as a fashionable brand, instead of an alien one.

Once a customer comes to the stores, IKEA keep up its brand communication efforts through other means. One of the most popular of these is its magazine, IKEA Family Live. This magazine is published quarterly and in a number of different languages (Anonymous, 2009a). It has a worldwide distribution of nearly 9 million copies. Through the use of this magazine IKEA is able to stay in touch with its customers and keep reminding them about their company, its mission, values, and products. The recipients of this magazine are often loyalty card holders, IKEA can map out their buying habits and measure the effect of its branding campaigns.

The IKEA brand is now no longer considered just a furnishing company, rather it has become a 'phenomenon' that is about the lifestyle of customers (Anonymous, 2006). In many places it has a cult-like following, with people going to IKEA as a place to enjoy and have a pleasurable shopping experience.

For IKEA, branding plays a vital role in creating a positive experience for its customers. This is the first link in the chain that leads to purchasing products. IKEA feels that if the first link is an enjoyable one, then the customer is likely to proceed further.

Customer focus

Another mean factor that leads to the success of IKEA is its customer focus. At IKEA, 'closeness to customers is considered a necessary condition for success in a new international market' (Tarnovskaya *et al.*, 2008). IKEA works hard on trying to understand its customers. Besides carrying out regular customer surveys, it also arranges home visits, which allow the company to get a better feel and understanding of its customers and their attitudes towards the brand.

The whole concept of the company arose from a focus on the customer. Currently, new products are developed with the customer in mind and start with the customer. For instance, when developing a new product the company first asks what will the customer pay for this and what levels of quality will the customer want? The rest of the product is then designed to meet these objectives. Hence, the company is able to produce one hit product after another.

Employees

The employees of the firm are a vital part in its success strategy. The employees are the main line of contact with the firm, and hence need to portray the company's brand image. IKEA has a flat organisational structure, which gives a higher level of responsibility to the employees (Arnold, 2002). This system gives the employees a sense of pride and purpose, which is crucial if a company wants its employees to deliver a pleasant experience for its customers.

IKEA focuses on a number of areas for its employees. First its recruitment policy is based on the values of 'cost-consciousness', 'simplicity' and 'leadership by example.' IKEA looks for employees that will 'dare to be different' and have a team attitude. Next, training plays a central role in the development of its employees. Like a majority of the customers, the employees too are not accustomed to the culture and lifestyle of the company, and hence training takes into account these factors. The training of the employees introduces them to the corporate culture and the IKEA way of doing things. Once the employees are hired, they are regarded as member of the IKEA family and are divided into teams. Working in teams gives the employees more responsibility and builds a friendly working environment. IKEA gives its employees good compensation and facilities. Employees are offered a reasonable salary, insurance, and even free lunches in some places.

IKEA's rapid growth and success is partly due to its employees. It is these employees that carry forward the vision of the company and help to deliver the level of experience that the company is seeking to provide.

Supply chain network

The supply chain of IKEA is critical to its objective of offering low prices and quality products. IKEA is based in Sweden, and has most of its operations in Europe and North America. All places with high costs. Thus, much of the supply chain of the company has shifted towards lower cost centres around the globe (Strand, 2009). IKEA's supply chain uses over 1,300 suppliers (Lloyd, 2009). It owns some of these operations; however it assists and guides the rest.

Part of the challenge of having a low cost strategy and a large number of suppliers is to ensure a standard level of quality. IKEA has managed this by having a strategy of 'cooperation with credible, well-informed partners' (IKEA, 2008; Strand, 2009). IKEA works closely with its suppliers and integrates them into its global supply chain network (Tarnovskaya et al., 2008). It provides support to the suppliers in terms of training, guidance, quality controls and even financial assistance (Tarnovskaya et al., 2008). Furthermore the company tries to build its relationship on trust. 'The threat of opportunistic behavior by suppliers is minimized through long-term orders, investments in production, and strict control over implementation' (Tarnovskaya et al., 2008).

Besides the supply side of the supply chain, IKEA also works on improving other areas. For instance, recently it has been continuously modernising its distribution centres (Anonymous, 2009b). The modernisation includes improved handling facilities, the use of automated systems, and better information systems to manage the operations. In one particular facility in the Washington DC area, turnaround time went down from 72 hours to 24 hours.

Furthermore, the retail outlets of the company are designed to reflect the company's lifestyle and help create an appropriate customer experience. The company focuses on things such as the store design, its layout, displays and technology in its retail outlets. A good combination can lead to stimulating and pleasant shopping experiences, which according to research are important in increasing impulse buying (Mattila and Wirtz, 2008).

Innovation

Innovation at IKEA incorporates all aspects of the company. The company first started off with an innovative business idea. Later the company incorporated an innovative supply chain and outsourcing strategy. The company also continuously innovates its product lines to offer customer products that are better, cheaper and more reliable.

IKEA has introduced to the customer innovative experiences. The self service concept adapted to a furniture outlet was very unique to most countries, as was the self assembled furniture sold in IKEA stores. Innovations in its advertising is also a key to the company's success (Arnold, 2002). Some of the recent innovations taking place at the company include, innovations in the use of new technology, environmentally friendly materials for the construction and packing of goods, innovations in production and delivery systems as well as innovations in quality control, training, and supply chain management (Ghauri et al., 2008).

Benefits of CEM at IKEA

A number of benefits and advantages have already been discussed. However there are several others worth mentioning. The company has a loyal customer base of about 1.8 million customers (Howell, 2009). This is a sizable base of customers that not only purchase frequently from the stores but also have increased their average transactions over time. Furthermore, the strong customer base has allowed the company to do something amazing; open up new stores in one of the worst financial downturns in the recent past (Lloyd, 2009). The company is working on opening several new stores in places like the United States.

Conclusion

IKEA's business idea was an innovative one. Since its inception, it has revolutionised the retail furnishings industry and introduced a number of important innovations. IKEA is currently the leading retailer of furnishings around the world and continues to grow. They have created a special experience for their customers, which has allowed them to be number one. There is much that other companies can learn from their experiences.

Case study 4: Singapore International Airlines

Introduction

Singapore International Airlines (SIA) is one of the leading airlines of the world (Wirtz and Johnston, 2003). It has won perhaps more awards for its outstanding customer service than any other airline. As one of the world's top airlines, and Singapore's best-known company it is also ranked by various business magazines as an 'admired' company (Chan, 2000). How did Singapore Airlines achieve this status, while others were struggling? This case looks at and examines SIA's rise to success and more importantly it examines the magic formula that SIA uses to maintain this status over time.

History

Singapore Airlines has its origins in Malayan Airways which was formed in 1947. In 1972, this airline gave birth to two different airlines companies: Malaysian Airways Limited and Singapore Airlines (Chan, 2000). Since then SIA has never looked back and has left its sister Malaysian Airways far behind. Initially SIA was owned by the government of Singapore, which looked at the airline as an investment (Chan, 2000). Since Singapore itself is a small city state, there are no domestic flights that SIA could dominate. Instead, right from the start, SIA had to come up with different strategies to not only survive but also prosper in the highly competitive airline industry.

Since its founding, SIA has achieved many remarkable milestones and has been at the forefront of adopting new technology. For instance in 1977, along with British Airways, it introduced the supersonic Concorde. More recently, in 2007 it became the first airline to introduce the super jumbo Airbus A380, the largest aircraft in the world today (SIA, 2008).

In 1985, SIA's shares were floated on the stock exchange. Since its inception, SIA has been a profitable company and achieved much success. The next segment briefly looks at some of these successes.

Success at SIA

SIA's main success can be measured in two ways, first its financial performance and second the recognition it gets in the industry. Looking at financial performance: it has a very impressive track record and is 'consistently one of the most profitable airlines in the world' (Wirtz and Johnston, 2003). In fact, it is so consistent that it has an uninterrupted profit record (Chan, 2000). Perhaps one of the reasons for this high degree of profitability is its high level of efficiency, which according to a 1993 study was one of the highest among passenger airlines (Schefczyk, 1993). Through this consistently high level of performance, SIA has been able to create a strategic competitive advantage which helps it to outperform its competition continuously (Heracleous *et al.*, 2004).

Looking back at the profitability of SIA, in the year 1992, it was ranked as the most profitable airline in the world (see Table 8.3).

Table 8.3 World's most profitable airlines in 1992

Rank	Airline	Profit (US$ million)
1	Singapore Airlines	522.4
2	Cathay Pacific Airways	385.6
3	British Airways	301.1
4	China Airways	145.2
5	Thai Airways International	120.8
6	Qantas Airways	105.6
7	Southwest Airlines (USA)	103.6
8	Swissair	80.3
9	Air New Zealand	63.7
10	Malaysia Airlines System	57.2
11	Britannia Airways	56.1
12	Gulf Air	47.6
13	El Al (Israel)	31.5
14	Belgium Airlines	11.1
15	Korean Air	1.5

Source: Mak & Go (1995)

About a decade later, it still ranked as the most profitable airline in the world (see Table 8.4). SIA outperforms all other airlines and does so quite comfortably.

More recently looking at its annual report, we can see that SIA will probably continue this trend. Its passenger revenues continue to rise, and outperform the competition (see Figure 8.3).

Table 8.4 SIA performance relative to competition

Performance metrics	SIA	United	Northwest	Continental	American	Delta	BA	Cathay	KLM	Quantas
Revenues $m	5,133	16,138	9,905	8,969	18,963	13,879	12,103	3,903	5,788	5,207
Net income (loss) $m	343.2	(2,145)	(423.0)	(95.0)	(1,762)	(1,027)	(206.1)	84.2	(138.2)	212.3
Net profit margin (%)	6.68	-----	-----	-----	-----	-----	-----	2.16	-----	4.08
Operational profit margin (%)	10.4	-----	-----	0.016	-----	-----	-----	2.73	-----	6.83
Revenue / cost ratio	1.12	0.81	0.92	1.02	0.88	0.93	0.99	1.03	0.99	1.07
Revenue per $1,000 labour cost	5,310	2,279	2,499	2,969	2,361	2,266	3,581	3,989	3,739	3,995
Net income per Load Tonne – Km $0.001	2.73	(10.53)	(3.06)	(1.02)	(8.64)	(6.27)	(1.55)	1.03	(1.35)	2.54

Source: Heracleous *et al.*, (2004)

Figure 8.3 Passenger revenue

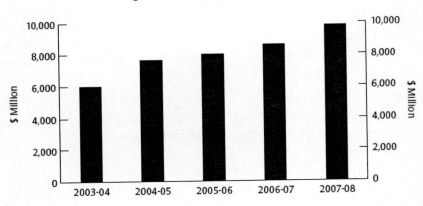

Source: SIA (2008)

The second important factor for success is recognition. SIA has been recognised by organisations all across the globe for its performance. Fortune recently ranked it as the 4th most admired airline in the world (Fortune, 2009a). It has been ranked as one of the top two airlines three years running at the world airline awards (WorldAirlineAwards, 2009). Moreover SIA routinely gets various top awards such as 'the best airline', 'best business class', 'best cabin crew service', or 'best in-flight food' (Wirtz and Johnston, 2003). Some of the recent awards include, 'Best Asian Airline', 'Airline of the Year' and 'Best First Class' (SIA, 2008).

Another important success factor is the ability of a company to create customer loyalty. SIA has been very successful at this. SIA has been able to charge premium prices, which is an element of emotional loyalty, or the highest degree of customer loyalty. Moreover, SIA has a high degree of repeat sales (as measured through its loyalty programme) and the customers of SIA give positive recommendations to others. This shows that SIA has been able to create a large group of loyal customers, and it appears that a large percentage of these customers would fall in the higher brackets of customer loyalty.

All of these factors show that SIA is one of the best companies in the world. However, this is not the important issue. Rather, we are interested in finding out how SIA achieved this? This question will be examined in detail in the next sections.

Creating a unique customer experience at SIA

The customer experience at SIA is a result of a number of important strategies. These strategies however, work in 'totality' according to Mr Yap Kim Wah, SIA's senior vice president responsible for product and service (Wirtz and Johnston, 2003). It is this unique blend, which must be together that has helped SIA succeed.

Branding

One of the most important things that SIA did after it split from Malaysian Airways was to rebrand itself. SIA introduced the

'Singapore Girl' (the air hostess) as its main branding strategy. SIA wanted to incorporate the feelings of being gentle and courteous in its image. This task was best symbolised by the Singapore Girl. According to Chan, the 'Asian woman does not feel she is demeaning herself by fulfilling the role of the gracious, charming and helpful hostess' (Chan, 2000). SIA claimed to be giving passengers the best service, provided by very hospitable stewardesses. Even their dress was specially designed by the famous fashion designer, Pierre Balmain (Chan, 2000). This was portrayed in its advertisements which showed the Singapore Girl in various settings helping out passengers. SIA wanted to show to its customers that it was delivering a premium quality service and not only was the service good but the service providers were also good at delivering hospitable service.

Superior customer service

Singapore Airlines also focused on providing high quality customer services. This was in partnership, of course, through the Singapore Girl. It is because of their focus on customer services that it has come to be known the world over as a provider of quality services (Frost and Kumar, 2000). SIA has been taking various steps to improve their services. For instance, back in 1972 they became the first airline to give free food and drinks to its customers on board (Chan, 2000). Since then they have taken various steps to improve their services.

SIA has had an organisation wide focus on customer services. All members of their organisation are focused towards providing the best quality of services, both at the front end as well as those working on back end support roles. It has been able to create a corporate culture that is focused on delivering the best services to its customers. This has led to the development of a strategic competitive advantage for SIA, which other airlines regularly set as their benchmarks. The commitment to customer services can be seen in the remarks of the Stephen Lee, the Chairman of SIA in its annual report,

> To our customers, I thank each of you for your ongoing support, and recommit all of us in the Company to striving harder each year to make your experiences with us as exceptional as you expect. (SIA, 2008)

SIA has been able to create this excellence in customer services through understanding its customers, focusing on its employees and through continuous innovations. SIA not only focuses on the onboard services, but looks at the whole customer experience. This starts at the booking process, and includes areas such as checking in, waiting lounges, onboard the plane itself, and other related services such as hotels, etc. SIA has been working on providing excellent customer services in all areas of the customer experience spectrum.

Not just excellent services but creating delight

SIA's goal is to not only provide excellent quality services, but to create customer delight. They try to create extraordinary experiences through outstanding service (Schmitt, 2003). They do this by creating what they call the 'wow effect.' SIA's long term reputation of providing great services means that customers have high expectations from them. SIA understands this, and works with this by going a step further. Mr Yap Kim Wah, the Senior Vice President for product and service says they want to create services where the customer walks away saying, 'Wow! That was something out of the ordinary' (Wirtz and Johnston, 2003). Delight or 'wow' comes from developing newer services, or offering newer products. SIA tries to give the customer what he/she would not expect, and hence be delighted by the experience. Customer research plays a big role in helping to achieve this. The trends that SIA study help them to develop short and long term projections for the next three to five years. From these trends they are able to identify areas for improvement and change, and hence are able to keep a step ahead of both the customers' expectations as well as the competition.

Knowing the customer

In order to build an excellent level of service, SIA makes an effort to understand the customer's needs. They not only listen to their customers but also try to understand their lifestyles. Listening to customers involves looking at both compliments as well as complaints (Wirtz and Johnston, 2003). SIA conducts much research into finding out customer needs and wants. There are a number of ways in which information is collected. Around one in ten passengers are surveyed for feedback. Moreover, SIA uses data from IATA surveys which helps SIA to compare itself with its competition. SIA also uses 'mystery shoppers' both on its own flights as well as competitors to get a feel of the quality of services and customer expectations. This is combined with actively listening to the front line employees. Moreover, SIA also takes verbal comments and complaints very seriously. SIA's SVP for product and service, Mr Wah, believes that customers who take the time out to give verbal comments should be taken seriously as they have most likely experienced a very good or very poor service (Wirtz and Johnston, 2003).

Understanding the lifestyles helps the company to anticipate future changes in needs, and to make changes before the customers even know they want it. For example Mr Sim Kay Wee, the Senior Vice President of the cabin crew of SIA observed from the change in lifestyle a shift towards health awareness and eating healthy. Consequently, SIA changed their food and started to offer healthier options (Wirtz and Johnston, 2003).

Employees and training

Besides focusing on the customer, Singapore Airlines also puts much attention on its employees. For instance it was reported in 1997 that Singapore Airlines was spending about $80 million annually on training its employees (Pfeffer, 1997). Employee training and development plays a key role in SIA's strategy to success and providing the customer with an exceptional experience. 'Training is a necessity, not an option. It is not to be dispensed with when times are bad. Training is for everybody. It embraces everyone from the office assistant and baggage handler to the chief executive officer. We do not stint on training. We'll use the best in software and hardware that money can buy. Because we take a long-term view of training, our investments in staff development are not subject to the vagaries of the economy' said the former CEO of SIA Dr. Cheong (Wirtz and Johnston, 2003; Heracleous et al., 2004).

From recruitment until leaving the company, all employees are given a variety of training throughout their career with the company. At the start, for instance, SIA hostesses are given four months of intensive training, which is considered to be the longest amount of training given by any airline (Heracleous et al., 2004). Some of the training a SIA hostess would receive includes technical, functional as well as interpersonal skills. SIA hostesses are trained on how to deal with customers in the best possible manner. The recruitment itself is a tough process which is highly demanding. Only the best of the best get selected to work at SIA. Choosing the 'right' people help to ensure that they fit into SIA corporate culture of providing excellent customer services. The SIA cabin crew is expected to be below 26 years of age when joining and are given a five year contract. Furthermore the intensive selection process, which proceeds through three different interviews, includes a social gathering (Chan, 2000).

Another example of employee focus is that SIA pilots are included in senior management training classes. This is despite the fact that SIA pilots will seldom move into senior management positions or take part in decision making at that level.

> *As a strong culture organisation, Singapore Airlines thought it was important to make the pilots feel a part of the organisation and to help them understand its operations; therefore, they were included in the class.* (Pfeffer, 1997)

This sort of a culture helps to ensure that all employees are motivated and working towards achieving the goals and objectives of customers.

SIA also continuously gets feedback from its employees. It conducts two 'Organisational Climate Surveys' every year (SIA, 2008). This ongoing process of getting feedback from employees accomplishes two main goals. First, it shows to the employees that the company cares about their opinions and two, it helps to identify areas for improvement. Recent surveys show that SIA is improving on all ten categories surveyed, which means that employee satisfaction is improving (SIA, 2008).

SIA manages and motivates a massive crew of over six thousand by grouping them into teams. Crew are organised into teams of about twelve to thirteen and are scheduled to fly as frequently as possible. Doing this helps to build a sense of community and membership to the organisation. Moreover, crew can help each other out as well as find out each other's strengths and weaknesses. This method allows SIA to have a great level of control over its employees while at the same time the employees feel a part of the greater SIA corporate community. Problems are easily identified, and thus employees can be sent for training accordingly. Moreover, this system helps to ensure a consistency in the high degree of service quality that SIA is famous for. Furthermore, employees work together in teams to work towards providing excellent service at a profit (Heracleous *et al.*, 2004).

Continuous innovation

SIA owes part of its success to innovation. The SIA management knows that in order for them to maintain a strategic competitive advantage they need to 'maintain continuous improvement' (Heracleous *et al.*, 2004). The innovation and improvements at SIA take place at every level and in every department. It is about a total innovation management approach.

Onboard is the place SIA is working hard to continuously improve and stay a step ahead of the competition. A recent example is the new First Class onboard the A380. This is described in detail in the SIA annual report as:

> *Featured exclusively onboard the A380, Singapore Airlines Suites is truly a class that goes beyond first. Designed for the most distinguished of customers, Singapore Airlines Suites offers unrivalled privacy and luxury. Each of the 12 Suites is the customer's very own private cabin in the sky in which to work, relax, dine and sleep. Doors can be closed and window screens lowered for greater privacy. Each cabin includes an 87.5-cm wide plush leather seat, which makes way for a separate mattress, converting into a full-flat, 1.98 meter bed. Customers traveling as a couple can also choose to be seated in two adjoining Suites which offer a double bed after conversion.* (SIA, 2008)

The annual report described first class. However, both the business and the economy classes also benefit from continuous improvement. These innovations will most certainly help SIA to create an unforgettable customer experience, and help to create customer delight.

SIA has been one of the leading airlines when it comes to using technology. It was one of the first to introduce electronic ticketing in 1997. Currently SIA is working on implementing a new e-ticketing system which will allow passengers to fly on multiple airlines on the same ticket. Other uses of technology include the in-flight system, which was one of the first of its kind in the world. The WISEMEN system, introduced in 1997, allows passengers to choose between movies, shows, play games, listen to music and do much more.

SIA looks at every aspect of the customer experience. Hence it has been one of the first airlines to concentrate on ground services. SIA has developed state of the art lounges for its passengers, making waiting for a flight a more enjoyable experience. More over they work with various organisations and departments to make sure that the customer experience from buying a ticket to reaching their destination is a pleasant one (Heracleous *et al.*, 2004).

Furthermore, SIA has been a leader when it comes to investing in aircraft. It has some of the youngest aircraft in the world. This means that SIA continuously gets hold of the 'world's most modern aircraft' (Chan, 2000). Recently, SIA became the world's first airline to purchase the Airbus A380, a plane 'which has won accolades from customers and commentators the world over' (SIA, 2008). The A380 is the largest aircraft in the world today, with a much larger seating capacity. A larger capacity has allowed SIA to introduce innovations such as the new first class cabins. Although buying new aircraft is a costly matter, over the long run this translates into benefits. The A380, for instance, is also a 'greener' aircraft, burning about 20% less fuel than the Boeing 747 (SIA, 2008). SIA invests in newer aircraft that are fuel efficient, faster, safer, have greater capacity and have less downtime. The recent acquisition of the A380 and the Boeing 777-300ER aircraft have made SIA the 'youngest, most modern and fuel-efficient aircraft [fleet] in the world' (SIA, 2008).

Conclusion

SIA is an amazing company. It is one of the best airlines in the world and has been consistently at the top of the industry. SIA is unique, because of its ability to provide consistently high levels of delightful customer experience. Research indicates that SIA is able to create these wonderful experiences through the use of a good branding strategy, listening to and focusing on the customer and employees and through continuous innovations in all areas.

Case study 5: Walt Disney Company

Introduction

The Walt Disney Company (Disney) is world renowned for a number of its popular products, which range from Mickey Mouse to the Disney theme parks. The name brings to mind good memories for both the young and old alike (Anonymous, 2007). It is one of the most creative companies in the world today. Ranked by Fortune as the leader in its industry and the most admired company, the Walt Disney Company is a huge organisation. The company owns film studios, production houses, theme parks, hotels, cruise ships and much more. Disney World in the US operates just about as many buses as the city where it is located (Anonymous, 1998). It can be considered to be a firm in a number of different industries, however the company believes that it is there for one reason, which is to make people happy (Collins and Porras, 2005).

Walt Elias Disney started off in the 1920s by creating animated cartoons. Since then the company has achieved phenomenal growth and success. Disney is now a household name around the globe. Walt Disney, who guided the company through the first few decades of the company, led it with passion and motivation. He had a quest for newer things and going after challenges, which has been embedded in the corporate culture of the company (Hightower, 1993). The Walt Disney Company has achieved much success since the 1920s, and there are several key reasons for this success. In the following paragraphs these success factors will be discussed in detail.

Leadership

One of the key factors for the success of the firm has been its leadership. Walt Disney led the company in the beginning and set up firm foundations for the company. As a visionary, he did a number of things which included hiring the best people (Hightower, 1993), that had a drive for challenges and a motivation to succeed. Walt himself said that one of the most important things he did was to coordinate the talent of all employees and to direct that talent towards a common goal (Chan, 2000). As an entrepreneur, Walt was careful not to create an organisation that was centred on him, rather one that would last far longer than he. He created a company that was focused on the power of the imagination, an institution that delivered magic (Collins and Porras, 2005).

The latest of the company's CEO's, Bob Iger is a strong leader and is following vision bringing joy and laughter to people around the world. Some of the things that make him a good leader include ruling with consensus and trust in his employees (Anonymous, 2007). Iger has been able to keep the company working towards the goal of creating joy. As a leader he keeps his office accessible to employees, and manages by walking around the company. He personally goes to meet and greet employees in all levels and shows his appreciation towards their work (Anonymous, 2007). Through his leadership, he has helped the company to increase its revenues. Hence, the first key factor for the success of the Walt Disney Company is a leadership that is committed to the goals of providing a high quality of service to the stakeholders.

People

The people working at Disney, also called crew members, are another major factor for its success. The company focuses on employees and activities centred around the employee, which helps it in fostering a culture that is customer friendly (Jerome and Kleiner, 1995). The Walt Disney Company looks at every aspect of the employees, from recruitment, to training through continuous motivation. It is important for employees to follow the philosophy of the company. If they believe in the philosophy and implement it in their daily job lives, they are able to provide the highest level of customer experience possible.

Disney is highly committed to training its employees. The company's focus on employee training has earned it an 'international reputation for excellence' (Miller, 1992). Everyone in the company is required to get customer service training, even employees that don't come in direct contact with the customers (Jerome and Kleiner, 1995). For example, at the Walt Disney World in Florida, one of the methods used in training is to get all of its employees to spend a day dressed as a Disney character (Anonymous, 1998). This helps the employees to stay focused on the company's main objective which is to make the customers happy and to ensure they have an enjoyable experience. Another example is the low rate of turnover the company has been able to achieve due to its employee policies and training. Disneyland in California has a turnover of 20%, as compared to the 500-600% industry average, which is very remarkable (Miller, 1992). Disney has been so successful with its training that now other organisations are looking to it to provide training to their employees. Disney University, the training section at Disney provides training to all sorts of organisations from across the globe.

In addition to selection and training the company also works on managing its people in the best possible manner. They try to facilitate employees so that they can then in turn provide the best possible experience to customers. The company places a great degree of trust in its employees. Moreover they are also given a high degree of autonomy in doing their jobs. Staff are empowered to take decisions. At a higher level, management can take important decisions without getting the top management involved. The company also works in teams at every level (Hightower, 1993). These factors have given employees at every level an incentive to work towards perfection. For example, Pixar, the film studio that produces animated movies, makes independent decisions on the type of projects they will work on, as well as how long they will take on delivering those projects. Pixar is currently working on only one project a year; however they are producing one hit movie after another.

Creativity

Just as innovation is important to companies producing physical products, creativity is important to Disney. For Disney, it is at the heart of its business, and everything and everyone is focused on being creative (Hightower, 1993). It was by being creative that Disney took its start. If Walt Elias Disney had not been creative and come up with ideas such as Mickey Mouse, the company would never have flourished. The company believes in the philosophy of 'demand the impossible' (Hightower, 1993). Walt's method of working was to challenge his staff, and to get them to think in new ways. To this day the company follows this strategy and thrives on creativity. As a result of a focus on creativity the company has not only been able to produce very popular cartoon characters, but also had technological innovations such as synchronised sound and colour in movies.

Creativity can be found at and is encouraged at all levels of the organisation. For instance, a parking lot attendant found a new way of helping customers find lost cars. Creativity is applied at every level and at every step of the customer's experience with the company, for instance, at a senior level, top management has held brainstorming sessions. Creativity has been one of the main reasons for the success of a company which has a very challenging job. Disney wants to make people happy, which can be one of the hardest things to do in the world. Moreover, the company has a good reputation, hence people interacting with the organisation's products and services have high expectations. The company gets around this by being creative, and thus pleasantly surprising its customers.

Focus on customer

Disney places a great deal of emphasis on the quality of the experience it provides to its customers. Many of the products and services of the organisation are focused towards younger audiences. Kids are said to be the harshest critics. If they don't like something they will simply not watch it. Hence the organisation focuses on its customers, and works to provide only the best quality of experiences.

Disney focuses on its customer by giving them what they want. From films to theme parks, the company tries to bring to life its customers' wildest dreams. The focus on the customer is at every step of the experience spectrum. For example, in the theme parks an average customer comes in contact with 75 employees during a day. For Disney, it is about making sure that each of those 75 encounters is great. A customer having one bad experience and 74 positive ones would remember the bad one (Jerome and Kleiner, 1995). Therefore the company makes sure that each and every encounter is a memorable one. For example, to achieve this, not only are front line employees given training in customer services, but even those employees that are never in contact with customers (Jerome and Kleiner, 1995). Adopting this philosophy has enabled the company to build a reputation for 'quality, courtesy, cleanliness and escapism' at its theme parks (Miller, 1992). The company wants to create 'lasting memories and bright smiles' (WaltDisney, 2008). Focusing on the customer allows the company to stay ahead of the competition and create loyalty.

Conclusion

As discussed earlier, Disney is a very successful company. Each year they move to new heights. In 2008 their revenue hit an all time record of $37.8 billion (WaltDisney, 2008). Their focus on the customer and providing the customer with the most enjoyable experience has created a high level of loyalty among its customers. It is estimated that about seventy percent of customers to the theme parks are repeat customers (Anonymous, 1998). Moreover the company has produced a number of hits including Beauty and the Beast, which was the first animated film to be nominated for the Academy Award's coveted best film category. The company has been able to achieve its success due to its strategies of creativity, strong leadership, through its people and a focus on the customer.

Table 8.5 Walt Disney revenues from 2004 to 2008

	2004	2005	2006	2007	2008
Revenue (in millions $)					
Media networks	11,299	12,722	14,186	15,104	16,116
Parks and resorts	7,750	9,023	9,925	10,626	11,504
Studio entertainment	8,713	7,587	7,529	7,491	7,348
Consumer products	2,414	2,042	2,107	2,269	2,875
	30,176	31,374	33,747	35,510	37,843

Source: Walt Disney (2008)

Case study 6: Zara

Introduction

Zara is the largest clothing retailer in the world (Anonymous, 2008). Zara is owned by Inditex, a Spanish firm and specialises in 'fast fashion.' Zara has been a pioneer within the retail sector. The company introduced cheap chic fashion and as a result created a competitive advantage that is difficult to mimic (Capell, 2008). The company is considered to be a leader in the fast fashion industry, an industry that produces high quality clothes at reasonable prices, and ships them to the market quickly (Bruce and Daly, 2006). The company has achieved much success through following two important strategies, first it has an amazing supply chain network, and second the company focuses on the customers' needs and wants. In doing so the company has been able to leave the competition far behind. We will examine some of the company's success and its magic formula for growth in the following paragraphs.

Zara's remarkable achievements

In a fast paced fashion world, Zara was quick to realise the importance of getting new fashions out quickly to the market, and hence pioneered the fast fashion concept (Park and Sternquist, 2008). This strategy has benefited Zara immensely. It has experienced rapid growth, for example, from 2001 to 2003 alone it expanded into 30 countries and added 250 stores (Park and Sternquist, 2008). The company is currently worth $13.8 billion and is continuing to expand at a fast pace (Capell, 2008). Recently the company overtook Gap as the leading clothing retailer in the world. Not only is the company expanding rapidly, but is also doing so profitably. Although no data is available for Zara itself, the parent company Inditex recently announced profits. The company had net profits of Euro 843 million, with sales of Euro 7.35 billion (Mulligan, 2008). This is certainly a remarkable feat considering the world's economy was in a slump and many retailers suffered heavily. However, the company is not resting on its laurels just as yet. It has major plans for further expansions. It plans to open stores in Russia, South Korea and China (Mulligan, 2008). It has plans for around 225 new stores this year which will create about 7,000 jobs (Rohwedder, 2009). Furthermore, with a loyal customer base, the company is not only able to charge slightly higher prices than competitors but also guarantee continued sales in its existing markets.

Focusing on the customer

The fashion industry is an interesting one and like no other. For customers the newest fashion is perhaps the most important factor. Other factors include availability and price. Zara has realised this and has been able to successfully design its business to suit its customers' needs. While most retailers start with the designer, Zara starts with the customer. Customers are monitored for what they are buying (Capell, 2008). This information is collected through a number of different means, including electronically and through feedback from managers and employees in the stores. Zara has learned that its customers demand well designed clothes that are up to date, of high quality and at low prices (Walters, 2008). As compared to the elite fashion houses, fast fashion costs approximately 90% less.

Since fashion changes quickly, customers demand the latest trends. Zara has hence created a system of releasing new products to the market within 1 to 2 weeks. Moreover the stock in its stores can be replenished all across the globe in 24 to 48 hours (Walters, 2008). This makes the customer happy as they are able to get the latest fashions. The company has also set up a system for ensuring that quality is at the highest level. The quality starts at production, where the factories are given clear guidelines on the level of quality required. This is backed-up by a double quality check, which helps the company to get high quality products out to the markets (Walters, 2008).

Zara's focus is on ensuring that the customers get a good experience. The experience starts at the store, where new designs and styles are readily available. The experience continues with the use of the product, as a high quality and new fashion product makes customers feel good about themselves. The experience continues with a continuous flow of fresh inventory and new designs to the stores.

Supply chain management

Zara has been able to provide its customers with the latest fashions, quickly, and at reasonable prices due to its amazing supply chain network. It has been argued that its supply chain network is 'so unique that no competitor has been able to completely imitate its superior production and delivery process' (Park and Sternquist, 2008). Inditex, Zara's parent company, has spent over thirty years 'perfecting its strategy' and 'along the way it has broken almost every rule in retailing' (Capell, 2008).

Zara has developed a unique supply chain network which has helped it in creating rapid stock turnarounds (Bruce and Daly, 2006). It has done this by keeping strict controls over all aspects of its supply chain. While other retailers produce much of their products in cheaper Asian markets, Zara keeps most of the production close to home. Much of its production is based in Spain, Portugal and Morocco. Although the wages are higher in these countries the company is able to save money on transportation costs. Furthermore, having production close to the demand centres allows the company to quickly respond to market changes.

The company also uses a just-in-time system, which was developed with the world's leading automobile manufacturer, Toyota. The company can get its stocks replenished in Europe within a remarkable 24 hours. It transports its stock to the Americas and Asia via air transport. Although, it is a more costly system as compared to sea transport, the company is able to get its goods out within 48 hours. For customers who have access to the latest fashion, paying a little extra is not a problem. Hence the company is able to not only recover these additional costs but also to make a profit.

The company's production is split into two different areas. For certain demand the company produces its merchandise well in advance of the seasonal sales. This is usually produced in larger quantities. For the uncertain demand, fashion that is likely to change quickly, the company produces goods in small quantities (Kaipia and Holmstrom, 2007). Producing goods in small quantities allows the company to do a number of things. First it is able to transport it quickly to the marketplace. Kaipia and Holmstorm explain the benefits of this strategy:

> During the season, speed, flexibility and responsiveness are required and used. To be able to respond to end-customer demand and taste changes, flexibility is left in each phase of Zara's supply chain. What is remarkable about this approach is the fact that the responsiveness is required for only half of the volume (Kaipia and Holmstrom, 2007).

Second, the company does not need to worry about overstocking its stores and later on selling it through massive reductions. The small batches are of new designs which are sold quickly. The limited range of clothing makes it exclusive, making it more attractive to its customers (Bruce and Daly, 2006). Moreover this also makes the customers want to return frequently to look at more new designs.

Most of Zara's production is outsourced to external workshops located near the Inditex factories (Walters, 2008). The fabrics are pre-cut into pieces, which make them easy to transport and easy to stitch. The company deals with 350 workshops that employ over eleven thousand workers. The company keeps a close eye on the workshops and works with them to ensure that the products are produced at the highest standard.

Conclusion

Zara is a great company that focuses on delivering great customer experiences. The company gives its customers great experiences by giving them the newest design products, frequently and at low prices. Zara also focuses on the quality of its products to make sure that they are up to the standards of its customers. Within a short span of time the company has become the global leader in clothing retailing, outpacing rival Gap just a short while ago. Zara has been able to achieve this success due to two main reasons. First is its focus on the customer. By understanding exactly what the customer wants Zara is able to stay ahead of the competition. Second, to deliver goods to the customer, the company had developed an amazing supply chain network which has been difficult to follow by others. Zara is continuing to grow at a fast pace and will probably be a market leader and an impressive example of customer experience management for the foreseeable future.

Developing exceptional customer experiences: the art of wooing

Companies that are successfully able to implement great CEM strategies reap many financial rewards. Developing an effective customer experience requires a number of steps that a company must take. If followed accurately, these factors will help companies to develop great systems that will produce exceptional experiences for their customer.

There are two levels of systems that companies need to consider. The inner circle consists of the core factors that companies will need to implement. Most of the time the customer will not see these; however there are factors that the customer will have interactions with (such as employees).

Leadership

First the company needs to have a strong leadership. Strong leadership has helped to build strong companies. SIA, Harley-Davidson, Apple, IKEA, and Walt Disney are all examples of companies that have benefited from great leaders. Some of these companies went into a decline and then were revived by the leadership. For example Apple benefited from the return of Steve Jobs. Leadership helps to set a corporate culture focused on the customer. Good leaders can create an environment where employees feel proud to work, are highly motivated and the whole organisation works to excel in its objectives.

Employees

The employees of an organisation are also a key factor in companies that want to create great experiences for their customers. For services organisations it is imperative as their employees have direct contact with customers. Often it is the employee who is the only link between a customer and the company in a service based organisation. For all firms, if the employees are motivated they will produce high quality of products and services. Employees will make sure that they can satisfy the customer's needs. A focus on the employee starts with selection. Walt Disney and SIA are examples of companies that spend considerable time finding the best possible employees for its organisation. Apple makes sure they get the best talent, so that they can produce new products.

Next, employee training is a crucial step. Successful companies make sure that their employees are trained to adapt to the corporate culture of the firm. Moreover these firms continuously train their employees. Continuous training allows the companies not only to retain their best employees but also helps them to quickly fix problems or implement new strategies. Finally, great companies trust their employees and create an environment which is friendly for them to work in. Companies have created teams, given more responsibility and have empowered their employees.

Innovation

Great companies stay great by focusing on innovation. Companies are working hard to continuously innovate in every aspect of the organisation. Without innovations Apple would never have been able to stay ahead of the competition and introduce advanced products. Zara uses innovation to continuously introduce new fashions into the marketplace. Disney uses creativity to ensure that the company can satisfy the harshest critics – kids. Companies not only innovate in the product/service side of the business, but in other aspects such as supply chain, processes, marketing etc.

Supply chain management

Supply chain management is another important area where companies can work on developing exceptional experiences for customers. SCM is not limited to retailers and manufacturers. Service oriented firms such as SIA have redesigned their ticket booking system, making it easier to book tickets. IKEA has used SCM to its advantage to offer customers a great shopping experience, high quality products at low prices. Zara uses SCM effectively to ensure its customers get the latest fashion clothing. Apple has innovated by controlling nearly the whole supply chain, making sure that the customer gets the best service and advice, from sales through to after-sales.

Quality focus

Furthermore, all great companies focus on quality. It does not matter whether these companies are selling exclusive and high class products such as Harley-Davidson motorbikes, or low priced clothing (Zara). These companies all focus on the quality of their products. The experience for customers starts after purchasing a product. If the quality is no good, the after sales experience will turn sour. Hence, these companies implement various quality strategies to ensure that the customer's quality expectations are met.

These inner-circle factors can be considered internal factors. Usually companies take care of these factors within the organisation and often do not have interaction with the outside world. The outer circle consists of factors that have a greater level of interaction with customers. These are usually the factors that the customer can see and experience firsthand.

Customer focus

Customer focus is crucial to the successful implementation of a great CEM strategy. If companies are not aware of their customer's needs, then how can they fulfil them? Companies need to first obtain an understanding of what their customers require. For instance, Zara has been able to succeed by churning out new fashion quickly, because that's what their customers want. Apple customers want help in buying products, and hence Apple trains its sales people. Knowing what the customer wants is the first key. A company must also continue to receive that feedback from customers on an ongoing basis. Harley Davidson gets its feedback by interacting with customers on a face to face basis. Singapore Airlines gets its feedback through customer surveys. Continuously monitoring customer feedback allows companies to constantly update its services/products, offer new ones and remove non popular ones. Furthermore, companies need to keep the customer in mind when designing all services. The customer experience needs to be at the forefront of everything in the business. For instance, Singapore Airlines and Walt Disney provide customer oriented training to all members of staff; even if they do have direct contact with customers. If the whole organisation is customer focused, everyone in the company will work towards satisfying the customer and developing exceptional experiences.

Community building

Community building is another important factor which helps organisations in creating a continuous positive customer experience. Harley Davidson and Apple are two good examples of companies that encourage and support the development of communities. Harley Davidson is the best known with its Harley Owners Group. The HOG provides support and facilitates interactions between owners of the bikes. Communities increase a sense of belongingness, and give customers a reason to use the product or service. Communities also help improve the experience of customers. Communities are now taking a different shape by going virtual. Many companies are meeting and interacting with customers online through specially created websites or through community portals such as Facebook, Twitter and MySpace.

Customer delight

Organisations need to think of not just satisfying the customer but going beyond that to creating customer delight. Disney goes that extra mile by making sure their customers are happy and enjoy their products and services. Singapore Airlines works hard to create a 'wow' effect for its customers by surprising them with new things. Apple works on exceeding customer expectations by creating ever new products that are not only friendly but also attractive. Zara creates delight by churning out new fashion before anyone else. Harley Davidson uses its HOG to create a delight factor for its customers. Building customer loyalty at the highest level, or emotional attachment, requires that companies go beyond the ordinary. To create an emotional attachment to the brand companies need to delight their customers. If the whole organisation is focused towards this goal, they will be better able to manage delight.

Brand focus

Finally, organisations need to focus on their brand and need to convey the message of their brand to their customers. IKEA promotes the IKEA way of life. IKEA has worked hard to show a positive image of its brand and has succeeded, even in countries where its products were not initially considered attractive. Apple has created a turnaround of its company by showing that its products are not for geeks but for 'cool' and 'hip' people. Singapore Airlines has used the Singapore Girl to hammer its point about Asian hospitality. It may get confusing for customers to distinguish between brands due to a high level of competition. Effective branding allows customers to learn about a company's products and services, and it helps to build a positive image of the brand. This positive image is a part of the customer's experience. Customers who feel good about using a particular brand are more likely to use it. Figure 8.4, shows a diagrammatic representation of these factors.

Figure 8.4 Developing exceptional customer experiences

Conclusion

Both the inner as well as the outer circle factors are crucial for developing positive customer experiences for customers. Organisations will find that they need to bring their own variations and modifications to these. There is no magic formula that will work for every company exactly as it has for some of these successful organisations. Just look at Zara, they got help from Toyota in developing their supply chain, however they modified it and adapted it according to their own organisation. If companies can adopt these strategies and can implement them effectively then they will create a continuous cycle which will persist in providing great experiences for customers, resulting in increased customer loyalty and leading to long term success.

References

Anonymous (1998) Can your college compete with the magic of Disney? *Education & Training*, 40(4), 151-152.

Anonymous (2006) Globalization's winners and losers: Lessons from retailers J.C. Penny, Home Depot, Carrefour, Ikea and others. *Strategic Direction*, 22(9), 27-29.

Anonymous (2007) From beast to beauty: The culture makeover at Walt Disney. *Strategic Direction*, 23(9), 5-8.

Anonymous (2008) Fashion Forward. *Foreign Policy*, 169(Nov/Dec), 28.

Anonymous (2009a) Creativity - Case study: Ikea Family Live. *Marketing Week*. London.

Anonymous (2009b) IKEA thinks global acts local. *Modern Materials Handling*, 64(1), 30.

APPLE (2008) *Apple Inc. Annual Report 2008*, Cupertino, CA, Apple Inc.

APPLE (2009) Biohazard Suit. Apple Inc., [Online] Available at http://www.apple.com/getamac/ads/ [Accessed on May 1, 2009].

Arnold, S. J. (2002) Lessons learned from the world's best retailers. *International Journal of Retail & Distribution Management*, 30(11), 562-570.

Barsch, P. A. (2005) The Demise of the 4 Ps Has Been Greatly Exaggerated. MarketingProfs http://www.marketingprofs.com/5/barsch3.asp?part=2 [Accessed on April 2, 2009]

Berry, L. (1995) Relationship Marketing of Services-Growing Interest, Emerging Perspectives. *Journal of Academy of Marketing Science*, 23(4), 236-245.

Bruce, M. & Daly, L. (2006) Buyer behavior for fast fashion. *Journal of Fashion Marketing and Management*, 10(3), 329-344.

Capell, K. (2008) Zara Thrives By Breaking All The Rules. *Business Week*. New York.

Chan, D. (2000) The story of Singapore Airlines and the Singapore Girl. *Journal of Management Development*, 19(6), 456-472.

Collins, J. C. & Porras, J. I. (2005) *Built to Last: Successful Habits of Visionary Companies*, Boston, MA, Random House Business Books.

D'Souza, S. (2004) Can Harley's Secret Weapon Revitalize Your Marketing? *MarketingProfs* http://www.marketingprofs.com/4/dsouza29.asp, [Accessed on April 20, 2009]

Davis, S. (2006) You're Only as Strong as Your Weakest Brand Touchpoint. MarketingProfs http://www.marketingprofs.com/6/davis1.asp, [Accessed on April 9, 2009]

Edvardsson, B., Enquist, B. & Hay, M. (2006) Values-based service brands: narratives from IKEA. *Managing Service Quality,* 16(3), pp. 230-246.

Elmer-Dewitt, P. (2009a) Apple: Only good. Dell: Poor and very poor. Fortune, http://apple20.blogs.fortune.cnn.com/2009/04/18/apple-only-good-dell-poor-and-very-poor/ [Accessed on April 29, 2009]

Elmer-Dewitt, P. (2009b) How the App Store got to 1 billion downloads. Fortune, http://apple20.blogs.fortune.cnn.com/2009/04/23/how-the-app-store-got-to-1-billion-downloads/, [Accessed on March 29, 2009]

Fortune (2009a) World's Most Admired Companies. Fortune, http://money.cnn.com/magazines/fortune/mostadmired/2009/full_list/, [Accessed on March 25, 2009]

Fortune (2009b) World's Most Admired Companies: Apple. Fortune, http://money.cnn.com/magazines/fortune/mostadmired/2009/snapshots/670.html, [Accessed on March 30, 2009]

Frost, F. A. & Kumar, M. (2000) Intservqual - an internal adaptation of the GAP model in a large service organisation. *Journal of Services Marketing,* 14(4), 358-377.

Ghauri, P., Tarnovskaya, V. & Elg, U. (2008) Market driving multinationals and their global sourcing network. *International Marketing Review,* 25(5), 504-519.

Harley-Davidson (2008) *Harley-Davidson 2008 Annual Report,* Milwaukee, WI, Harley-Davidson Inc.

Harley-Davidson (2009) http://www.harley-davidson.com/wcm/Content/Pages/home.jsp?locale=en_US [Accessed on April 4, 2009]

Hartley, R. F. (2004) *Management Mistakes and Successes,* Chichester, John Wiley and Sons, Ltd.

Heracleous, L., Wirtz, J. & Johnston, R. (2004) Cost-effective service excellence: lessons from Singapore Airlines. *Business Strategy Review,* 15(1), 33-38.

Hightower, D. F. (1993) Creativity is your business too! *Planning Review,* 21(5), 54.

Howell, N. (2009) Customer Relationship Management: Stick with who you know. *New Media Age.* London.

Ikea (2008) Ikea Facts & Figures - Ikea Group 2008 http://193.108.42.168/repository/documents/1562.pdf, [Accessed on April 25, 2009]

Ikea (2009) Ikea Facts & Figures - Ikea Group 2009. http://193.108.42.168/repository/documents/1562.pdf, [Accessed on April 25, 2009]

Jerome, L. & Kleiner, B. H. (1995) Employee morale and its impact on service: What companies do to create a positive service experience. *Managing Service Quality,* 5(6), 21-26.

Kaipia, R. & Holmstrom, J. (2007) Selecting the right planning approach for a product. *Supply Chain Management: An International Journal,* 12(1), 3-13.

Kumar, N., Scheer, L. & Kotler, P. (2000) From market driven to market driving. *European Management Journal,* 18(2), 129-142.

Lloyd, M. E. (2009) Ikea Sees Opportunity During Hard Times – As Expansion in U.S. Continues, Swedish Retailer Expects Its Value Furnishings to Appeal to Shoppers Amid Economic Slump. *Wall Street Journal.* New York, NY. Feb 18, 2009

Lowenstein, M. W. (2005) *One customer, divisible: linking customer insight to loyalty and advocacy behavior,* Crawfordsville, IN, Thompson Higher Education.

Mak, B. & Go, F. (1995) Matching global competition: Cooperation among Asian airlines. *Tourism Management,* 16(1), 61-65.

Mattila, A. S. & Wirtz, J. (2008) The role of store environmental stimulation and social factors on impulse purchasing. *Journal of Services Marketing,* 22(7), 562-567.

McAlexander, J. H., Schouten, J. W. & Koenig, H. F. (2002) Building Brand Community. *Journal of Marketing,* 66(1), 38-54.

Miller, B. W. (1992) It's a kind of magic. *Managing Service Quality,* 2(4), 191-193.

Mininni, T. (2006) Brand Loyalty – How to Build It, How to Keep It. MarketingProfs, http://www.marketingprofs.com/6/mininni5.asp, [Accessed on April 7, 2009].

Mulligan, M. (2008) Zara owner to continue store expansion plans. *Financial Times.* London. Dec 12, 2008

Muniz, A. & O'Guinn, T. (2001) Brand Community. *Journal of Consumer Research,* 27(March), 412-432.

Nonaka, I. & Kenney, M. (1991) Towards a new theory of innovation management: A case study comparing Canon, Inc. and Apple Computer, Inc. *Journal of Engineering and Technology Management,* 8, 67-83.

Park, Y. & Sternquist, B. (2008) The global retailer's strategic proposition and choice of entry mode. *International Journal of Retail & Distribution Management,* 36(4), 281-299.

Pfeffer, J. (1997) Pitfalls On The Road To Measurement: The Dangerous Liaison Of Human Resources With The Ideas Of Accounting And Finance. *Human Resource Management,* 36(3), pp. 357-365.

Pugliese, M. J. & Cagan, J. (2002) Capturing a rebel: modeling the Harley-Davidson brand through a motorcycle shape grammar. *Research in Engineering Design,* 13, 139-156.

Rodger, M. (2008) Harley-Davidson's branding gets my motor running. *Scotland on Sunday.* Edinburgh, Johnston Press Digital Publishing 31 August 2008

Rohwedder, C. (2009) Earnings: H&M Is Forging Ahead, Despite Retail's Misery. *Wall Street Journal (Eastern Edition).* New York, N.Y. Jan 30, 2009

Schefczyk, M. (1993) Operational performance of airlines: an extension of traditional measurement paradigms. *Strategic Management Journal,* 14(4), 301-317.

Schmitt, B. H. (2003) *Customer Experience Management,* Hoboken, N.J., John Wiley & Sons Inc.

SIA (2008) Singapore Airlines Annual Report 2007/08. Singapore, Singapore Airlines.

Strand, R. (2009) Corporate Responsibility in Scandinavian Supply Chains. *Journal of Business Ethics,* 85, 197-185.

Tarnovskaya, V., Elg, U. & Burt, S. (2008) The role of corporate branding in a market driving strategy. *International Journal of Retail & Distribution Management,* 36(11), 941-965.

Walt Disney (2008) The Walt Disney Company Annual Report 2008. Los Angeles, CA, Walt Disney Co.

Walters, D. (2008) Demand chain management + response management + increased customer satisfaction. *International Journal of Physical Distribution & Logistics Management,* 38(9), 699-725.

Wirtz, J. & Johnston, R. (2003) Singapore Airlines: What It Takes To Sustain Service Excellence - A Senior management perspective. *Managing Service Quality,* 13(1), pp. 10-19.

World Airline Awards (2009) Airline of the Year 2009. Skytrax World Airline Awards, http://www.worldairlineawards.com/ [Accessed on April 11, 2009].

Chapter 9

How to measure emotional fulfilment of online customer experiences

Introduction

Following the early contributions of consumer behaviour scientists and marketers in the 1980s, which introduced the experiential perspective of consumer behaviour (Hirschman and Holbrook, 1982; Hirschman, 1984), the concept of customer experience has been increasingly perceived in the literature as a fundamental factor in today's economy (Pine and Gilmore, 1999), a central element of consumers' lives (Carù and Cova, 2003a) that is paramount for understanding their needs and expectations (Holbrook, 2000).

The importance of paying attention to the measurement of customer experience has been increasingly picked up by researchers and practitioners in recent years (Novak *et al.*, 2000; Chang, 2006; Minocha *et al.*, 2006).

Study of the contributions of the different bodies of knowledge indicates that existing quality management literature – except perhaps for a few studies (Fundin and Nilsson, 2003; Zairi, 2007) – seems to overlook customers' hedonic needs and the whole experiential perspective in the online environment. Existing perceived quality, satisfaction and loyalty models seem to suffer from some significant conceptual and methodological limitations that need to be reconsidered to address the emerging and ever-growing online environment.

This study attempts to bridge the gap between the marketing and quality management studies by proposing a model for the integrated measurement of online experience.

Underpinning theories for the measurement of online customer experience

Two bodies of literature were reviewed to propose a model for integrated online customer experience; the customer experience literature in the marketing discipline, and measurement studies in the quality management literature, particularly for the online environment.

Online customer experience in the consumer behaviour and marketing literature

Early consumer behaviour literature emphasised that customer motivations go beyond the utilitarian motives of mere product or service acquisition to include hedonic motives such as feelings, emotions, aesthetics, pleasure and enjoyment that satisfy the experiential needs of customers (Holbrook and Hirschman, 1982; Hirschman, 1984). As a result of that, the experiential behaviour model emerged to advocate the fact that customers are triggered by the need to enjoy the experience by itself, in addition to the mere need to obtain a product, or complete a mission (Hirschman, 1984; Babin *et al.*, 1994; Addis and Holbrook, 2001).

Utilitarian motivation means that customers start from a mission or task which is the need to acquire a product/service, and the acquired benefit depends on whether the mission is completed or not, or whether the mission is completed efficiently and more effortlessly (Holbrook and Hirschman, 1982; Batra and Ahtola; 1991; Babin *et al.*, 1994; Hirschman, 1984).

Hedonic motivation on the other hand refers to consumption behaviours in fulfilment of happiness, fantasy, awakening, sensuality and enjoyment needs (Hirschman, 1984). Values gained from hedonic motivation are experiential and emotional (Babin *et al.*, 1994).

A stream of research advocating the need to emphasise the experiential perspective of consumer behaviour and experience management emerged in the last two decades (Gilmore and Pine, 2002; Addis and Holbrook, 2001; Forlizzi and Ford, 2000; Milligan and Smith, 2002; LaSalle and Britton, 2003; Caru and Cova, 2003b; Prahalad and Ramaswamy, 2004; Smith and Wheeler, 2002; Shaw and Ivens, 2002).

The online environment in contrast to conventional fronts, represents a significant change in customer experience (Parsons, 2002; To et al., 2007). Online customers are not passive recipients of marketing campaigns, they are central players who value experiencing increased control and freedom (Wolfinbarger and Gilly, 2001).

The literature is witnessing an emergence of recent studies advocating that online customers are motivated with more than gathering information and purchasing products. All online customers are about the experience even if at different levels (Mäenpää et al., 2006); they appreciate the online experience for its own sake (Monsuwe et al., 2004); value the fun and play associated with the online experience (Hoffman et al., 2000; Hoffman and Novak, 1996); and look for emotional and experiential satisfaction (Kim and Shim, 2002).

Measurement of the online customer experience in quality management and marketing studies

The significance of measuring and monitoring customer perceived quality and satisfaction in the online environment has been recognised through an increasing number of studies (Santos, 2003; Bauer et al., 2005; Fundin and Nilsson, 2003; Parasuraman et al., 2005; Birgelen et al., 2005). The literature is also in general agreement that loyal customers are a key source of different positive returns for the firm (Oliver, 1999; Reichheld, 1994; Jiang and Rosenbloom, 2005; Hoisington and Naumann, 2003; Berry 1995).

Nevertheless, literature on customer perceived quality, customer satisfaction and loyalty in the online environments is characterised by a number of conceptual and measurement issues that were perhaps inherited from the literature of conventional business settings.

In the area of customer perceived quality, a critical question remains unanswered on whether quality should be measured as a perception or as a disconfirmation. Research that advocates the first approach suggests that perceived quality is equivalent to customer perception or evaluations of the different dimensions of the service provided (e.g. Cronin and Taylor, 1992, 1994). The disconfirmation-based measurement suggest that quality can be measured by identifying the difference between customer perceptions and expectation of services provided (Parasuraman *et al.*, 1985, 1988).

The expectation-based theory seems to be dominating (see for example Gefen and Devine, 2001; Zeithaml *et al.* 2002; Jayawardhena, 2004; Long and McMellon, 2004; Lee and Lin, 2005; Parasuraman *et al.* 2005) followed by the performance-based theory (see for example Santos, 2003; Bauer *et al.*, 2005; Ibrahim *et al.*, 2006). The KANO model has also been used to identify quality attributes in the online environment (see for example Zhang and von Dran, 2002; Fundin and Nilsson, 2003; Bauer *et al.*, 2005; Nilsson-Witel and Fundin, 2005) in addition to the quality function deployment (QFD), the theory of reasoned action and the technology acceptance model (TAM) (Loiacono *et al.* 2002).

As a result, and by adopting the expectation-based theory, the bulk of customer perceived quality literature in online environments continues to conceptualise factors associated with the perceived online quality as dimensions (or components) of the construct rather than as antecedents. Unfortunately, this view does not regard perceived quality as a separate construct, rather its components are summed to obtain an estimate of service quality (Dabholkar, 1996).

Interestingly, the perceived quality construct has been wrongly equated with the customer satisfaction construct (Dabholkar, 1996; Dahlsten, 2003); customer satisfaction and perceived quality were not always seen as distinct constructs (Dabholkar, 1996).

The literature has also witnessed different views on the relationship between both constructs. Brady and Cronin Jr (2001) summarised the three competing theories evident in the literature in addressing the relationship between customer perceived quality and satisfaction, and therefore the relationship between satisfaction and customer behaviour intentions. According to the authors, the first theory advocates that perceived quality is an antecedent of satisfaction where the cognitive quality evaluation leads to a primarily emotive satisfaction assessment, which, in turn, drives behavioural intentions. The theory is based on the fact that the cognitive orientation of customer perceived quality will lead to the generation of satisfaction which due to its emotive nature can affect behavioural intentions. This theory also acknowledges the mediating role of satisfaction on quality. Examples of studies in support of this theory include Dabholkar (1996) and Fynes and Voss (2001).

The second theory hypothesises a non-recursive path between the two constructs; the effect between the two constructs is situation-specific and the temporal sequence would depend on transaction-specific variables, which means that factors such as the nature of the service, the type of customer, etc. may drive the nature of the relationship between the quality and satisfaction link. For instance, cognitively oriented customers are more likely to evaluate the service quality first then develop a satisfaction judgment. While on the other hand, emotionally driven customers are more likely to begin with affective oriented assessments before they judge the service quality, and therefore draw a relationship that makes satisfaction an antecedent to service quality.

The third theory suggests that satisfaction acts as an antecedent of service quality and therefore assumes a direct link between service quality and consumer behavioural intentions, where perceived service quality is seen as a global construct that directly affects behavioural intentions.

In addition to the variant theories that seed the foundation for measurement of the online environment, there also seems to be a great debate in the literature on what should be measured and the best tools that firms should focus on, whether in online or offline environments.

Brady and Cronin Jr (2001) explain that despite agreement on the importance of delivering superior quality and achievement of customer satisfaction, the debate rests on whether the focus should be on quality including all its technical, functional and environmental components or on significance of the more emotional satisfaction assessment.

Cronin and Taylor (1992) and Dabholkar (1996) argue that consumers may not buy products with highest quality, price, convenience, etc., they may look for other factors that affect their satisfaction and therefore influence their purchase intentions.

Customer satisfaction surveys for instance and customer satisfaction indices are considered to have serious flaws as they fail to consistently demonstrate connection to real customer loyalty and growth despite the resources and efforts invested in their design and administration (Reichheld, 1994). Part of the problem with existing customer satisfaction surveys or indices, is that the score is determined by customers' past experience on, for instance, the functionality of the computer or the cleanliness of the hotel room (Applebaum, 2001) and never addresses the emotional connection with customers, which is seen an important indicator of how healthy the relationship between the customer and the firm is (Applebaum, 2001; McEwen and Fleming, 2003) or their intentions to recommend the brand to others (Reichheld, 1994; Applebaum, 2001).

On another hand, existing loyalty measurement may not be sufficient to address today's business needs. Bourdeau (2005) explains that customers may buy again and again from a firm because they are trapped by inertia, indifference or existing switching barriers. While loyal customers may buy less of a product or service due to their reduced need for it, or as their lifestyles change (Reichheld, 1994); retention rates therefore may provide a valuable link to profitability but not to growth. On a similar note, McEwen and Fleming (2003) outline the fact that repeated purchase behaviour is usually motivated, or bribed, by the firm's offer of gifts, discounts and rewards, the authors therefore explains that behavioural measures of loyalty such as repeat purchase are often misleading, and do not differentiate between loyal customers and those with no commitment.

The need for a revolutionary and integrated approach

The significant change in the business environment is due to the introduction of online technologies, accompanied by the existing gap between the marketing and quality management literature in addressing measurement of the online customer experience, which calls for an integrated model for the measurement of online customer experience.

The integrated measurement model should address at least the following four dimensions:

- Hedonic perspective of the customer experience in the online environment in addition to the utilitarian perspective.

- All stages of the online experience.

- The self-driven and firm-driven factors that are important to customers.

- Holistic types of measurement that show relationships between measures.

The following section details each one of these dimensions and considers how they contribute to the development of an integrated model for the measurement of online customer experience.

Figure 9.1 Gap in the literature

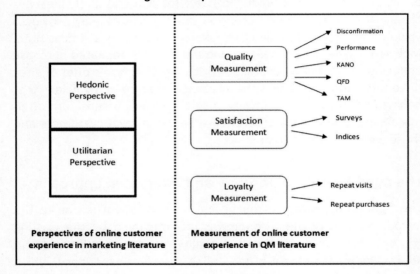

Integration between hedonic versus utilitarian perspective

An increasing amount of recent research suggests that drivers of online buying are not exclusive to functional attributes and as e-customers become more experienced, they increasingly seek hedonic value through online means too (Bridgesa and Florsheimb, 2008; Monsuwe *et al.*, 2004; Hoffman *et al.*, 2000; Hoffman and Novak, 1996).

Nevertheless, studies that address the hedonic view of customer online experience are still few. Examples of which include the studies of Alpar (1999), Loiacono *et al.* (2002) and Kim *et al.* (2004) who emphasise the importance of the entertainment value in impacting customer satisfaction with the website. Other hedonic factors included in perceived quality or satisfaction studies in the online environment included emphasis on factors like the e-scape by Birgelen *et al.* (2005), attractiveness of site design (Evanschitzky, Iyer *et al.,* 2004; Hsu, 2008), sensation (Janda *et al.,* 2002), playfulness (Liu and Arnett, 2000), aesthetics (Madu and Madu, 2002; Yang and Fang, 2004), enjoyment (Zhang and von Dran, 2002) and novelty (Huang, 2003).

According to Gentilea *et al.* (2007):

Its evaluation depends on the comparison between a customer's **expectations** *and the* **stimuli** *coming from the interaction with the company and its offering in correspondence of the different* **moments of contact or touch-points**

Figure 9.2 Perspectives of customer experience

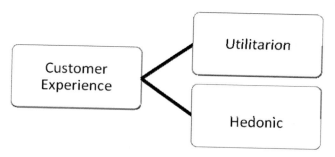

All stages of the online customer experience

A customer's online experience consists of many important stages ranging from information search, evaluation of range of products, decision making, transaction, and post purchase stages related to delivery, returns and customer service (Wolfinbarger and Gilly, 2003).

Studying customer perceived quality of his/her online experience at all stages has been found to be particularly important due to the important role each stage plays in comprising an overall quality experience. Minocha *et al.* (2006) explains that the pre-purchase stage is important as it plays an important role in changing browsing or potential customers into customers who are willing to make a purchase. Additionally, obstacles that may be faced by a customer at the e-purchase and post purchase stages are likely to prevent a negative customer perception.

The nature of the service experience, and the perception of the customer on his/her evaluation of the entire experience is likely to vary depending upon the activities being completed through his/her engagement which ranges from information collection through to customer support to transactions and shopping (Rowley, 2006).

Generally, existing models for the measurement of perceived quality in online environments seem to overlook this perspective, except for the study of Minocha *et al.* (2006).

Integration between self-driven and firm-driven perspectives

The advanced and more sophisticated technologies provided now on the web allow for a differentiated experience that is richer and requires a high level of customer involvement (Lawler and Joseph, 2006). The more 'involving' nature of the online medium causes customers to be in a 'lean forward' mode, as opposed to a 'lean backward' mode during exposure to traditional media messages (Cleary, 1999 cited in Patwardhan, 2004).

Online consumers experience self-service which 'can be conceptualised as the transference of control to the customers' where customers drive their own experience by figuring out how to reach for information they require, how to select and compare between products, and how to complete the product purchase transaction by themselves (Rowley, 2006).

More importantly, today's websites include advanced features that allow customers to drive their own experience through a high level of involvement in personalisation, customised products/services, simulations (Lawler and Joseph, 2006) or support from virtual communities around users (Hagel and Armstrong, 1997), and highly involved customer bases of hobbyists and enthusiasts (Wolfinbarger and Gilly, 2001).

Active participation and customer involvement at various touchpoints in the service or product value chain, adds value to customers not only through the more useful, convenient and state-of-the-art product but also through the competitive experience of co-creating the product with the company so that it suits exactly the customers' needs and expectations (Mascarenhas *et al.*, 2006).

Consequently, and due to the immersive and interactive qualities of online exchanges, recent literature has started to emphasise involvement as an important factor for pleasant or compelling online experience (Hoffman and Novak, 1996; Childers *et al.*, 2001; Patwardhan, 2004; Huang, 2006; Demangeot and Broderick, 2007) but with no clear link to customers' perceived quality, satisfaction or loyalty.

Unfortunately, factors that address customer engagement and self-driven experiences have been generally overlooked from existing models that measure customer perceived quality in the online environment.

Figure 9.3 Types of quality factors in the online experience

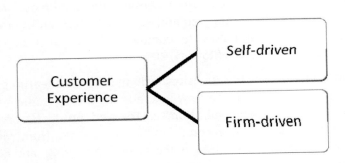

An integrated model for the measurement of online customer experience

Overlapping in the use of perceived quality, satisfaction and loyalty for measurement of online customer experience is evident. Some studies have identified lists of attributes as antecedents or components for the customer satisfaction construct without referring to the relationship with the perceived quality construct (Alpar, 1999; Ho and Wu, 1999; Szymanski and Hise, 2000; van Riel et al., 2001; Evanschitzky et al., 2004; Kim et al., 2006). On a similar note, Srinivasan et al. (2002) also developed a list of attributes as antecedents for the loyalty construct without referring to the relationship with the perceived quality or satisfaction constructs. Given the fact that contributions of such studies do not suggest distinct antecedents for the satisfaction or the loyalty constructs, that are completely different from the perceived quality components or antecedents; such studies and despite their useful contribution add to the confusion in the literature by not supporting the fact that the perceived quality and customer satisfaction constructs (Dabholkar, 1996; Dahlsten, 2003) as well as the loyalty constructs are separate constructs, and therefore do not create a better understanding of the relationship among them.

For instance, some studies propose that perceived quality is an antecedent to delight (Herington and Weaven, 2007) or satisfaction (Jun and Cai, 2001; Rotondaro, 2002; Kim *et al.*, 2004; Ribbink *et al.*, 2004; Birgelen *et al.*, 2005; Bai *et al.* 2008) which mediates the relationship with purchase intentions (Lee and Lin, 2005; Bai *et al.*, 2008) or loyalty (Ribbink *et al.*, 2004; Birgelen *et al.*, 2005). Others assume that there is a direct relationship between perceived quality and purchase intentions (Loiacono *et al.* 2002; Lee and Lin, 2005) or loyalty (Gefen and Devine, 2001) and mediated by value (Zeithaml *et al.*, 2002; Parasuraman *et al.* 2005). Other studies did not address the perceived quality construct at all and proposed the satisfaction as an antecedent to purchase intentions not a mediator (Kim *et al.*, 2006).

Brady and Cronin Jr (2001) argue that the many studies which consider the effect of either customer perceived quality only or satisfaction only on consumer behaviour intentions or loyalty and do not test models that include both of these constructs may lead to biased results, which may overstate the importance of the impact of one or both of these variables on consumers' intentions and hence haze the antecedent role of service quality and satisfaction that should be studied.

A model that identifies attributes and key factors for perceived quality, customer satisfaction and loyalty to measure the online customer experience is necessary; taking into consideration the fact that the three constructs are separate – yet highly interrelated.

Accordingly, the model outlined below was developed to provide a holistic view of the measurement of online customer experience that integrates three types of measurement: performance measurement using the XQual measure, transaction measurement using the satisfaction measure and outcome measurement using the loyalty measure.

Figure 9.4 Integrated model of measurement

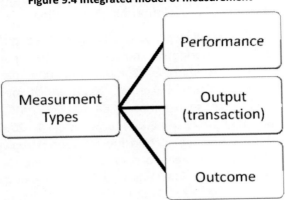

Experience quality: performance measure

Performance-based measurement of perceived quality can be performed by asking customers to evaluate how they feel about the service provider performance in relation to specific features or factors (Cronin and Taylor, 1992).

The performance-based measurement was used as an underpinning foundation for this measure as it is believed to: outperform the disconfirmation approach (Parasuraman *et al.*, 1994); offer more solid theoretical and empirical evidence (Cronin and Taylor, 1992; Cronin and Taylor, 1994); give a more complete understanding of perceived quality (Dabholkar, 1996) in a shorter (Carrillat *et al.*, 2007), simpler and more efficient way (Hudson *et al.*, 2004; Jain and Gupta, 2004); provides better validity of results (Teas, 1993) and is a stronger indicator of service quality than expectations (Page Jr and Spreng, 2002); and proved to be a superior approach compared to the disconfirmation approach (Brady and Cronin Jr 2001).

The performance-based measurement of perceived quality adopts the antecedents conceptualisation model where the judgment of quality follows consumers' evaluation of certain performance dimensions of the service provider (Cronin and Taylor, 1992; Cronin and Taylor, 1994). This approach for quality measurement allows consumers to evaluate different factors related to the service but also form a separate overall evaluation of its quality that is not a straightforward sum of the components.

Analogous to the service quality literature, measurement of experience quality can be performed using the customers' evaluation of the performance of certain factors related to their experience with the website. Performance measurement of online customer experience refers to customers' perceptions of the performance of certain factors that are recognised as antecedents of the experience quality. The term XQual will be used to indicate the measurement of customers' perceived quality of their online experience. The XQual measure integrates all types of factors that apply to the special nature of the online environment as outlined below.

Factors for all stages of the online customer experience

Customer experience relates to all touchpoints between a customer and an organisation, across all events of contacts or 'moments of truth' (Schmitt, 1999). Dunn and Davis (2003) gathered possibilities of interaction with a brand around the purchasing process and called it a 'Brand Touch Point Wheel'.

The wheel defines three distinct components of the customer experience:

- Pre-purchase experience, where the customer interacts with the brand through a website, advertising material or collaterals.

- Purchase experience, where customers interact with the brand during product/service assortment, points of display purchase, product performance and parts delivery.

- Post purchase experience, where customers interact with the brand by experiencing product quality during consumption, loyalty programmes, billing and customer service.

These three stages constitute the direct encounter or interaction between the firm and the customer in the online business environment as the following (Minocha *et al.* 2006).

- Pre-purchase stage: during this stage, the customer chooses a website, carries out the necessary searches for a product or service and makes a decision about whether or not to make a purchase. Decisions are influenced by several factors, such as website usability, information provided, price, credibility of the website, delivery mechanisms and refund policies, etc.

- E-purchase: During this stage, the customer selects the product/service and completes the transaction; this usually involves entering personal details, billing and delivery information, and payment details.

- Post-purchase: this stage involves tracking the order and the receipt of the products/services. During this stage, the customer may need to query an order, complain about the state of the delivery, or question his payment handling. He might need to contact the organisation at a touchpoint other than the website.

Figure 9.5 Stage of the online customer experience

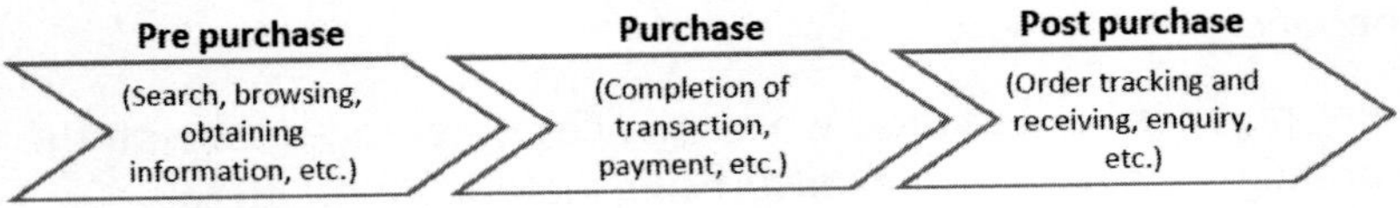

Pre purchase	Purchase	Post purchase
(Search, browsing, obtaining information, etc.)	(Completion of transaction, payment, etc.)	(Order tracking and receiving, enquiry, etc.)

Integrated factors

Online users seem to appreciate escapism (Monsuwe *et al.,* 2004; Birgelen *et al.,* 2005) and entertainment (Alpar, 1999; Loiacono *et al.,* 2002; Kim *et al.,* 2004; Bauer *et al.,* 2005); it is not surprising to predict that playfulness can be a strong factor in creating pleasant customer experience and quality online presence (Chen and Yen, 2004).

Customer experience is believed to consist of functional clues, that affect customer perceptions of the calculative quality, mechanic clues and humanic clues that affect customers' perception of the emotional quality (Berry *et al.* 2002). Those clues are driven by the firm to enrich the customer experience (Berry *et al.* 2006). Where the functional clues relate to the so called technical quality of offerings, reliability and competence of the service, the mechanic component of the experience refers to sensory presentation of the service such as smells, sounds, sights, textures, etc. and the humanic component is generated from the behaviour and appearance of face-to-face service providers – choice of words, tone of voice, level of enthusiasm, body language, neatness, and appropriate dress, etc.

Obviously, the humanic clues do not apply in the context of the online environment (Monsuwe *et al.,* 2004). However, and in compensation of that, the online environment allows for self-driven experiences (Lawler and Joseph, 2006; Rowley, 2006; Wolfinbarger and Gilly, 2001) where the customer is engaged in the creation of the value chain through different means. Involvement is reported to produce hedonic value to the customer as well as utilitarian value, but to a lesser extent (Demangeot and Broderick, 2007).

Accordingly, performance factors can be classified, as in Figure 9.6 below, where functional and sensory clues are driven by the firm, and where customer involvement clues are driven by the customer. Functional clues will impact the utilitarian quality perception, while both the sensory and involvement factors will impact the hedonic quality perception.

Figure 9.6 Integrated perspective of quality factors

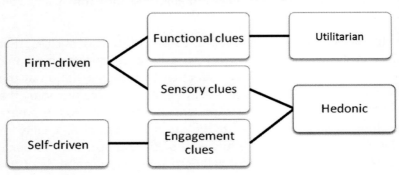

In conclusion, the measure XQual will be used to indicate the measurement of customers' perceived quality of their online experience and will refer to the result of the customer evaluation process regarding how they perceive the performance of the website in relation to certain factors that address both the utilitarian and hedonic, self driven and firm driven aspects of the experience.

Through an intensive scan of the literature (see Appendix), and results of the qualitative analysis of the content of an online blog that was created for the sake of this research, the following seven attributes and 25 critical factors were found to be important in impacting customers' evaluations of perceived quality and therefore will be considered antecedents to the XQual measure. The XQual attributes consist of: ease of use, reliability, functionality, appearance, responsiveness, price competitiveness, customer involvement/engagement.

Analogous to the definition of quality attributes for a service or product which refers to the characteristics or features that must be built in a product/service design in order to fulfil customer needs (Juran, 1977), quality attributes for the online experience refer to the characteristics or features that must be ensured in the design of experiences in order to fulfil customer needs. Critical factors on the other hand refer to the specific aspects that are found to have significant impact on the perception of each attribute. Critical factors act as second level and sub-dimensions for each attribute.

A matrix of the attributes, their corresponding factors and the type of factor perspective they belong to is outlined in Table 9.1.

Ease of use

Ease of use is considered an important factor in evaluating customers' perceived quality (Childers *et al.,* 2001; Jun and Cai, 2001; Loiacono *et al.,* 2002; Santos, 2003; Ribbink *et al.,* 2004; Yang and Fang, 2004; Baia *et al.,* 2008), in affecting customer satisfaction (Alpar, 1999; Ho and Wu, 1999; Baia *et al.* 2008) and in creating more loyal customers (Rajgopal *et al.,* 2000; Loiacono *et al.,* 2002; Ribbink *et al.,* 2004).

Ease of use was originally emphasised in the literature addressing the technology adoption dynamics in workplace contexts. Davis *et al.* (1989) developed a technology acceptance model (TAM) to understand workplace adoption of new technology and found that ease of use and usefulness were the main identified determinants. The model stipulates however, that the first determinant of a person's attitude toward using new technology in the workplace, is perceived 'usefulness' of the technology which refers to the degree to which using the technology will enhance and improve the user's job performance.

Table 9.1 Matrix of the XQual factors

Experience stage	Attribute	Critical factor	Utilitarian Functional	Hedonic Sensory	Hedonic Engagement
Pre Purchase	Ease of use	Ease of understanding	□		
	Ease of use	Ease of navigation	□		
	Reliability	Availability and accessibility	□		
	Reliability	Promptness to enquiries	□		
	Quality of information	Clarity of information	□		
	Quality of information	Accuracy of information	□		
	Quality of information	Extensiveness of information	□		
	Quality of information	Up-to-dateness of information	□		
	Security	Privacy of information	□		
	Appearance	Site aesthetics and attractiveness		□	
	Appearance	Professional appearance		□	
	Appearance	Site novelty		□	
	Customer engagement	Content participation (reviews and feedbacks) and socialize			△

326

During Purchase				
Customer engagement	Synchronous interaction with staff through chat			△
Customer engagement	Demonstration and simulation			△
Customer engagement	Personalisation			△
Customer engagement	Customisability			△
Customer engagement	Explorability			△
Customer engagement	Site playfulness			△
Ease of use	Ease of transaction		□	
Ease of use	Speed of transaction		□	
Reliability	Availability and accessibility		□	
Reliability	Accuracy of transaction		□	
Security	Privacy of information		□	
Security	Financial security		□	
Customer engagement	Personalisation			△
Reliability	Availability and accessibility		□	
Reliability	Accurate delivery of order		□	
Reliability	On time delivery of order		□	

Post Purchase					
Reliability	Ability to solve problems	□			
Reliability	Ease of order return	□			
Reliability	Timely updates of order status	□			
Appearance	Aesthetics of order packaging		□		
Customer engagement	Synchronous interaction with staff			△	
Customer engagement	Content participation (reviews and feedback) and socialising			△	

Korgaonkar and Wolin (1999) employed the TAM to examine the impact of online service quality on portal site usage and found that perceived ease of use influences actual portal site use, attitude toward using the portal site and behavioural intention to reuse the portal site. Additionally, their findings indicated that perceived ease of use is more important than perceived usefulness.

Literature has reported that ease of use or 'usability' in the online contexts means the ability of customers to get an overview of the structure, as well as ease of navigation (Madu and Madu, 2002), it is related to and affected by the site's search functions and organisation, overall design and download speed (Zeithaml et al., 2002) as well as response speed and navigation support (Alpar, 1999).

Similarly, Loiacono et al. (2002) consider that usability includes ease of understanding of the web pages through display of information being easy to read and understand, as well as ease of operating and navigating between pages or intuitive operations.

Szymanski and Hise (2000) outlined in their study that well-designed websites through the use of uncluttered screens, providing easy-to-follow search paths and fast downloading of information not only assures an easy to use website but also provides pleasurable experiences and positively impacts customer satisfaction.

Demangeot and Broderick (2007) explored the sense-making of the site and outlined that the ability of the site: to match prevalent web conventions (web intuitiveness); to provide links that lead to the pages and information the customer expects (links relevance); to respond effectively to the consumers' moves and provides the user with progressively more relevant content (content relevance); to use clear visual and textual material; and to generally behave in a way that is anticipated by the user (clarity of screen) are factors that affect sense making of the website and therefore its ease of understandability and navigation.

Obviously, ease of use is an attribute related to the website design that the company chooses to apply in order to make it easy for customers to understand, navigate through and operate. Therefore ease of use will be defined in this study as the degree to which the site is easy to understand (website understandability), easy to navigate (website navigability) as well as easy to operate or perform required transactions (ease of transactions).

Reliability

Reliability (fulfilment or consistency in performance) is an important factor in impacting customers' perceived quality (Cox and Dale, 2001; Gefen and Devine, 2001; Jun and Cai, 2001; Madu and Madu, 2002; Rotondaro, 2002; Zeithaml *et al.*, 2002; Fundin and Nilsson, 2003; Li *et al.*, 2003; Wolfinbarger and Gilly, 2003; Long and McMellon, 2004; Yang and Fang, 2004; Lee and Lin, 2005; Ibrahim *et al.*, 2006; Rowley, 2006), satisfaction (Rotondaro, 2002; Fundin and Nilsson, 2003; Lee and Lin, 2005; Trabold *et al.*, 2006) and loyalty (Gefen and Devine, 2001).

Reliability or fulfilment is the dominant dimension of service quality in traditional business settings (Zeithaml *et al.*, 2002). Similarly, it has been also reported to be an important determinant of customer e-satisfaction (Wolfinbarger and Gilly, 2003).

According to Madu and Madu (2002), reliability is also concerned with availability of the website, its accessibility, speed and ability to quickly download information, as well as reliability of information and customer transactions.

Santos (2003) explained that reliable websites process their online orders accurately, charge customers correctly, deliver products on time, and deliver products similar to those described in the website and in the same condition.

Yang and Fang (2004) outlined that reliability means keeping the service and promotion promise, accurate order fulfilment, accurate record and quote, accuracy in billing and accurate calculation of commissions.

The attribute of reliability overlaps in many cases with 'fulfilment' and 'performance'. (Janda *et al.*, 2002) defines fulfilment (which overlaps according to the authors with reliability dimensions in the e-SERVQUAL) as the firm's ability to deliver products accurately as well as its willingness to rectify mistakes occurring during the transaction.

Quality and availability of customer support was one of the reliability or fulfilment factors highlighted by Chen and Chang (2003) who used this term to refer to delivery schedule and options, warranty services, return and exchange policies and charges, availability and quality of technical support and availability of post-sales services.

Cox and Dale (2001) define reliability as consistency of performance and dependability. This definition is closely related to the performance attribute by Janda *et al.* (2002) which refers to the 'firm's ability to confirm, process and deliver their online order correctly and speedily', to indicate customer perception of the amount of time required to complete an entire sales transaction as well as its accuracy. Additionally, the authors added that this attribute also means the ability and willingness of the firm to rectify mistakes when occurring with minimal hassle to the customer.

Lim and Dubinsky (2004) outlined, in determining reliability of an online firm, that customers tend to evaluate the firm reputation, the website security and privacy policies.

Although the meaning of the word 'reliability' may seem self-evident, it has been defined in many different ways that apply to widely divergent phenomena. By synthesising the main factors presented in the different definitions of the term, as in the Appendix, reliability in this study means the ability of the website to function whenever needed, to process the transaction accurately and speedily, make on time delivery of the order, have accurate delivery of the order, the ability to rectify mistakes whenever they happen and ease of order return if needed.

Information quality

Information quality with its different aspects has been emphasised in impacting customer perceived quality (Liu and Arnett, 2000; Li *et al.,* 2003; Rowley, 2006), their satisfaction (Alpar, 1999; Szymanski and Hise, 2000; Trocchia and Janda, 2003; Evanschitzky *et al.,* 2004) and loyalty.

The advantage provided by the web in providing information services, makes quality of the information an important factor to evaluate the online experience (Rowley, 2006). Rowley also believes that quality of information enhances the online experience by reducing the uncertainty and risk associated with the web.

Loiacono *et al.* (2002) outlined that customers seek information for one of two reasons, either as an ongoing search on a relatively frequent basis, independent of particular purchase needs, or as a pre-purchase search where information is sought to facilitate a purchase decision. However they added that regardless of the reason for seeking information, certain characteristics are important to assure quality of information. In this study those characteristics are information extensiveness, accuracy, clarity, and up-to-dateness.

Security

The security attribute has been reported as one of the main barriers to customers' use of the online channel (Szymanski and Hise, 2000; Cox and Dale, 2001).

Financial security and non-financial security (privacy) are important factors that impact customers' perceived quality (Jun and Cai, 2001; Janda *et al.,* 2002; Loiacono *et al.,* 2002; Madu and Madu, 2002;

Fundin and Nilsson, 2003; Santos, 2003; Wolfinbarger and Gilly, 2003; Jayawardhena, 2004; Yang and Fang, 2004; Bauer *et al.*, 2005; Birgelen *et al.*, 2005; Rowley, 2006; Hsu, 2008), satisfaction (Szymanski and Hise, 2000; Gefen and Devine, 2001; van Riel *et al.*, 2001; Fundin and Nilsson, 2003; Evanschitzky *et al.*, 2004; Birgelen *et al.*, 2005; Kim *et al.*, 2006; Trabold *et al.*, 2006) and loyalty (Gefen and Devine, 2001; Birgelen *et al.* 2005).

Janda *et al.* (2002) found that security has two forms: financial and non-financial. Financial security relates to the risks associated with conveying financial information online while non-financial security relates primarily to the risks associated with revealing customers' personal information such as his/her contact details.

Appearance

Sensory stimulation coming from colour, sound and scent are believed to be critical dimensions that motivate consumers to shop and enhances the consumption experience in traditional settings (Tauber, 1972) and in the online environment (Parsons, 2002).

Multimedia friendliness produced by voice effects, pictures and visuals creates an appealing appearance of the electronic environment, and hence enhances the overall customer experience by increasing the enjoyment and entertainment of customers (Mäenpää *et al.*, 2006).

Appearance is defined as 'the proper use of colour, graphics, images, and animations, together with the appropriate size of the web pages', it is usually the first factor observed by customers (Santos, 2003). Birgelen *et al.* (2005) refer to website appearance/ attractiveness as e-scape and define its sub-features as the attractive display of information, appealing of layout and colour and attractiveness of design.

Website aesthetics, attractiveness and visual appeal in the online experience is believed to increase perceived service quality, customer satisfaction (Birgelen *et al.*, 2005), joy (Birgelen *et al.*, 2005; Mäenpää *et al.*, 2006) and customer entertainment (Loiacono *et al.*, 2002). Appealing aappearance of the site is believed to attract customers during their first or repeat visits, even if the actual product was less appealing (Santos, 2003).

Synthesis of existing literature and the online blog showed that this attribute can include four factors: appealing website aesthetics, professional appearance of the site and website novelty.

Involvement/engagement

The advanced and more sophisticated technologies provided now on the web allow for differentiated experiences that are richer and require a high level of customer involvement (Lawler and Joseph, 2006). Marketers consider the internet to be the fourth marketing channel on account of its potential to attract, engage, and involve customers (Chen and Yen, 2004).

Conventionally, consumer involvement in the consumption process exceeds the typical personal relevance multiplicity of cognitive responses to include attention, interest and excitement, by emphasising the degree of activation or arousal. Involvement is therefore more emotional and is associated with the right brain. This phenomenon means that consumers are engaged in the activity in pursual of immediate pleasure or gratification (Holbrook and Hirschman, 1982).

Similarly, and due to the immersive and interactive qualities of online exchanges, recent literature started to emphasise involvement as an important factor for pleasant or compelling online experience (Hoffman and Novak, 1996; Childers *et al.*, 2001; Patwardhan, 2004; Huang, 2006; Demangeot and Broderick, 2007) but with no clear link to customers' perceived quality, satisfaction or loyalty. Involvement is reported to produce hedonic value to the customer as well as utilitarian value but to a lesser extent (Demangeot and Broderick, 2007).

Patwardhan (2004) defines involvement in the online setting as a 'psychological state of the participatory experience' that is multidimensional in nature and represents a heightened cognitive (rational, thinking) and emotional engagement during exposure to each online activity.

Demangeot and Broderick (2007) believe that involvement is a state that results from the interaction between the customer and the content of the site. Therefore he classifies involvement into 'cognitive involvement' which relates to the extent to which customers attend, think about, focus or exert mental effort during their engagement with a certain online activity, while 'emotional involvement' refers to the extent to which customers feel emotionally involved or affected during their engagement to drive a certain online activity.

McEwen (2004) outlines that customer involvement through interaction and participation, continuous feedback, co-creation and co-ownership of products have a dual positive impact, both on customers and the firm.

In addition to influencing the quality of the online experience (Cox and Dale, 2001; Gefen and Devine, 2001; Madu and Madu, 2002; Zeithaml, 2002; Jayawardhena, 2004; Kim et al., 2004; Lim and Dubinsky, 2004; Long and McMellon, 2004; Ribbink et al., 2004; Yang and Fang, 2004; Bauer et al., 2005; Parasuraman et al., 2005; Ibrahim et al., 2006), customer satisfaction (Alpar, 1999; Kim et al., 2004; Birgelen et al., 2005) and loyalty (Gefen and Devine, 2001; Srinivasan et al., 2002; Ribbink et al. 2004), interactivity of websites were reported to influence positively joy of the experience (Gefen and Devine, 2001; Birgelen et al., 2005).

Accordingly, customer online engagement includes factors such as interaction with the website through asynchronous or synchronous communication, personalisation, customisation, exploration, demonstration and simulation, as well as website playfulness.

Satisfaction: transaction measurement

The understanding of satisfaction in online environments, including the exploration of dimensions and determinants, is at a relatively nascent stage (Evanschitzky *et al.,* 2004).

Anderson and Srinivasan (2003) defined e-satisfaction as 'the contentment of the customer with respect to his or her prior purchasing experience with a given electronic commerce firm'.

Customer satisfaction matters because it affects customers' behavioural outcomes (Zeithaml *et al.,* 1996); considerable emphasis in the literature has been put on linking perceived service quality, customer satisfaction and behavioural intentions and financial results (Oliver *et al.,* 1997).

Consequently, recent studies have theorised that there may be other levels beyond mere customer satisfaction and adequate quality (referring to the mere evaluation of performance of product attributes) that could impact customers' behavioural consequences (Oliver *et al.,* 1997).

Kano *et al.* (1984) for instance outlined in their 'attractive quality' theory that the fulfilment of unspoken and unexpected features of a product will lead to customers' delightfulness.

Recent thinking has begun to focus on delight as a higher level of satisfaction which may create exceptional outcomes (Oliver *et al.,* 1997) such as unshakable customer loyalty (Arnold *et al.,* 2005).

Although not addressed enough in the literature, satisfaction/ dissatisfaction has a uni-dimensional continuum that can entertain extreme positive states of emotional responses and highly positive satisfaction states such as positive surprise (Oliver *et al.,* 1997).

Based on the above, the feeling of satisfaction will be presented as a continuum that starts with feeling of fulfilment of basic needs, and continues to feeling of enjoyment, to pleasant surprise. Customers experience the upgrade of these feeling to reach a state of delight as the ultimate satisfaction feeling.

Feeling of fulfilment of basic needs

Traditionally, Oliver (1980) defined satisfaction as an affective, emotional reaction growing and resulting out of confirmation or disconfirmation of product expectations. It is a complex emotional response following experience with a product (Oliver, 1981).

Based on the expectancy-disconfirmation theory satisfaction is also defined as 'the summary psychological state resulting when the emotion surrounding disconfirmed expectations is coupled with a consumer's prior feelings about the consumer experience' (Oliver et al., 1997). Satisfaction is a transaction-based measure that is related to a specific exchange with the product/service (Parasuraman et al., 1991, 1994).

The expectancy-disconfirmation model as explained by Oliver (1981) has been recognised for its success in explaining the satisfaction dynamics (Phillips, 1999). In brief the model illustrates that satisfaction happens in a series of well-defined steps that start with the consumer forming certain expectations about the likely performance of a product, i.e. consumers are expected to form pre-consumption expectations before they observe the product attribute performance, later the consumer evaluates the product actual performance and then compares the actual performance to his/her own expectations.

Naturally, confirmation happens if consumer expectations match (are equal) to the actual performance of the product. Positive disconfirmation takes place if product actual performance is greater than customers' expectations, and negative disconfirmation is experienced if expectations were greater than the product actual performance.

According to this model (Oliver 1981), satisfaction happens when customers perceive the performance of the product attribute to be fulfilling of their needs and according to their pre-defined expectations. In this study, this feeling of fulfilment will be considered the first step on the satisfaction continuum.

Therefore, fulfilment of basic needs relates to customers' feelings about the quality of the experience (performance of certain factors) in relation to their pre-determined needs.

Obviously, customer needs in the online environment differ from one customer to another. Wolfinbarger and Gilly (2001) argue that utilitarian shoppers are committed the accomplishment of a goal of product acquisition as effortlessly and efficiently as possible, experiential shoppers focus on the experience as much as they focus on the product acquisition. Some customers expect to exert control on the virtual world through their self-initiated activities (Hoffman *et al.*, 2000).

Enjoyment and pleasant surprise

Disconfirmation of customer expectations against the performance of specific product attributes may not be sufficient enough to address the entire concept of customer satisfaction. Affect or emotions have been found to be an important component in the satisfaction judgment process (all), satisfaction is a function of positive affect and disconfirmation (Oliver *et al.* 1997).

Customers can experience different levels of satisfaction and express different emotional profiles when they evaluate their experience with a product or a service (Westbrook and Black, 1985). Customer delight represents an extreme positive emotional state on the satisfaction continuum (Arnold *et al.*, 2005).

Customer delight is defined as a '...profoundly positive emotional state generally resulting from having one's expectations exceeded to a surprising degree' (Herington and Weaven, 2007).

Herington and Weaven (2007) stipulated that there is general agreement in the literature that delight is considered a second level emotion. Delight is characterised by a blend of lower order emotions like pleasure and surprise (pleasant surprise) (Westbrook and Black, 1985), or a mixture of joy and surprise (Plutchik, 1980), or a function of surprising consumption, positive affect (joy) and arousal (Oliver et al., 1997). Westbrook and Black (1985) labelled customers of the highest levels of joy and positive surprise as 'delighted customers'.

Oliver et al. (1997) stipulate that 'satisfaction may be best understood as an ongoing evaluation of the surprise inherent in a product acquisition and/or consumption experience', they then add that the unexpected high levels of satisfaction or service performance initiate positive affect (joy), which in turn causes the delight sequence.

It takes a large positive discrepancy between the product/service performance and expectations to generate the feeling of surprise (Oliver, 1989). Surprise arises when the performance differs significantly from expectations, or when features of a service, or some combination of them show the capacity to perform exceptionably well (Oliver et al., 1997).

The appreciation of enjoyment and pleasant surprise by customers fits the context of the online environment. Generally, some of the reasons that were found to be substantial in motivating customers to use the online environment were not directly linked to the acquisition of a product or service. Customers use the online environment for an opportunity to be distracted from the problems and stresses of their daily life routine, due to a need for reward after a long hardworking job for instance, where emotional states and moods lead to rationalisation of shopping behaviours or to enjoy bargaining for a lower price or getting a better value which provides a unique form of enjoyment for some shoppers (Parsons, 2002). Laukkanen (2006) believe that the internet has generated additional dimensions for the exchange business; fun and enjoyment seem to enhance the overall customer experience (Koufaris, 2001; Koufaris and Hampton-Sosa, 2002) and encourage customers' repeat visits to the site (Rice, 1997).

Loyalty: outcome measure

Loyalty is defined 'as the enduring psychological attachment of a customer to a particular service provider' (Butcher *et al.*, 2001).

Loyalty is 'a deeply held commitment to rebuy or repatronise a preferred product/service consistently in the future, thereby causing repetitive same-brand or same brandset purchasing, despite situational influences and marketing efforts having the potential to cause switching behavior' (Oliver, 1999). Oliver conceptualised three hierarchical phases corresponding to the loyalty continuum moving from shallow to deep levels of loyalty. The stages are:

- A cognitive preference over other competitive brand attributes resulting from customer belief of brand superiority.

- An affective preference toward the product.

- A greater intention (conation) to purchase the product beyond that for competing products.

This cognitive-affective-conative hierarchal phase of loyalty explains the differing levels of loyalty. Customer loyalty builds up as each of those phases are realised – starting by establishing a belief about a superior brand, then liking it more than any other offering, developing by that a clear affective preference, then intending to buy the brand as opposed to other competitive brands (Oliver *et al.*, 1997).

According to Oliver (1999) customers develop a cognitive preference for a brand or 'cognitive loyalty' based on the service intrinsic attribute performance and shallow information on the brand, or a recent experience with the firm; this kind of loyalty is generally reserved for low involvement and mundane purchases.

The affect loyalty on the other hand is deeper. Through this customers begin to like the brand and form a commitment to the firm. The more intense the level of customer affect, the higher the level of their commitment to the brand. Conative loyalty is obviously the most desirable target for the firm, where customer commitment is deeper causing strong motivations to rebuy, and resulting from repeated positive cognitive and affective experiences with the service.

As a customer's commitment to a service provider evolves and deepens moving from one stage to another, loyalty outcomes become stronger and more prevalent (Bourdeau, 2005). According to this study, customer loyalty can be presented on a continuum where loyalty evolves through time to create emotional attachment; the ultimate state of loyalty.

Identification

Consumers identifying with or relating to brand or a service provider occur when they affiliate themselves with the firm or share certain values with it (Bourdeau, 2005), and take a sense of ownership over the service (Butcher *et al.,* 2001).

Butcher *et al.* (2001) explains that identification is implicit in the intuitive notions of customers expressing themselves through the service provider they choose or visit regularly. This means that service providers will be seen by the loyal customer as an extension of one's self identity, identifying a service provider as 'my service provider' or acknowledging collective representations with the service provider using 'us' and 'we' (Jones and Taylor, 2007).

Advocacy

Butcher *et al.* (2001) outline that loyal customers who become active advocates for the service may provide positive word-of-mouth (Zeithaml *et al.*, 1996; Johnson *et al.*, 2001; Jones and Taylor, 2007), may recommend the service to other prospective customers (Fisk *et al.*, 1990; Reichheld, 1994) or encourage others to use the service or even defend the virtues of the service provider (Kingstrom, 1983).

Reichheld (1994) believes that customer willingness to recommend a product/service to someone else, like a friend or a colleague, is one of the best indicators of loyalty. In this case a customer acts as a reference and puts his/her own reputation on the line. Literature supports the fact that advocacy reflects a higher level of customer commitment to a service provider (Bourdeau, 2005).

High preference or strength of preference

This involves the factors related to customer preference for choosing a brand over its competitors (Jones and Taylor 2007). Some recent studies have argued that deficiencies of existing customer behaviour and decision making process theories come from emphasising the cognitive factors only, and call for more attention to the affect-related factors for better understanding of the human-computer interaction dynamics in the online environment (Hwang and Kim, 2007).

Trust

Trust in online environments, or e-trust is defined 'as the degree of confidence customers have in online exchanges, or in the online exchange channel' (Ribbink *et al.*, 2004).

The role of trust in affecting customer intentions to purchase online has been emphasised by the literature (see for example, Rajgopal *et al.*, 2000; Koufaris and Hampton-Sosa, 2002; Madu and Madu, 2002;

Ribbink *et al.*, 2004; Hsu, 2008). Customers' perceived trust in a website affects their willingness to take the risk of buying something virtually (Hsu, 2008). Lack of trust has been reported as one of the most frequently cited reasons for not making online purchases by customers (Lee *et al.*, 2001). It is therefore reasonable to expect that customers would have to trust a website before becoming or remaining customers (Herington and Weaven, 2007).

The online medium is relatively new and is still a challenge to many customers who do not have enough experience in it (Monsuwe *et al.*, 2004). The online medium is considered to be more risky and uncertain compared to conventional business settings. Online transactions are conducted at a distance with no physical product inspection, or discussions with salespersons (Hsu, 2008) and there is uncertainty about privacy and security of information (Lee *et al.*, 2001) which in turn creates a sense of powerlessness among online shoppers (Monsuwe *et al.*, 2004).

Generally, customers' level of trust, whether interpersonal (between the website and the customer) or institutional (between the customer and the computer system or internet), affects customers' intentions to purchase and re-purchase online (Monsuwe *et al.*, 2004).

Trust was reported to be an outcome of online service quality (Herington and Weaven, 2007) to directly affect loyalty (Ribbink *et al.*, 2004).

According to Madu and Madu (2002), trust is closely associated with security as well as system integrity. Customers' trust of a website affects their willingness to purchase online or even disclose personal information. The authors outlined that online sites can build customers' trust by being highly reliable and dependable in the way they respond to customers' requests, inquiries and complaints.

A study carried out by Koufaris and Hampton-Sosa (2002) showed that a positive customer experience with a website, through perceived ease of use and usefulness will lead to a favourable customer perception of the site in terms of being more trustworthy. They also confirmed that customers' trust in a website is an important determinant of customer intentions to buy and in later loyalty.

Functionality and usability of website design is a very important determinant to earn the trust of customers as, with a lack of salespersons, the website becomes the most important factor to customers.

Leading firms in trust or 'customer confidence' (as called by (Rajgopal *et al.*, 2000) maintain highly reliable websites as well as knowledgeable and accessible customer service and offer quality and security guarantees. The authors mention other factors that contribute to customer confidence and trust, such as the firm's technological abilities and independence, years in business, as well as years in the online business, in addition to memberships in trade organisations.

A high level of security and privacy of a site lowers customer perceptions of risk involved in the transaction (Monsuwe *et al.*, 2004) and therefore has a positive impact on customer trust (Lee *et al.*, 2001).

Conclusion

The chapter proposed a model for the integrated measurement of online customer experience by conceptualising three constructs, namely: online experience quality (or XQual), online customer satisfaction and customer loyalty, as in Figure 9.7.

Online experience quality refers to customers' perceived performance of a certain website in relation to specific factors that address the utilitarian and hedonic aspects of their pre-purchase, purchase and post-purchase experience.

The XQual construct consists of 34 integrated factors that were categorised under six main attributes: ease of use, reliability, quality of information, security, appearance and engagement. The construct integrates self-driven factors and firm driven factors, as well as functional, sensory and engagement factors that satisfy customers' hedonic and utilitarian needs.

Figure 9.7 An integrated model for the measurement of customer online experience

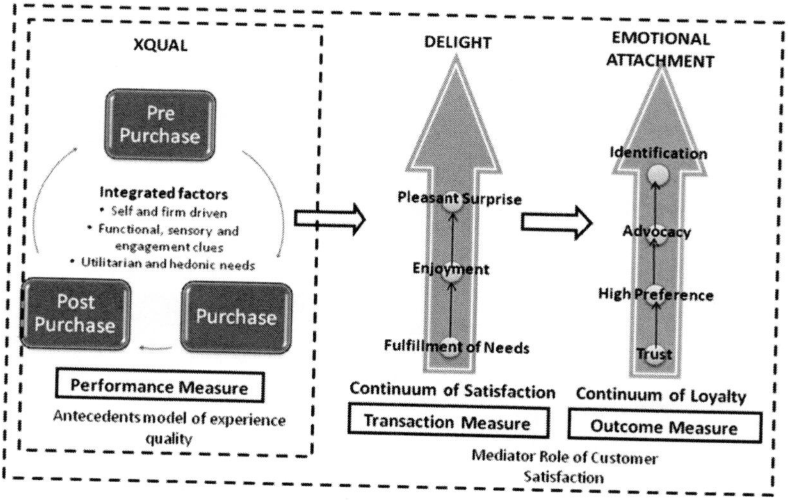

Satisfaction of online customers on the other hand refers to a transaction-based measure that is related to a specific exchange between the customer and the online environment and is based on what customers expect compared to what they receive.

The satisfaction construct consists of three main components: fulfilment of basic needs, enjoyment and pleasant surprise. The construct is built based on a progressive conceptualisation representing the growth of customer satisfaction to reach its ultimate emotional state, i.e. delight.

Loyalty of online customers entails customers' progressive commitment to buy from a certain website. The loyalty construct consists of four progressive components, namely: trust, strength of preference, advocacy and identification. The construct advocates that the higher the level of customer loyalty as progressing from component one to another, the higher the emotional attachment customers generate.

Appendix

1. Ease of use	Navigability	Alpar 1999; Baia *et al.* 2008; Long and McMellon 2004; Birgelen *et al.* 2005; Szymanski and Hise 2000; Tih and Ennis 2006; Yang and Fang 2004; Zhang and von Dran 2002; Loiacono *et al.* 2002; Li *et al.* 2003; Tan *et al.* 2003; Zeithaml 2002; Parasuraman *et al.* 2005; Cox and Dale 2001; Jayawardhena 2004
	Ease of understanding	Baia *et al.* 2008; Evanschitzky *et al.* 2004; Herington and Weaven 2007; Ho and Wu 1999; Loiacono *et al.* 2002; Long and McMellon 2004; Szymanski and Hise 2000; Tih and Ennis 2006; Yang and Fang 2004; Zhang and von Dran 2002; Li *et al.* 2003; Zeithaml 2002; Parasuraman *et al.* 2005
	Ease of transaction	Tih and Ennis 2006; Wolfinbarger and Gilly 2003; Lui and Arnett 2000
	Speedy transaction	Janda *et al.* 2002; Yang and Fang 2004; Tih and Ennis 2006; Ibrahim *et al.* 2006; Trabold *et al.* 2006
2. Reliability	Website functionality	Parasuraman *et al.* 2005; Zeithaml 2002; Bauer *et al.* 2005; Cox and Dale 2001; Jayawardhena 2004; Bauer *et al.* 2005; Yang and Fang 2004; Kim *et al.* 2006; Rotondaro 2002
	Accurate transactions	Tih and Ennis 2006; Yang and Fang 2004; Ibrahim *et al.* 2006
	On-time delivery	Ho and Wu 1999; Janda *et al.* 2002; Wolfinbarger and Gilly 2003; Long and McMellon 2004; Yang and Fang 2004; Parasuraman *et al.* 2005; Rowley 2006; Tih and Ennis 2006; Trabold *et al.* 2006; Hsu 2008
	Accurate delivery	Zeithaml *et al.* 2002; Santos 2003; Wolfinbarger and Gilly 2003
	Ability to solve problems	Trabold *et al.* 2006; Lui and Arnett 2000; Yang and Fang 2004
	Ease of return	Parasuraman *et al.* 2005; Trabold *et al.* 2006

	Responsiveness of customer support	Alpar 1999; Bauer *et al.* 2005; Birgelen *et al.* 2005; Cox and Dale 2001; Gefen and Devine 2001; Ho and Wu 1999; Ibrahim *et al.* 2006; Kim *et al.* 2004; Jun and Cai 2001; Lee and Lin 2005; Li *et al.* 2003; Lim and Dubinsky 2004; Loiacono *et al.* 2002; Long and McMellon 2004; Madu and Madu 2002; Ribbink *et al.* 2004; Rowley 2006; Yang and Fang 2004; Parasuraman *et al.* 2005; Zeithaml 2002; Huang 2003
	Promptness in communication	Santos 2003; Cox and Dale 2001; Long and McMellon 2004; Rotondaro 2002; Yang and Fang 2004
3. Quality of information	Accuracy	Birgelen *et al.* 2005; Kim *et al.* 2006; Jun and Cai 2001; Li *et al.* 2003; Liu and Arnett 2000
	Timeliness	Alpar 1999; Hsu 2008; Kim *et al.* 2006; Jun and Cai 2001; Li *et al.* 2003; Tih and Ennis 2006
	Extensiveness	Bai *et al.* 2008; Bauer *et al.* 2005; Janda *et al.* 2002; Kim *et al.* 2006; Li *et al.* 2003; Liu and Arnett 2000; Long and McMellon 2004; Wolfinbarger and Gilly 2003; Huang 2003
	Clarity	Kim *et al.* 2006; Long and McMellon 2004
4. Security	Financial	Bauer *et al.* 2005; Wolfinbarger and Gilly 2003; Trabold *et al.* 2006; Zhang and von Dran 2002; Parasuraman *et al.* 2005 ; Zeithaml 2002; Janda *et al.* 2002; Kim *et al.* 2006; Liu and Arnett 2000; Szymanski and Hise 2000; Evanschitzky *et al.* 2004; Lim and Dubinsky 2004; van Riel *et al.* 2001
	Non-financial privacy	Wolfinbarger and Gilly 2003; Trabold *et al.* 2006; Zhang and von Dran 2002; Parasuraman *et al.* 2005; Zeithaml 2002; Janda *et al.* 2002; Kim *et al.* 2006; Lim and Dubinsky 2004; van Riel *et al.* 2001
5. Appearance	Website attractiveness and aesthetics	Birgelen *et al.* 2005; Hsu 2008; Loiacono *et al.* 2002; Long and McMellon 2004; Madu and Madu 2002; Yang and Fang 2004; Zhang and von Dran 2002; Jun and Cai 2001; Kim *et al.* 2004
	Professional appearance of	Hsu 2008; Cox and Dale 2001; Kim *et al.* 2004;

	the site	Santos 2003
	Website novelty - innovativeness	Loiacono *et al.* 2002; Huang 2003
6. Involvement	Responsiveness	Alpar 1999; Bauer *et al.* 2005; Birgelen *et al.* 2005; Cox and Dale 2001; Gefen and Devine 2001; Ho and Wu 1999; Ibrahim *et al.* 2006; Kim and Stoel 2004; Jun and Cai 2001; Lee and Lin 2005; Li *et al.* 2003; Lim and Dubinsky 2004; Loiacono *et al.* 2002; Long and McMellon 2004; Madu and Madu 2002; Ribbink *et al.* 2004; Rowley 2006; Yang and Fang 2004; Parasuraman *et al.* 2005; Zeithaml 2002; Huang 2003
	Participation	Alpar 1999; Bauer *et al.* 2005; Huang 2003
	Synchronicity	Alpar 1999; Long and McMellon 2004; Huang 2003
	Personalisation and customisation	Alpar 1999; Bauer *et al.* 2005; Birgelen *et al.* 2005; Ibrahim *et al.* 2006; Jayawardhena 2004; Lim and Dubinsky 2004; Ribbink *et al.* 2004; Loiacono *et al.* 2002; Wolfinbarger and Gilly 2003; Long and McMellon 2004; Huang 2003
	Demonstrability	Janda *et al.* 2002; Huang 2003
	Exploration	Liu and Arnett 2000; Parsons 2002; Mäenpää *et al.* 2006; Demangeot and Broderick 2007
	Playfulness	Liu and Arnett 2000; Chen and Chang 2003; Laukkanen 2006

References

Addis, M. and Holbrook, M. B. (2001) On the Conceptual Link Between Mass Customisation and Experiential Consumption: An Explosion of Subjectivity. *Journal of Consumer Behaviour*, 1(1): 50-66.

Alpar, P. (1999) Satisfaction with a Web Site: Its Measurement, Factors and Correlates. *Electronic Business Engineering*: 4. Internationale Tagung Wirtschaftsinformatik 1999.

Anderson, R. E. and Srinivasan, S. S. (2003) E-satisfaction and e-loyalty: A contingency framework. *Psychology and Marketing*, 20(2): 123-138.

Applebaum, A. (2001) The Constant Customer. *Gallup Management Journal*, 1(2): 1-5.

Arnold, M. J., Reynolds, K. E. and Ponder, N. (2005) Customer delight in a retail context: investigating delightful and terrible shopping experiences. *Journal of Business Research*, 58(8): 1132-1145.

Babin, B., Darden, W. and Griffin, M. (1994) Work and/or Fun: Measuring Hedonic and Utilitarian Shopping Value. *Journal of Consumer Research*, 20(4): 644.

Bai, B., Lawb, R., *et al.* (2008) The impact of website quality on customer satisfaction and purchase intentions: Evidence from Chinese online visitors, *International Journal of Hospitality Management* 27(3): Pages 391-402.

Batra, R. and Ahtola, O. T (1991) Measuring the hedonic and utilitarian sources of customer attitudes. *Marketing Letters*, 12(2): 159-170.

Bauer, H. H., Hammerschmidt, M. and Falk, T. (2005) Measuring the quality of e-banking portals. *International Journal of Bank Marketing* 23(2): 153-175.

Berry, L. L. (1995) Relationship marketing of services - Growing interest, emerging perspectives. *Journal of the Academy of Marketing Science* 23(4): 236-45.

Berry, L.L., Carbone, L. P. & Haeckel, S. H. (2002) Managing the total customer experience. *MIT Sloan Management Review* (Spring) 85-89.

Berry, L.L., Berry, V., Shankar, J. T. Parish, S., Cadwallader and Dotzel, T. (2006) Creating new markets through service innovation, *MIT Sloan Management Review*, 47 (2) 56-63.

Birgelen, V. M., Ghijsen, P. and Semeijn, J. (2005) The added value of web innovation for customer satisfaction. *Managing Service Quality*, 15(6): 539-554.

Bourdeau, B. (2005) *A new examination of service loyalty: identification of the antecedents and outcomes of an additional loyalty framework.* Department of Marketing, Florida State University PhD 240.

Brady, M. K. and Cronin, J. J. Jr (2001) Some New Thoughts on Conceptualizing Perceived Service Quality: A Hierarchical Approach. *Journal of Marketing,* 65(3): 34-49.

Bridgesa, E. and Florsheimb, R. (2008) Hedonic and utilitarian shopping goals: The online experience. *Journal of Business Research* 61(4): 309-314.

Butcher, K., Sparks, B. and O'Callaghan, F. (2001) Evaluative and relational influences on service loyalty. *International Journal of Service Industry Management,* 12(4).

Carrillat, F. A., Jaramillo, F. and Mulki, J. P. (2007) The validity of the SERVQUAL and SERVPERF scales: A meta-analytic view of 17 years of research across five continents. *International Journal of Service Industry Management,* 18(5): 472-490.

Caru, A. and Cova, B. (2003a) A critical approach to experiential consumption: Fighting against the disappearance of the contemplative time. *Third International Critical Management Studies Conference,* Lancaster University.

Caru, A. and Cova, B. (2003b) Revisiting Consumption Experience: A More Humble But Complete View of the Concept. *Marketing Theory,* 3(2): 267-86.

Chang, C. Y. C. (2006). *What Customers Perceive During Their Online Shopping Experience.*

Chen, K. and Yen, D. C. (2004) Improving the quality of online presence through interactivity. *Information & Management* 42(1): 217-226.

Chen, S. J. and Chang, T. Z. (2003) A descriptive model of online shopping process: some empirical results. *International Journal of Service Industry Management,* 14(5): 556-569.

Childers, T. L., Carr, C. L., Peck, J. and Carson, S. (2001) Hedonic and utilitarian motivations for online retail shopping behavior. *Journal of Retailing,* 77(4): 511-535.

Cox, J. and Dale, B. G. (2001) Service quality and e-commerce: an exploratory analysis. *Managing Service Quality,* 11(2): 121-31.

Cronin, J. J. and S. A. Taylor (1992) Measuring Service Quality: A Reexamination and Extension. *Journal of Marketing* 56(July): 55-68.

Cronin, J. J. and S. A. Taylor (1994) SERVPERF Versus SERVQUAL: Reconciling Performance-Based and Perceptions-Minus-Expectations Measurement of Service Quality. *Journal of Marketing* 58(January): 125-131.

Dabholkar, P. A. (1996) Consumer evaluations of new technology-based self-service options: An investigation of alternative models of service quality. *International Journal of Research in Marketing*, 13(1): 29-51.

Dahlsten, F. (2003) Avoiding the Customer Satisfaction Rut. *MIT Sloan Management Review*, 44(4): 72-77.

Davis, F. D., Bagozzi, R. P. and Warshaw, P. R. (1989) User acceptance of computer technology: a comparison of two theoretical models. *Management Science* 35(8): 982-1003.

Demangeot, C. and Broderick, A. J. (2007) Conceptualising consumer behaviour in online shopping environments. *International Journal of Retail & Distribution Management*, 35(11): 878-894.

Dunn, M. and Davis, S. (2003) Building brands from the inside. *Marketing Management,* Chicago 12.

Evanschitzky, H., Iyer, G.R., Hesse, J. and Ahlert, D. (2004) E-satisfaction: a re-examination. *Journal of Retailing*, 80(3): 239-247.

Fisk, T. A., Brown, C. J. Cannizzaro, K. and Naftal, B. (1990) Creating patient satisfaction and loyalty. *Journal of Health Care Marketing*, 10(2): 5-15.

Forlizzi, J. and Ford, S. (2000) The building blocks of experience: an early framework for interaction designers. *Proceedings of the conference on Designing interactive systems: processes, practices, methods, and techniques*: 419-423.

Fundin, A. and Nilsson, L. (2003) Using Kano's theory of attractive quality to better understand customer experiences with e-services. *Asian Journal on Quality*, 4(2): 32-49.

Fynes, B. and Voss, C. (2001) A Path Analytic Model of Quality Practices, Quality Performance, and Business Performance. *Production and Operations Management*, 10(4): 494-513.

Gefen, D. and Devine, P. (2001) Customer Loyalty to an Online Store: The Meaning of Online Service Quality. *Proceedings of the International Conference on Information Systems*: 613-617.

Gentilea, C., Spillera, N. and Noci, G. (2007) How to Sustain the Customer Experience: An Overview of Experience Components that Co-create Value With the Customer, *European Management Journal* 25(5): 395-410

Hagel, J. and A. Armstrong (1997) *Expanding Markets through Virtual Communities,* Harvard Business School Press.

Herington, C. and Weaven, S. (2007) Can banks improve customer relationships with high quality online services? *Managing Service Quality,* 17(4): 404-427.

Hirschman, E. (1984) Experience Seeking: A Subjectivist Perspective of Consumption. *Journal of Business Research,* 12: 115-136.

Hirschman, E. C. and Holbrook, M. B. (1982) Hedonic consumption: Emerging concepts, methods and propositions. *Journal of Marketing Science,* 46 (Summer): 92-101.

Ho, C. and Wu, W. (1999) Antecedents of Customer Satisfaction on the Internet: An Empirical Study of Online Shopping. *Proceedings of the 32nd Hawaii International Conference on System Sciences,* IEEE Institute of Electrical And Electronics.

Hoffman, D.L. and Novak, T. (1996) Marketing in Hypermedia Computer-Mediated Environments: Conceptual Foundations. *Journal of Marketing* 60: 50-68.

Hoffman, D. L., Novak, T. P. and Schlosser, A. (2000) Consumer Control in Online Environments. *Elab. vanderbilt. edu,* February.

Hoisington, S. and Naumann, E. (2003) The loyalty elephant. *Quality progress,* 36(2): 33-41.

Holbrook, M. B. (2000) The millennial consumer in the tests of our times: experience and entertainment. *Journal of Macromarketing* 20(2): 178-92.

Holbrook, M. B. and Hirschman, E. C. (1982) The experiential aspects of consumption: Consumer fantasies, feelings, and fun. *Journal of Consumer Research,* 9(September): 132-40.

Hsu, S. H. (2008) Developing an index for online customer satisfaction: Adaptation of American Customer Satisfaction Index. *Expert Systems With Applications,* 34(4): 3033-3042.

Huang, M. H. (2003) Designing website attributes to induce experiential encounters. *Computers in Human Behavior,* 19(4): 425-442.

Huang, M.-H. (2006) Flow, enduring, and situational involvement in the Web environment: A tripartite second-order examination. *Psychology and Marketing* 23(5): 383 - 411.

Hudson, S., Hudson, P. and Miller, G. A. (2004) The Measurement of Service Quality in the Tour Operating Sector: A Methodological Comparison. *Journal of Travel Research,* 42: 305-312.

Hwang, Y. and D. J. Kim (2007) Customer self-service systems: The effects of perceived Web quality with service contents on enjoyment, anxiety, and e-trust. *Decision Support Systems* 43(3): 746-760.

Ibrahim, E. E., Joseph, M. and Ibeh, K. I. N. (2006) Customers' perception of electronic service delivery in the UK retail banking sector. *The International Journal of Bank Marketing*, 24(7): 475-493.

Jain, S. K. and Gupta, G. (2004) Measuring Service Quality: SERVQUAL vs. SERVPERF Scales. *VIKALPA* 29(2): 25.

Janda, S., Trocchia, P. J. and Gwinner, K. P. (2002) Consumer perceptions of Internet retail service quality. *International Journal of Service Industry Management*, 13(5): 412-431.

Jayawardhena, C. (2004) Measurement of Service Quality in Internet Banking: The Development of an Instrument. *Journal of Marketing Management*, 20(1-2): 185-207.

Jiang, P. and B. Rosenbloom (2005) Customer intention to return online: price perception, attribute-level performance, and satisfaction unfolding over time. *European Journal of Marketing* 39(1/2): 150-174.

Johnson, M. D., Gustafsson, A., Andreassen, T. W., Lervik, L. and Cha, J. (2001) The evolution and future of national customer satisfaction index models. *Journal of Economic Psychology* 22(2): 217-245.

Jones, T. and Taylor, F. S. (2007) The conceptual domain of service loyalty: how many dimensions? *Journal of Services Marketing*, 21(1): pp. 36-51.

Jun, M. and Cai, S. (2001) The key determinants of Internet banking service quality: a content analysis. *International Journal of Bank Marketing*, 19(7): 276-91.

Juran, J. M. (1977) *Quality Control Handbook*, McGraw Hill, New York.

Kano, N., Seraku, N., Takahashi, F. and Tsuji, S. (1984) Attractive quality and must-be quality. *The Journal of the Japanese Society for Quality Control*, April: 39-48.

Kim, J. I., Lee, H. C. *et al.* (2004) Factors Affecting Online Search Intention and Online Purchase Intention. *Seoul Journal of Business* 10(2).

Kim, W. G., Ma, X. and Kim, D. J. (2006) Determinants of Chinese hotel customers' e-satisfaction and purchase intentions. *Tourism Management,* 27(5): 890-900.

Kim, Y. M. K. and Shim, K. Y. (2002) The influence of intent shopping mall characteristics and user traits on purchase intent. *Iris Marketing Review*, 15 (2): 25-34.

Kingstrom, P. O. (1983) Patient ties to ambulatory care providers: the concept of provider Loyalty. *Journal of Health Care Marketing*, 3(2): pp.27-34.

Korgaonkar, P. K. and D. Wolin (1999) A multivariate analysis of web usage. *Journal of Advertising Research* (March/April): 53-68.

Koufaris, M. (2001) Consumer Behavior in Web-Based Commerce: An Empirical Study. *International Journal of Electronic Commerce*, 6(2): 115-138.

Koufaris, M. and Hampton-Sosa, W. (2002) Customer trust online: examining the role of the experience with the Web-site. *Department of Statistics and Computer Information Systems Working Paper Series, Zicklin School of Business,* Baruch College, New York.

LaSalle, D. and Britton, T. (2003) *Priceless: Turning Ordinary Products Into Extraordinary Experiences*, Harvard Business School Press.

Laukkanen, T. (2006) Customer-perceived value of e-financial services: a means-end approach. *International Journal of Electronic Finance*, 1(1): 5-17.

Lawler, J. and Joseph, A. (2006) A Study of Apparel Dress Model Technology on the Web. *Journal of Information, Information Technology, and Organizations*, 1: 59-73.

Lee, D., Park, J and Ahn, B. S. (2001) On the explanation of factors affecting e-commerce adoption. *Twenty-Second International Conference on Information Systems*. New Orleans,Louisiana, USA.

Lee, G. G. and Lin, H. F. (2005) Customer perceptions of e-service quality in online shopping. *International Journal of Retail & Distribution Management*, 33(2): 161-76.

Li, Y. N., Tan, K. C. and Xie, M. (2003) Factor analysis of service quality dimension shifts in the information age. *Managerial Auditing Journal*, 18(4): 297-302.

Lim, H. and Dubinsky, A. J. (2004) Consumers' perceptions of e-shopping characteristics: an expectancy-value approach. *Journal of Services Marketing* 18(7): 500.

Liu, C. and Arnett, K. P. (2000) Exploring the factors associated with Web site success in the context of electronic commerce. *Information & Management*, 38(23): 33.

Loiacono, E. T., Watson, R. T. and Goodhue, D. L. (2002) WEBQUAL: measure of web site quality. *2002 Marketing Educators Conference: Marketing Theory and Applications*, 13: 432-7.

Long, M. and McMellon, C. (2004) Exploring the determinants of retail service quality on the Internet. *Journal of Services Marketing*, 18(1): 78-90.

Madu, C. N. and Madu, A. A. (2002) Dimensions of e-quality. *International Journal of Quality & Reliability Management,* 19(3): 246-258.

Mäenpää, K., Kanto, A., Kuusela, H. and Paul, P. (2006) More hedonic versus less hedonic consumption behaviour in advanced internet bank services. *Journal of Financial Services Marketing*, 11(1): 4-16.

Mascarenhas, O. A., Kesavan, R. and Bernacchi, M. (2004) Customer value-chain involvement for co-creating customer delight. *The Journal of Consumer Marketing*, 21(7): 486.

McEwen, W. J. (2004) Why Satisfaction Isn't Satisfying: Car dealers aren't the only ones bemoaning the inadequacy of customer satisfaction programs. *Gallup Management Journal* November.

McEwen, W. J. and Fleming, J. H. (2003) Customer satisfaction doesn't count. *Gallup Management Journal*, March.

Milligan, A. and Smith, S. (2002) *Uncommon Practice: People who Deliver a Great Brand Experience*, Financial Times Prentice Hall.

Minocha, S., Dawson, L., Blandford, A. and Millard, N. (2005) Providing Value to Customers in E-Commerce environments: The Customer's Perspective, in *Contemporary Research in E-Marketing*, IDEA Group, PA, USA.

Monsuwe, T. P., Dellaert, B. G. C. and De Ruyter, K. (2004) What drives consumers to shop online? A literature review. *International Journal of Service Industry Management*, 15(1): 102-121.

Nilsson-Witel, L. and Fundin, A. (2005) Dynamics of service attributes: a test of Kano's theory of attractive quality. *International Journal of Service Industry Management* 16(2): 152-69.

Novak, T. P., Hoffman, D. L. and Yung, Y. (2000) Measuring the Customer Experience in Online Environments: A Structural Modeling Approach. *Marketing Science*, 19(1): 22-42.

Oliver, R. L. (1980) A Cognitive Model of the Antecedents and Consequences of Satisfaction Decisions. *Journal of Marketing Research*, 17(460-9)

Oliver, R. L. (1981) Measurement and Evaluation of Satisfaction Processes in Retail Settings. *Journal of Retailing*, 57: 25-48.

Oliver, R. L. (1989) Processing of the Satisfaction Response in Consumption: A Suggested Framework and Research Propositions. *Journal of Consumer Satisfaction, Dissatisfaction and Complaining*, 2: I-16.

Oliver, R. L. (1999) Whence consumer loyalty? *Journal of Marketing* 63 (Special Issue): 33 - 44.

Oliver, R. L., Rust, R. T. and Varki, S. (1997) Customer delight: Foundations, findings, and managerial insight. *Journal of Retailing*, 73(3): 311-336.

Page, T. J. Jr. and Spreng, R. A. (2002) Difference Scores versus Direct Effects in Service Quality Measurement. *Journal of Service Research*, 4(3): 184.

Parasuraman, A., Berry, L. L. and Zeithaml, V .A. (1991) Refinement and reassessment of the SERVQUAL scale. *Journal of Retailing*, 67(4): 420-50.

Parasuraman, A., Zeithaml, V. A. and Berry, L. L. (1985) A Conceptual Model of Service Quality and Its Implications for Future Research. *Journal of Marketing*, 49(4): 41-50.

Parasuraman, A., Zeithaml, V. A. and Berry, L. L. (1988) SERVQUAL: A Multiple Item Scale for Measuring Consumer Perceptions of Service Quality. *Journal of Retailing*, 64(1): 12-39.

Parasuraman, A., Zeithaml, V. A. and Berry, L. L. (1994) Reassessment of expectations as a comparison standard in measuring service quality: implications for further research. *Journal of Marketing*, 58: 111- 24.

Parasuraman, A., Zeithaml, V. A. and Berry, L. L. (2005) E-SQUAL: a multiple-item scale for assessing electronic service quality. *Journal of Service Research*, 7(3): 213-34.

Parsons, A. G. (2002) Non-functional motives for online shoppers: why we click. *Journal of Consumer Marketing* 19(4/5): 380-392.

Patwardhan, P. (2004) Exposure, Involvement and Satisfaction with Online Activities: A Cross-National Comparison of American and Indian Internet Users. *International Communication Gazette,* 66(5): 411.

Phillips, D. M. (1999) *The role of consumption emotions in the satisfaction response.* The Pennsylvania State University, The Pennsylvania State University. Doctoral dissertation.

Pine, B. J. and Gilmore, J. H. (1999) *The Experience Economy.* Boston, Massachusetts, Harvard Business School Press.

Plutchik, R. (1980) Emotion: *A psychoevolutionary synthesis.* New York.

Prahalad, C. K. and Ramaswamy, V. (2004) Co-creation experiences: The next practice in value creation. *Journal of Interactive Marketing,* 18(3): 5-14.

Rajgopal, S., Venkatachalam, M. et al. (2000) *Does online customer experience affect the performance of e-commerce firms.* University of Washington, Seattle, September, Retrieved December 2007.

Reichheld, F. F. (1994) Loyalty and the renaissance of marketing. *Marketing Management,* 2(4): 10.

Reichheld, F. F. (1994) Loyalty and the renaissance of marketing. *Marketing Management,* 2(4): 10.

Ribbink, D., van Riel, A. C. R. Liljander, V. and Streukens, S. (2004) Comfort your online customer: quality, trust and loyalty on the internet. *Managing Service Quality,* 14(6): 446-456.

Rice, M. (1997) What makes users revisit a Web site? *Marketing News,* 31(6): 12.

Rotondaro, R. G. (2002) Defining the customer's expectations in e-business. *Industrial Management and Data Systems,* 102(8): 476-82.

Rowley, J. (2006) An analysis of the e-service literature: towards a research agenda. *Journal of Internet Research,* 16(3): 339-359.

Santos, J. (2003) E-service quality: a model of virtual service quality dimensions. *Managing Service Quality,* 13(3): 233-246.

Schmitt, B. H. (1999) *Experiential Marketing: How to Get Customers to SENSE, FEEL, THINK, ACT and RELATE to Your Company and Brands.* New York: The Free Press.

Shaw, C. and Ivens, J. (2002) *Building Great Customer Experiences,* Palgrave, New York.

Smith, S. and Wheeler, J. (2002) *Managing the Customer Experience: Turning Customers Into Advocates,* Financial Times/Prentice Hall.

Srinivasan, S. S., Anderson, R. and Ponnavolu, K. (2002) Customer loyalty in e-commerce: an exploration of its antecedents and consequences. *Journal of Retailing,* 78(1): 41-50.

Szymanski, D. M. and Hise, R. T. (2000) E-satisfaction: an initial examination. *Journal of Retailing,* 76(3): 309-322.

Tauber, E. M. (1972) Why do people shop? *Journal of Marketing* 36(Oct): 46-59.

Teas, C. (1993) Expectations, Performance Evaluation, and Consumers' Perceptions of Quality. *Journal of Marketing,* 57: 18-34.

Tih, S. and Ennis, S. (2006) Cross-industry analysis of consumer assessments of internet retailers' service performances. *International Journal of Retail & Distribution Management,* 34(4): 290-307.

To, P. L., Liao, C. and Lin, T. H. (2007) Shopping motivations on Internet: A study based on utilitarian and hedonic value. *Technovation,* 27(12): 774-787.

Trabold, L. M., Heim, G. R. and Field, J. M. (2006) Comparing e-service performance across industry sectors. *International Journal of Retail & Distribution Management* 34(4/5): 240-257.

Trocchia, P. J. and S. Janda (2003) How do consumers evaluate Internet retail service quality? *Journal of Services Marketing* 17(3): 243-253

van Riel, A. C. R., Liljander, V. and Juriens, P. (2001) Exploring consumer evaluations of e-services: a portal site. *International Journal of Service Industry Management,* 12(4): 359-77.

Westbrook, R. A. and Black, W. C. (1985) A motivation-based shopper typology. *Journal of Retailing* 61(1): 78-103.

Wolfinbarger, M. and Gilly, M. C. (2001) Shopping Online for Freedom, Control, and Fun. *California Management Review,* 43(2): 34-55.

Wolfinbarger, M. and Gilly, M. C. (2003) eTailQ: dimensionalizing, measuring and predicting etail quality. *Journal of Retailing,* 79(3): 183-198.

Yang, Z. and Fang, X. (2004) Online service quality dimensions and their relationships with satisfaction. *International Journal of Service Industry Management,* 15(3): 302-26.

Zairi, M. (2007) *Creating Value Through Innovation: Gauging Customer Reaction Through a Simulated Shopping Experience,* ASQ Conference.

Zeithaml, V. A. (2002) Service excellence in electronic channels. *Managing Service Quality,* 12(3): 135-138.

Zeithaml, V. A., Berry, L. L. and Parasuraman, A. (1996) The Behavioral Consequences of Service Quality. *Journal of Marketing,* 60 (April): 3 I-46.

Zeithaml, V. A., Parasuraman, A. and Berry, L. L. (2002) Service quality delivery through web sites: a critical review of extant knowledge. *Journal of the Academy of Marketing Science,* 30(4): 362-75.

Zhang, P. and von Dran, G. M. (2002) User Expectations and Rankings of Quality Factors in Different Web Site Domains. *International Journal of Electronic Commerce,* 6(2): pp. 9-33.

Index

benchmarking, 63, 169-192

best practice, 131, 170

brand orientation, 228, 268

business process management, 80, 188

customer experience management (CEM), 4, 197-206, 209-228, 251, 258, 262, 272, 295, 298

critical success factors (CSFs), 59-92, 170, 186, 188, 189

customer relationship management (CRM), 21-45, 51-103, 111-166, 169-192, 197, 219

customer centric, 1, 2, 3, 11, 67, 165, 219

customer experience, 1-10, 11, 27, 36, 80, 81, 145, 149, 198, 201, 202, 204, 206, 209, 216, 217, 219, 220, 225, 226, 227, 231, 232, 233, 234, 237, 239, 240, 251, 253, 254, 255, 257, 272, 277, 279, 283, 284, 285, 287, 295, 298, 307, 308, 309, 313, 314, 315, 316, 318, 319, 321, 322, 323, 333, 340, 344, 358

customer loyalty, 358

customer orientation, 18, 227, 228, 229

customer service (CS), 1, 23, 30, 31-33, 35, 44, 63, 70, 82, 91, 93, 95, 98, 111, 133, 134, 142, 148, 153, 162, 166, 210, 220, 235, 237,

238, 273, 278, 287, 316, 322, 344

disconfirmation-based measurement, 310

e-business, 358

e-CRM, 25, 27-28, 29, 44, 98, 99

employee relationship management (ERM), 85

enterprise resource planning (ERP), 23, 43, 44, 57, 63, 91, 92, 93, 94, 95

expectation-based theory, 310

experience management, 200, 201, 202, 309

experiential services, 201

field service (FS), 30, 31, 32, 45, 98

Hedonic motivation, 308

KANO model, 310

loyalty, 3, 15, 23, 31, 35, 36, 39, 41, 42, 67, 68, 77, 83, 99, 113, 122, 124, 125, 127, 131, 132, 147, 150, 151, 198, 203, 204, 205, 206, 211, 221, 225, 227, 231, 242, 244, 258, 261, 269, 277, 289, 290, 299, 301, 307, 310, 312, 313, 317, 318, 319, 322, 330, 332, 333, 334, 335, 336, 340-344, 346

marketing automation (MA), 30, 32, 98, 131

partner relationship management (PRM), 28

perceived quality, 307, 309, 310, 311, 315, 316, 317, 318, 319, 320, 321, 324, 325, 330, 332, 334

performance-based measurement, 320

product orientation, 201

quality function deployment (QFD), 310

quality orientation, 227, 228

relationship marketing, 25, 26, 37, 77

sales force automation (SFA), 26, 30, 31, 43, 89, 129, 131, 133

satisfaction, 3, 33, 34, 36, 40, 41, 69, 99, 122, 133, 148, 204, 211, 224, 245, 254, 267, 282, 307, 309, 310, 311, 312, 315, 317, 318, 319, 325, 329, 330, 332, 333, 334, 335, 336, 337, 338, 339, 344, 345, 350

service orientation, 197, 201, 226

strategic management, 197

supply chain management (SCM), 23, 92, 95, 96, 255, 272, 297

technology acceptance model (TAM), 310, 325, 329

theory of reasoned action, 310

total customer experience (TCE), 198, 201, 202, 227, 255, 260

total quality management (TQM), ix, 165

tribal customer, 1, 8, 17

utilitarian motivation, 308

XQual, 319, 321, 324, 326, 344, 345